DATE DUE

DEMCO 38-296

The Marshall Cavendish Illustrated History of

POPULAR MUSIC

Volume 14
1976-1977

MARSHALL CAVENDISH
NEW YORK, LONDON, TORONTO, SYDNEY

Reference Edition Published 1990

on

. Vicenza.

Reference edition produced by DPM Services.

© Orbis Publishing Ltd.MCMLXXXIX
© Marshall Cavendish Ltd.MCMLXXXIX

Set ISBN 1-85436-015-3

Library of Congress Cataloging in Publication Data

The Marshall Cavendish history of popular music.
    p.   cm.
  Includes index.
  ISBN 1-85435-093-5 (vol. 14)
    1. Popular music – History and criticism. 2. Rock music – History
and Criticism. I. Marshall Cavendish Corporation. II. Title:
History of popular music.
ML 3470. M36 1988
784. 5' 009 – dc19   88-21076
                                        CIP
                                        MN

Editorial Staff

Editor	Ashley Brown
Executive Editors	Adrian Gilbert
	Michael Heatley
Consultant Editors	Richard Williams
	Peter Brookesmith
Editorial Director	Brian Innes

Reference Edition Staff

Reference Editor	Mark Dartford
Revision Editor	Fran Jones
Consultant Editor	Michael Heatley
Art Editor	Graham Beehag

CONTENTS

CONTRIBUTORS

CLIVE ANDERSON

Co-author of *The Soul Book* and contributor to *Encyclopedia of Rock*, he has also written for *Black Music, Black Echoes, New Kommotion* and other magazines.

STEPHEN BARNARD

Has contributed to *Atlantic Rock, Melody Maker* and the *Rock Files* series. He also lectures at the City University, London.

DICK BRADLEY

Completed his PhD thesis on *British Popular Music in the Fifties* at the Centre of Contemporary Cultural Studies in Birmingham, England, and has also written articles for *Media, Culture & Society*.

JOHN BROVEN

Author of *Walking to New Orleans* and *South of Louisiana*, he has also contributed to *Nothing but the Blues* and *Encyclopedia of Rock*. He writes for *Blues Unlimited* and has also compiled several New Orleans rhythm and blues anthologies

ROB FINNIS

Author of *The Phil Spector Story* and *The Gene Vincent Story*, he has contributed to the major rock journals and runs a specialist record shop.

SIMON FRITH

A lecturer at the University of Warwick, England, he has built up a reputation over the last 15 years as one of the leading international commentators on rock music. He has co-edited the *Rock File* series, and written *The Sociology of Rock*.

PETER GURALNIK

Author of *Feel Like Going Home, Lost Highway* and *Nighthawk Blues*, his articles on blues, country and rock have appeared in *Rolling Stone*, the *Village Voice, Country Music, Living Blues*, the *New York Times* and the *Boston Phoenix*.

BILL HARRY

Founder member of UK's *Mersey Beat*, he later became news editor of *Record Mirror* and music columnist for *Weekend*. He is currently an independent PR for such artists as Suzi Quatro and Kim Wilde.

MARTIN HAWKINS

An acknowledged expert on the Sun era of rock'n'roll (author of *The Sun Story*), he writes for *Melody Maker, Time Barrier Express* and *Country Music*

BRIAN HOGG

Publisher of *Bam Balam*, which concentrates on US and UK bands of the Sixties, he has also written for such magazines as *New York Rocker* and *Record Collector*.

PETER JONES

Was editor of UK's *Record Mirror* from 1961 to 1969. He then became UK News editor of *Billboard* in 1977 and later UK and European Editor.

ROBIN KATZ

After 10 years in the Motown Press Office, she now writes freelance for *New Sound, New Styles, International Musician* and *Smash Hits*.

JOE McEWEN

An acknowledged authority on soul music, he has written for *Rolling Stone, Phonograph Record, Black Music*, the *Boston Phoenix* and Boston's *Real Paper*.

BILL MILLAR

As a freelance journalist he writes for *Melody Maker* and other rock papers. He is the author of *The Drifters* and *The Coasters*.

DAVID MORSE

Author of *Motown*, he lectures at the School of English and American Studies at Sussex University, England.

TONY RUSSELL

Editor of *Old Time Music* from 1971, he contributes regularly to *Blues Unlimited* and *Jazz Journal* and is the author of *Blacks, Whites and Blues*.

ROBERT SHELTON

Has written about blues, country and folk for the *New York Times* , London *Times, Listener, Time Out* and *Melody Maker*.

NICK TOSCHES

Author of *Hellfire*, a biography of Jerry Lee Lewis, he also writes for *New York Times* and *Village Voice*.

MICHAEL WATTS

Writes on popular arts for *The Los Angeles Times* and London *Times* and is rock columnist for *Records and Recording Magazine*.

ADAM WHITE

Has written about Motown for *Music Week* and *Black Echoes*, and scripted a six-hour documentary about the company and its music for US radio. Also worked as managing editor of *Billboard* magazine in New York.

Work in Progress

**Ambitious new musical ideas
heralded the age of progressive rock**

*Virtuoso guitarist Robert
Fripp, founder member and
mainstay of acclaimed UK
progressives King Crimson.*

Jethro Tull (above) forged on through the Seventies with greater commercial recognition than Van Der Graaf Generator (below).

PROGRESSIVE MUSIC – a title encompassing a wide spectrum of styles influenced by other sources, from blues, modern and free jazz to classical music (and any mixture of all these) – was an aberration from the mainstream of popular music. Although progressive bands like Yes and Pink Floyd enjoyed sustained success in the Seventies, the greater part of rock in the Eighties carried on as it had before the late Sixties.

Recondite rockers

In the summer of 1967 the Beatles' *Sgt Pepper's Lonely Hearts Club Band* made poetry and dream/nightmare songs the latest hot property. All at once, Oxford undergraduates and virtuosi from the Royal Academy of Music joined ex-soul band musicians to concoct unlikely mixtures of Stravinsky, Mingus, James Brown, Brubeck and Bo Diddley, often with an approving glance at what Americans like Frank Zappa and Terry Riley were doing.

One particularly welcome fresh development was the sudden upsurge of keyboard-players. From the Fifties the electric guitar – at first a wonderful new sound but, after exposure in thousands of groups, in danger of becoming just another part of the musical wallpaper – had been the standard rock and pop instrument. It is quite easy to achieve a passable level of accomplishment on the six-string guitar. Unfortunately many guitarists of the period never progressed beyond the passable; outstanding players like Hendrix and Clapton simply confirmed how ordinary the majority were.

Perseverance and practice, however, is needed to master any form of keyboard. Survivors of childhood piano lessons have inevitably absorbed plenty of music theory and possess genuine technical ability. Not all the organists and pianists of the great psychedelic era were over-endowed with talent and inspiration; however, the good ones, such as Traffic's Steve Winwood, Curved Air's Francis Monkman, Soft Machine's Mike Ratledge, Van Der Graaf Generator's Hugh Banton and the Nice's Keith Emerson came up with music and new sounds that were a much-needed change. It should also be said that classically-trained keyboard players often found themselves at loggerheads with more instinctive, less disciplined drummers, singers and bassists. There was plenty of conflict within progressive bands, despite the media's flower-power propaganda about bands living together in perfect peace.

In particular, organists introduced the sound of long, sustained notes and thereby relieved many songs of the time-honoured accompaniment of staccato guitar-strumming. More sinuous arrangements thus became possible, causing songwriters and vocalists to rethink their styles.

Enigmatic variations

Writers used to listening to jazz or classical music had no desire to limit songs to the regulation three minutes; the then-fashionable term 'extended composition' covered a multitude of sins and virtues. In the right hands a 15-minute instrumental section could be a wonderful experience, but in the wrong ones could seem so interminable that audiences might expire from acute boredom. The extended solo entered rock; musicians who had listened to modern and avant-garde jazz players like Ornette Coleman and John Coltrane now soloed away in the middle of songs for chorus after chorus, disdaining the neat, prearranged eight-bar lead breaks of Hank Marvin and George Harrison.

Most significantly, however, there was for the first time in rock a genuine and vigorous cross-fertilisation of musical styles. Instead of the blinkered views of the blues fanatics, jazzers sneering at rock's simplicity or white British musicians laughing at so-called weird Indian sounds, many bands embraced all these different ingredients. Jethro Tull, basically a blues-oriented band, featured a singer who soloed on flute in the manner of jazz multi-instrumentalist Roland Kirk; not content with this advance, the band had a hit single, 'Living In The Past', with the same five-four time signature as Dave Brubeck's million-selling pop-jazz hit, 'Take Five'. It was all very confusing for the staid record companies who had controlled Britain's music output for so long. Independents sprang up to rush out the new sounds, but few survived.

By the end of 1968, many of the prize blooms of flower-power had wilted. The bands still together had discarded their looser elements and were generally tighter, more professional (and often less joyful). You could expect to hear musically excellent performances from many bands virtually every night, but without the idiosyncratic weirdness that had originally been such an important part of their attractiveness. King Crimson usually managed to supply the bizarre, thanks to Robert Fripp, but even then the song that made them famous, '21st Century Schizoid Man', was a Mingus-like arrangement that incorporated tight, fast passages in six-eight time.

Unusual time-signatures abounded – Soft Machine's Mike Ratledge came up with elevens, thirteens and fifteens in highly-arranged tunes such as 'Slightly All The Time' and 'Out-Bloody-Rageous'. One American musician commented on a Ratledge score, 'You guys must be affiliated to Einstein!'

Back in the groove

This second stage of progressive music lasted until the mid Seventies, when American jazz-funk began to influence the majority of the bands in another of rock's incestuous cross-breeds. Meanwhile the 'pomp-rockers' mounted bigger and more expensive shows, employing more and more roadies and truck drivers, their live tours usually serving as loss-making promotions for platinum discs.

But rock was resuming its more natural beat. In the late Seventies and Eighties Euro-rock, computerised synthesiser singles and disco hits kept closely to basic four-four time and simple melodies, for all their electronic wizardry. The late Seventies in Britain also saw the creative focus of rock abruptly shift from college campuses to small pubs and clubs. Audiences there were more concerned with drive and aggression than having their fancies tickled by musical sophistication and eclecticism – the very qualities that had been the hallmark of the best 'progressive' rock.   HUGH HOPPER

Soft Machine (above) took their inspiration from jazz, while Curved Air reflected the classical training of Francis Monkman (below).

IN THE COURT OF
KING CRIMSON

Robert Fripp's band joined the rock aristocracy

KING CRIMSON, who first entranced fans of progressive music when they supported the Rolling Stones in Hyde Park in July 1969, sprang from unlikely origins. Self-taught guitar virtuoso and English eccentric Robert Fripp (born 1946) from Wimborne, Dorset, joined up with Mike and Peter Giles in nearby Bournemouth to form Giles, Giles and Fripp in 1967; after a move to London, they released two unsuccessful singles and an album – *The Cheerful Insanity Of Giles, Giles And Fripp* – on Deram, before Fripp took the reins and the group evolved into King Crimson. Peter Giles was replaced on vocals by another Bournemouth friend, Greg Lake. Also involved was Ian McDonald who, besides being an accomplished reeds and keyboard player, introduced Fripp to Peter Sinfield; Sinfield became the group's lyricist, roadie and, eventually, its light-show operator.

Following intensive rehearsals in the basement of a cafe on the Fulham Palace Road, the group played a number of warm-up gigs in Newcastle before making their London debut at the Speakeasy on 9 April 1969. On the basis of a small but growing

reputation, King Crimson were signed up by David Enthoven and John Gaylord of EG Management, and a contract was secured with Island Records. After the success at Hyde Park, their debut album, *In The Court Of The Crimson King*, was enthusiastically promoted by luminaries such as John Peel and Pete Townshend ('an uncanny masterpiece') and raced up the UK charts to reach Number 5 in October.

In The Court Of The Crimson King was one of 1969's most exciting exercises in excess, from the nightmarish cover artwork, through the sententious lyrics of Pete Sinfield to the long group improvisation on 'Moonchild'. It also provided two famous Crimson anthems in '21st.Century Schizoid Man' and the title track.

An American tour in October and November was critically acclaimed, but was not a financial success. On returning to England both McDonald and Giles quit, unhappy with both the American trip and

the musical direction of the group. In 1970 they released their own album, *McDonald And Giles*, a pleasant enough collection of songs that made little progress in the charts.

The Poseidon adventure

Undaunted by this setback, Fripp pressed ahead with a follow-up album, roping in friends and associates, including McDonald and Giles. During recording Greg Lake announced his departure to work with Keith Emerson in Emerson, Lake and Palmer, so Peter Giles guested on bass and Gordon Haskell completed the vocals. Released early in 1970, *In The Wake Of Poseidon* did well in the charts – Number 4 in the UK – but in many ways it was a faint imitation of its predecessor. Although disfigured by a number of empty mellotron workouts, it was not totally without merit: 'Cadence And Cascade' showcased two new Crimson talents, free-jazz pianist Keith Tippett and Mel Collins, a versatile flautist and sax-player.

The jazz influence first heard on *Poseidon* pointed the way ahead. In the

and stage-lighting were increasingly at variance with the band's new hard-jamming style – was sacked. A fourth album was released in December 1971: like its predecessors, *Islands* was something of a mixed bag; its conflicting stylistic approaches bewildered audiences, and sales were correspondingly poor. Conflicts again developed between Fripp and the rest of the band, who departed after another American tour, leaving Fripp with an indifferently recorded live album, *Earthbound* (1972).

Fripp returned to Dorset to form a new line-up, and in July 1972 a new King Crimson came into being. The group was based around the trio of Fripp, drummer

summer of 1970, Fripp, Sinfield, Collins, Haskell (now on bass) and new drummer Andy McCullough went into the studio to record *Lizard*. More considered than the previous album, *Lizard* was characterised by Fripp's carefully 'mannered' approach to its production, and contributions from a number of session men – especially Tippett – as well as a vocal track by Jon Anderson of Yes.

There were to be no live dates, however, as Haskell left immediately after *Lizard*'s release, to be followed a few days later by McCullough. Determined to resume touring, Fripp looked for replacements. Drummer Ian Wallace was quickly signed up, and after a number of auditions (the candidates included Bryan Ferry) Fripp settled on Boz (Burrell) as vocalist, and for convenience chose him as bass-player as well, teaching him the rudiments over the succeeding days.

In April 1971 Crimson was back on the road and for the remainder of the year carried out a heavy touring schedule in Europe and the States. On the group's return from America, Sinfield – whose lyrics

Opposite: Rhapsody in blue – 1974-vintage Crimson, from left David Cross, John Wetton, Bill Bruford and Robert Fripp. Above: The first (left) and third LPs. Below: Fripp with two earlier colleagues, Greg Lake (left) and Peter Giles (right).

Two faces of Fripp: the young hippie teaching Boz to play bass (below right), and the maestro with his guitar synthesiser in the Eighties (left).

Bill Bruford (rejecting the financial and popular success of Yes) and bass-player/vocalist John Wetton, previously of Family. Fripp was delighted: 'This band is more King Crimson than it's ever been. All the original ideals and aspirations are there – love, respect and compatible ideas. It's a magic band!' The line-up was completed by the inclusion of avant-garde percussionist Jamie Muir, who quickly developed a fruitful relationship with Bruford, and David Cross, a classically-trained violinist who also doubled on mellotron.

A British tour was launched in October 1972 and was greeted by enthusiastic applause. The new outfit specialised in complex, often improvised, ensemble passages played against razor-sharp arrangements delivered with daunting speed and panache.

The group began recording in January 1973, and a couple of months later released

Larks' Tongues In Aspic, Crimson's most complete record to date. Wetton proved himself a forceful but intelligent bassist and the combination of Bruford and Muir was a revelation to those listeners bored with the clichés that then passed for rock drumming. With Fripp given the space and encouragement to go full out on guitar, the results were memorable.

Magic and disenchantment
On the release of *Larks' Tongues*, Jamie Muir retired, reportedly to a monastery, claiming that success raised barriers 'to the kind of alternatives that interest me'. A whirlwind of manic energy on stage, Muir had left his mark: Bruford had learned much from him, as he demonstrated on the next release. *Starless And Bible Black* (1974) consolidated the new musical territory discovered in *Larks' Tongues*, and was even more accomplished than its predecessor. 'The Night Watch' was a gem: violin and shimmering percussion introduced the song, creating a near-magical setting for Robert Palmer-James' atmospheric lyrics and a poignant guitar

solo from Fripp. The title track and 'Fractures' stood out as bleak – though brilliantly performed – extended compositions.

The tensions within the music were paralleled by growing conflict within the group itself. After the 1974 US tour came to an end with a gig at Central Park, New York on 1 July, David Cross slipped out of the line-up leaving Fripp, Bruford and Wetton to begin recording a new album. Fripp was becoming increasingly disenchanted with the music business, and just after the release of *Red* stated

Left: Fripp and Eno in Paris, 1975. Below: Crimson on one of their gruelling early Seventies tours; from left Mel Collins (sax/keyboards), Ian Wallace (drums), Boz (bass) and Robert Fripp (guitar).

categorically: 'King Crimson is completely over. For ever and ever.'

Red maintained the standards of its predecessors and with the aid of old Crimson hands, including Ian McDonald, the final track 'Starless' formed a suitably elegiac conclusion. Early in 1975, *USA*, a live album of the last American tour, was issued, followed in 1976 by *A Young Person's Guide To King Crimson*, a double album of tracks chosen by Fripp.

Bruford and Wetton were soon playing in a succession of other bands, while Fripp

Right: Reformed characters – the Eighties Crimson, from left Belew, Fripp, Bruford and Levin. Below right: Larks' Tongues In Aspic. *Below far right:* In The Wake Of Poseidon.

went into retirement, although continuing to work with Brian Eno – a collaboration that produced two LPs, *No Pussyfooting* (1973) and *Evening Star* (1975). Back home in Dorset, Fripp was able to find fresh inspiration in the teachings of the unorthodox social and religious thinker J. C. Bennett.

Gentlemen Americans
The retirement did not last long, however. Fripp moved to New York and involved himself in production, as well as playing guitar on records by Peter Gabriel, David Bowie and Blondie. Three solo albums were released, and Fripp undertook a series of solo dates at restaurants, record shops and other non-musical venues before forming a touring group, the League of Gentlemen. Following a tour of Europe and North America in the summer of 1980, an album, *The League Of Gentlemen*, was issued before the group disbanded.

Revived by a new enthusiasm for the music scene, Fripp formed a new band, Discipline, in 1981. The line-up consisted of former Crimson drummer Bill Bruford and two Americans, bass-player Tony Levin and a second guitarist, Adrian Belew, also responsible for vocals and lyrics. Fresh from stints with Frank Zappa and Talking Heads, Belew's extrovert approach and loose guitar style complemented the more meticulous Fripp.

Discipline's debut took place in the summer of 1981, and Fripp was sufficiently impressed by the response to rename the group King Crimson and release an album, *Discipline*. Seven years on from the last incarnation, the new Crimson had its own, generally cooler sound. The two guitars worked closely together, while Tony Levin was freed from a supportive bass role by virtue of the 'stick'; an electric multi-stringed instrument capable of an extensive tonal range, it enabled him to venture forward alongside Belew and Fripp.

The line-up recorded a second album, *Beat* (1982), that was very much a development of the ideas laid down on *Discipline*. The trilogy of albums was completed by the appropriately titled *Three Of A Perfect Pair* in 1984. Despite reaching Number 30 in the LP charts—Crimson's best for a decade—Fripp retired the group again, marrying punk rocker Toyah Willcox and releasing the occasional solo offering.

ADRIAN GILBERT

**King Crimson
Recommended Listening**

In The Court Of The Crimson King (Island ILPS 9111) (Includes: 21st Century Schizoid Man, I Talk To The Wind, Epitaph, Moonchild, The Court Of The Crimson King); *Larks' Tongues In Aspic* (Island ILPS 9230) (Includes: Easy Money, Larks' Tongues In Aspic Part One, Book Of Saturday, Exiles, Easy Money, Larks' Tongues In Aspic, Part Two).

IN PRAISE OF LEARNING

Above: Henry Cow in concert in 1975 with Robert Wyatt – confined to a wheelchair following a fall – and (inset) in 1973 with Geoff Leigh on sax. Right: Fred Frith, who, after leaving the band, moved to the US to become a noted session guitarist.

Henry Cow took music into new pastures

HENRY COW, Britain's most politically radical band of the progressive era, were born in 1968 – a year of widespread social unrest in Europe and the USA. The band's early line-ups were fluid, but centred on the nucleus of Fred Frith and Tim Hodgkinson, both ex-public schoolboys and students at Cambridge University. They were eclectic multi-instrumentalists eager to experiment: Fred described their early efforts as 'neo-Hiroshima-style music'.

After working as a duo, they were joined by John Greaves on bass. It was this line-up (plus a temporarily recruited heavy-rock drummer, Sean Jenkins) that in 1971 sent a demo tape to BBC Radio 1 producer John Walters and thereby unwittingly entered (and won) DJ John Peel's Rockortunity Knocks contest on his show 'Top Gear'.

Alternative structures

Intrigued by his ad in *Melody Maker* describing himself as a 'Wyatt-Varèse peculiar', the band gained the considerable services of drummer Chris Cutler. During his lengthy experience with such experimental outfits as Louise, Egg and Khan, he had developed a complex rhythmic percussive style well-suited to Henry Cow's music. When Geoff Leigh joined on tenor sax, the line-up featured on their first album *Leg End* (1973) was complete. Gigs were now becoming increasingly numerous, but as well as playing their own music Henry Cow were also busy promoting the work of other experimental musicians via the Cabaret Voltaire and the Explorers Club and working with such figures as saxophonist Lol Coxhill and free-jazz guitarist Derek Bailey. The band attempted to organise their own affairs as much as possible, choosing to sign with the only British record company (at that time) remotely in tune with their principles – Virgin Records.

The musical influences of *Leg End* were clear (Frank Zappa, the German avant-garde band Faust and modern classical composers such as Stravinsky and Varèse, for example), but the music was uniquely their own. Complex time signatures, unconventional instrumentation, variable tape speeds and backward-running tape combined to produce a sound as fresh and stimulating today as ever. More opportunity for improvisation (and a chance to reach a wider public) was provided by their contribution to the 1973 *Greasy Truckers: Live At Dingwalls Dance Hall* album. However, Henry Cow were not really a 'free band', as Fred pointed out in *Time Out* in 1976: 'We're playing probably a larger proportion of formally structured music than any other rock group has ever done. No-one else has attempted to do what we do since Zappa.'

In 1973 Geoff Leigh left to be replaced by Lindsay Cooper (flute, oboe, bassoon). This line-up produced the second album, *Unrest* (1974). The compositions were developed more fully, with greater exploration of texture and shape. There was also a striking sense of internal unity and balance – despite its amazing diversity, the album hung together brilliantly, with the improvised (or improvised-sounding) sections dovetailing perfectly with unison passages. Side two in particular showed the band making highly creative use of the studio – using it like an instrument, in fact.

In August 1974 Lindsay Cooper left, partly due to her dissatisfaction at being requested to play only Geoff Leigh's old parts. The strains of commercial involvement were beginning to tell on the rest of the band. More touring and recording meant less time to write and rehearse, less time to consider what they were actually doing.

There followed a period of collaboration with label-mates Slapp Happy, resulting in the release in February 1975 of a joint album, *Desperate Straights*. For a while it seemed that the two bands might merge permanently, but musical differences finally prevailed. Their second collaborative venture was thus released as Henry Cow's third album, *In Praise Of Learning* (1975). Around this time Slapp Happy's vocalist, Dagmar Krause, was recruited as a full-time member, while Lindsay Cooper rejoined the group.

Given Henry Cow's interest in various themes, and especially politics, the addition of a singer seemed only logical. Their first album with sustained vocals, *In Praise Of Learning*, was an astonishingly well-integrated work, frequently recalling Kurt Weill's music. Nor were the lyrics simply propagandist slogans; on the contrary, they were quite as complex as the musical structure. As Fred commented in *Impetus* in 1976: 'We don't make political statements in a passive way. We're doing what most so-called revolutionary artists aren't doing, which is expanding the form we're working in. Music is our skill, our craft, we change the music and incorporate our statements and in the long term that has a revolutionary effect.'

The next couple of years were to see some memorable collaborations: in particular with the Mike Westbrook Orkhestra and Robert Wyatt. If gigs in the UK were thin on the ground, those abroad were numerous, especially in Italy where they often played benefits for the Communist Party. In 1976 John Greaves left (to be replaced by cellist Georgie Born) and eventually Dagmar's persistent ill-health forced her out, too. The band split completely with Virgin, as a result of mutual dissatisfaction; in particular, the group no longer wished to shoulder the conventional rock band's responsibility for the promotion of their records.

Last round-up

By 1978, however, musical differences within the group resulted in its break-up, following the release of their densely-textured, instrumental *Western Culture*. Some of the material from the recording sessions for this powerful and innovative album was also put out as the Art Bears' *Hopes And Fears* (1978), mainly featuring Fred, Chris and Dagmar, and the release of these two contrasting records clearly demonstrated the different directions in which band members were pulling at the time. As part of their final press release put it: 'In our tenth year we are ceasing to operate as a permanent group although the musicians in the group are certain to work variously together in the future. Our own relations are still those of admiration and respect. It is only the group as a corporate and separate entity which can progress no further.'

JULIAN PETLEY

Henry Cow
Recommended Listening

Leg End (Virgin V 2005) (Includes: Nirvana For Mice, Teenbeat Introduction, Teenbeat, Teenbeat Reprise); *Western Culture* (Broadcast BC1) (Includes: On The Raft, Industry, Falling Away, Gretel's Talk, Look Back, Half The Sky).

Ian Anderson: the Pied Piper of Jethro Tull

IT WAS IN 1967 that Ian Anderson, accepting a shabby overcoat as a leaving-home present from his father, set off in a clapped-out van for London to become a musician. He had already played guitar with a Blackpool school band and had traded in his electric guitar for a microphone and a flute because he could carry these around in his pocket.

Born in Scotland on 10 August 1947, the itinerant Anderson put art-school behind him to join a seven-piece blues combo called variously the John Evan Band or the John Evan Smash. Anderson's drive led the band to seek gigs in the larger Midland towns; he approached Chris Wright, then working for a Manchester booking agency. Wright was busy at the time with Ten Years After, but, recognising Anderson's potential, he advised him to recruit a good blues guitarist. Luton-based Mick Abrahams – formerly of the Toggery Five and McGregors Engine – joined the band, but by November 1967 a shortage of cash and gigs had reduced them to a three-piece outfit: Anderson, Abrahams and bass-player Glenn Cornick. Drummer Clive Bunker, an old friend of Abrahams, was brought in to swell the numbers. At that time, they were an out-and-out blues band with Anderson's distinctive flute winding in and out of the mélange. They adopted a string of different names, including the Bag of Blues, before finally arriving at Jethro Tull – the name of an eighteenth-century agriculturalist.

In early 1968 Chris Wright moved to London and started Chrysalis Records with Terry Ellis, aiming to promote blues and underground bands in Britain. Chrysalis put Jethro Tull on modest wages, enabling Anderson to give up his job as sweeper-up at a Luton cinema and concentrate on his flute practice, which he did standing on one leg like a deranged flamingo while neighbours banged on the thin walls and threatened retribution. The band secured a residency at London's Marquee and consolidated their growing popularity with an appearance at the 1968 National Jazz and Blues Festival.

The same year saw the release of Jethro Tull's debut album, *This Was*. The LP contained energetic blues-based rock songs, tied together by Anderson's snarling

Right: The wild frontman plays the pied piper amid the swirling smoke of a colourful Tull set. Inset: A rustic pose from the bearded band; from left John Evan, Jeffrey Hammond-Hammond, Ian Anderson, Barriemore Barlow and Martin Barre.

vocals and breathy flute-playing, while a definite jazz influence could be heard in the Roland Kirk number 'Serenade To A Cuckoo' – apparently the first piece Anderson had learned to play. The album received favourable reviews and the single 'Love Story' crept into the Top Thirty at the beginning of 1969.

Mad dog Fagin

There was only room for one leader in the band, however, and tensions were growing between Anderson and Abrahams. Abrahams left to form Blodwyn Pig, being temporarily replaced by Tony Iommi of Earth (later Black Sabbath) before Martin Barre was recruited on a permanent basis. The new line-up pulled itself together under Anderson's energetic and firm leadership and produced the albums *Stand Up* (1969) and *Benefit* (1970). These featured Anderson's brilliant flute-playing, which owed little to convention, but borrowed from many styles, including baroque and folk; despite such unorthodoxy, he managed to exchange licks with the guitars and fit neatly into the rock format. Meanwhile, Jethro Tull's single 'Living In The Past' reached Number 3 in the UK, and two further singles made the Top Ten – 'Sweet Dream' in 1969 and 'Witches Promise' in 1970.

This period was to see Jethro Tull discarding their underground tag and emerging as one of the biggest progressive bands on the rock circuit. Both sophisticated and heavy enough to capture the same markets as Pink Floyd and Led Zeppelin, they also had a unique English quality that would later come to dominate their sound. But in 1970 and 1971, it was extensive gigging, a cult *flavour* (if, in fact, a much broader appeal), Anderson's Dickensian dervish image and initial popularity with the music press that brought their music to a vast audience in both Britain and America.

Anderson was working with composer/arranger David Palmer, a Royal Academy of Music graduate who had an interest in sixteenth-century English music. The singer was beginning to move towards more thematic songwriting, but what caught the public's attention was the bearded frontman's increasingly flamboyant stage act. Adopting the 'mad dog Fagin' posture, he would hop around in tights and a tattered overcoat, brandishing his silver flute. By 1971 two former members of the original John Evan Band had been recruited to Jethro Tull: John Evan on keyboards, and Jeffrey Hammond-Hammond, who replaced Glenn Cornick on bass. Cornick went on to form Wild Turkey.

When the theatrical element looked like becoming more important than the music, Jethro Tull moved towards more prolonged

studio recording and their first two concept albums followed. *Aqualung* (1971) dealt with Anderson's views on organised religion and the fate of life's luckless rejects – the singer's seedy on-stage persona was worked into the LP's cover illustration, depicting an old tramp whose wheezing had earned him the nickname 'Aqualung'. The album sold well and 'Life Is A Long Song' gave them a UK Top Twenty single hit. In comparison, *Thick As A Brick* (1972) was poorly received; it featured sides of continuous concept music held together with superfluous jamming and was lacking in both feel and inspiration. The band's subsequent album, *A Passion Play* (1973), was panned by the critics; Anderson had taken the concept as far as performing the set as an orchestrated stage show with an integrated film, which he wrote and directed himself.

The reaction to the album seemed to question its aspirations and pretensions rather than musical quality. Like *Thick As A Brick*, *A Passion Play* was one complete song divided into several reasonably discernible movements. The theme centred on the after-life, with the tale of a deceased person's traumatic experience at the gates of heaven and Lucifer bemoaning his fall from his former status as the 'old God' of Merrie England. Elaborately packaged, *A Passion Play* boasted the pinnacle of Anderson's pun-laden lyrics, coupled with music that threatened to sever the links with R&B in favour of an indigenously English style – a style that again manifested itself on the album *Songs From The Wood* four years later. *A Passion Play* was an intense album, with frequently incomprehensible lyrics, and perhaps its reception had much to do with the fact that it did not fit into any rock category.

Sticks and stones

Complaining of 'press abuse', Anderson announced in 1973 that the band were to suspend touring indefinitely. Ironically, it coincided with *A Passion Play* topping the American album charts and a *Melody Maker* report that called the band 'one of the world's top five live attractions'.

Tull were not long out of the public eye, however. They emerged the following year with a new album, *War Child*, which saw a return to individual songs and sold over a million copies. A rigorous tour schedule subsequently covered Australia, New Zealand, Japan and the States, where they broke their existing record for audience attendance, selling out 100,000 seats over five nights at the Los Angeles Forum. After three months Stateside, Tull descended upon Europe and did great business until Ian injured his ankle on stage in Kiel, Germany.

It was while in Europe that the album *Minstrel In The Gallery* was assembled – the first fruits of the group's mobile recording unit, Maison Rouge. It was an unexpectedly mellow creation in many respects, a lot of it acoustic and pretty, but still packing an electric punch in places,

especially the pulsating title track. It had an appealing freshness, but did not abandon the Tull tradition of focusing on down-and-outs, nor Ian's ability to be pensive, lewd and self-mocking in one line.

As 1976 dawned, a compilation album, hand-picked by Ian, was released, bearing the mysterious title *MU*. After numerous guesses about these initials had been made, Anderson revealed that they simply stood for the Musicians' Union. His choice of songs emphasised the quality of Tull melodies, with ballads strongly represented, but also included what *Melody Maker* called 'the ultimate in JT rock', 'Locomotive Breath', as well as examples of the ingenious dialogues between Anderson on flute and Martin Barre on guitar.

Songs of an old rocker

New work came together in 1976 on the album *Too Old To Rock'n'Roll: Too Young To Die,* which included several songs Ian had initially conceived for a stage musical to feature Adam Faith. Faith, however, was already committed to another stage production, so Ian expanded the project for Tull to record. The LP told the tale of rocker Ray Lomas (based on a real character whom Tull-arranger David Palmer knew). Ian survived the inevitable attempts by press to treat the album's title and theme as autobiographical, although the cartoon-strip artwork on the sleeve was an obvious caricature of Ian. To help promote the Lomas saga, Anderson appeared on TV shows such as 'Supersonic' and the 'Old Grey Whistle Test', while in July 1976 a special video presentation of the album was arranged with a stereo linkup between London Weekend Television and Capital Radio. The LP brought Tull's gold album total up to 11, and the success story kept on running . . . 1978 saw a satellite transmission of a Tull concert to 26 million people, while the live album *Bursting Out* presented a set laced with Anderson's salty banter and a mixture of ballads and exciting improvisations.

Prolific as ever, Tull kept turning out the albums for their loyal fans – *Stormwatch* (1979), *A* (1980) and *Broadsword And The Beast* (1982). The personnel changes have been many over the years, Anderson remaining the constant factor. The hermit-like existence he adopted, breeding salmon on a remote Scottish island, is mirrored in the rural themes of the late-Seventies albums *Songs From The Wood* (1977) and *Heavy Horses* (1978), celebrating, in title and content, the pleasures of the country life in acoustic ballads that owed much to Britain's folk heritage.

Ian Anderson continues in his much-quoted quest to 'justify the place on my passport where it says "Occupation: musician"'. In 1987, *Crest Of A Knave* took him back to the UK Top Twenty, while the group celebrated 20 years of Jethro Tull in 1988 with a multi-album set of the same title. Judging by the failure of his 1983 solo LP *Walk Into Light,* to the public Ian Anderson *was* Jethro Tull.

JETHRO TULL
Discography to 1982

Singles

Aeroplane/Sunshine Day (MGM 1384, 1967); Song For Jeffrey/One For John Gee (Island WIP 6043, 1968); Love Story/Christmas Song (Island WIP 6048, 1968); Living In The Past/Driving Song (Island WIP 6056, 1969); Sweet Dream/17 (Chrysalis WIP 6070, 1969); Witches Promise/Teacher (Chrysalis WIP 6077, 1970); Inside/Alive And Well (Chrysalis WIP 6081, 1970); Bungle In The Jungle/Back Door Angels (Chrysalis CHS 2054, 1974); Minstrel In The Gallery/Summerday Sands (Chrysalis CHS 2075, 1975); Living In The Past/Requiem (Chrysalis CHS 2081, 1976); Too Old To Rock And Roll/Rainbow Blues (Chrysalis CHS 2086, 1976); The Whistler/Strip Cartoon (Chrysalis CHS 2135, 1976); Moths/Life Is A Long Song (Chrysalis CHS 2214, 1978); A Stitch In Time/Sweet Dream (Chrysalis CHS 2260, 1978); North Sea Oil/Elegy (Chrysalis CHS 2378, 1979); Working John, Working Joe/Flyingdale Flyer (Chrysalis CHS 2468, 1980); Fallen On Hard Times/Broadsword (Chrysalis CHS 2619, 1982).

EPs

Life Is A Long Song (Chrysalis WIP 6106, 1971); *Ring Out Solstice Bells* (Chrysalis CXP2, 1976); *King Henry's Madrigal (Theme From Mainstream)* (Chrysalis CH3 2394, 1979).

Albums

This Was (Island ILPS 9085, 1968); *Stand Up* (Island ILPS 9103, 1969); *Benefit* (Island ILPS 9123, 1970); *Aqualung* (Island ILPS 9145, 1971); *Thick As A Brick* (Chrysalis CHR 1003, 1972); *Living In The Past* (Chrysalis CJT 1, 1972); *A Passion Play* (Chrysalis CHR 1040, 1973); *War Child* (Chrysalis CHR 1067, 1974); *M.U. – Best Of Jethro Tull* (Chrysalis CHR 10, 1975); *Minstrel In The Gallery* (Chrysalis CHR 1082, 1975); *Too Old To Rock And Roll, Too Young to Die* (Chrysalis CHR 1111, 1976); *Songs From The Wood* (Chrysalis CHR 1132, 1977); *Repeat – Best Of Jethro Tull, Volume 2* (Chrysalis CHR 1135, 1977); *Heavy Horses* (Chrysalis CHR 1175, 1978); *Live – Bursting Out* (Chrysalis CJT 4, 1978); *Stormwatch* (Chrysalis CDL 1238, 1979); *A* (Chrysalis CDL 1301, 1982); *Broadsword And The Beast* (Chrysalis CDL 1380, 1982).

A scarecrow stance for Anderson as he acknowledges another ovation for a triumphant Jethro Tull concert.

AIR CONDITIONED

The fresh but classical sounds of Curved Air

AT FIRST, Curved Air's sound was a complex mixture of electric rock and classical music, and its cool, liquid surface was sometimes touched with an eerie beauty. Sonja Kristina's ethereal vocals effectively elaborated on the wailing violin of Darryl Way and sweeping keyboards of Francis Monkman to create a moody but melodious blend. Later, the sound coarsened; that crystalline voice gave way to a harsh and grating rock singer's shout – in the same

way that the singer's sensual stage act was made more obvious by her appearing in ever scantier costumes – and Curved Air went the way of all flesh. But, for a brief moment in 1970-71, they fulfilled all the expectations of their progressive-rock audience.

In 1969 violinist Darryl Way left the Royal College of Music and began to work with Nick Simone, a virtuoso American pianist. Although both classically-trained, Way and Simone wanted to explore the possibilities of rock, and Way accordingly tried out a number of systems of violin

Above: Sonja Kristina performs the dance of the seven veils at an open-air concert late in Curved Air's career.

amplification. It was while testing such a system in a London music shop that he first met Francis Monkman, who was studying organ and harpsichord at the Royal Academy of Music but was concurrently experimenting with electric guitar. With Simone, bassist Rob Martin and drummer Pat Deneen, Monkman and Way formed Sisyphus.

Deneen quit early on, however, and a violent personality clash between Monkman and Simone resulted in the latter's departure around the same time. With Florian Pilkington-Miksa coming in on drums, the group continued to rehearse their predominantly instrumental repertoire as a four-piece. In the autumn of 1969, Sisyphus made their live debut supporting the Aynsley Dunbar Retaliation at Klook's Kleek in Hampstead.

A series of club dates followed, and later in the year the group answered an advertisement for a rock band whose members could read music, as a result being engaged by Galt MacDermot to provide the music for his play 'Who The Murderer Was' at the Mercury Theatre, Notting Hill Gate. Now calling themselves Curved Air (a name taken from avant-garde musician Terry Riley's *A Rainbow In Curved Air* album), the group was approached in January 1970 by Mark Hanau, a photographer working on the play, who put himself forward as manager and suggested that they should enlist Sonja Kristina, a beautiful Swedish-American singer-actress who had been appearing for 18 months in another of MacDermot's ventures, the musical *Hair*.

Heading out ...

Despite initial scepticism, Kristina was quickly accepted as lead singer and, with Hanau as manager, Curved Air began work on fresh material, rehearsing at the Cabin in Shepherds Bush. On March 5th they made their first public appearance, at the Royal College of Music, and in April played for the first time outside London at Manchester's Electric Circus. During June and July, Curved Air appeared frequently at venues such as the Roundhouse, the Marquee and the Lyceum in London, building up a small but enthusiastic following. When Rob Martin left the band, Ian Eyre was selected as his replacement on bass and made his debut with the group on their session for John Peel's Sunday radio show on 3 September.

While the group visited Holland and Germany and toured universities and polytechnics at home, Hanau was busy taking the album that they had recorded round the record companies, eventually signing the band to Warner Brothers for a massive £100,000 advance. *Air Conditioning* appeared late in 1970, and with the aid of a big promotional campaign and the gimmick of printing track information and an elaborate design on the record itself, provoked reactions ranging from curiosity to accusations of hype.

The music contained in the album was both competent and unorthodox, providing a variety of contexts in which Way's fluid, haunting violin and Monkman's powerful guitar and keyboard-work could be heard, although the poor quality of Mark Edwards' production meant that the full impact of the music was lost. This problem was worsened on the early pressings by appalling sound reproduction attributable to the record's picture-disc format.

After the release of *Air Conditioning*, which rose to Number 8 in the album charts in December 1970, Curved Air supported Black Sabbath on their UK tour and were very well-received, fans loving Kristina's shimmering presence and Way's shuddering solos on his perspex violin. At the same time, early in 1971, 'It Happened Today' and Way's extraordinary 7½-minute instrumental showcase 'Vivaldi' were coupled with the otherwise unreleased 'What Happens When You Blow Yourself Up' on a maxi-single, but it failed to chart.

Curved Air then recorded a new album, after which they toured the USA supporting Jethro Tull, Deep Purple, B. B. King and Edgar Winter. However, Warners were unhappy with some of the tracks that had been laid down and requested the group to return to England to re-record them. Some of the group members had found the American experience traumatic and, following arguments with Hanau, the group pulled out of a date at the Fillmore West and caught the plane home, abandoning their manager. They subsequently re-recorded the necessary material and signed with Clifford Davies Management, who organised a headlining tour of the UK. 'Back Street Luv' was simultaneously issued as a single; in August, it began a 12-week run in the charts which, with Curved Air's appearance on 'Top Of The Pops', saw it reach Number 4.

The LP, known simply as 'Second Album', was released shortly afterwards and made Number 9 in the charts in October. Its two sides emphasised the fact that Monkman and Way were becoming less collaborative. Way's material, on side one, demonstrated his skill in providing classically melodic backdrops for Kristina's lyrics, and afforded him ample opportunity to embellish his ideas with violin motifs and passages of considerable beauty, notably on 'Young Mother' and 'Puppets'. Monkman's preoccupation with composition and musicianship led to an altogether more complicated second side, with moods ranging from the jazz-oriented to the symphonic; his long, melodramatic 'Piece Of Mind' was the LP's masterpiece.

In the autumn of 1971, Curved Air returned to the States, where they were again warmly greeted. But Way and Monkman were clashing more and more over material and presentation, and legal arguments between Hanau and their new management caused further problems. At the end of the year Ian Eyre left and was replaced by Mike Wedgewood. During March 1972, Curved Air recorded their third album, *Phantasmagoria*. Once again,

Way's compositions were confined to side one of the record and Monkman's filled side two. Kristina's 'Melinda More Or Less', a song that dated from her time on the folk-circuit in the late Sixties, was also included and subsequently became a live favourite.

Air in short supply

By now, Monkman and Way had independently decided to leave, as had Pilkington-Miksa, tired of the constant disagreements. Kristina and Wedgewood decided to keep the name going, recruiting drummer Jim Russell and two teenage musical prodigies, Eddie Jobson on violin and synthesiser and Kirby on guitar, to record *Air Cut*, released in 1973. This band played live successfully, with maximum use of stage effects, but it was a short-lived version of Curved Air: Jobson left to replace Eno in Roxy Music and Wedgewood became bassist for Caravan. Kristina attempted a solo recording career before returning to the cast of *Hair* for a three-month spell in the summer of 1974.

In the meantime, Darryl Way had formed Wolf, a classical/jazz-rock outfit that had little commercial success during its 18-month existence, releasing three largely ignored albums before disbanding in 1974. Later that year Curved Air was revived when Kristina, Monkman, Way and Pilkington-Miksa decided to play a one-off college tour to clear the group's tax debts, bringing in Phil Kohn as bassist. From this tour, ironically their most successful, came the album *Curved Air Live*, released in early 1975. Afterwards, with their debts cleared, Monkman and Pilkington-Miksa decided not to continue and Kohn also quit. Kristina and Way brought in bassist Tony Reeves, guitarist Mick Jacques and drummer Stewart Copeland to record two further albums, *Midnight Wire* (1975) and *Airborne* (1976), before Curved Air finally disbanded in January 1977.

Kristina subsequently returned to the theatre, toured with her own group, Escape, and recorded a solo album, *Sonja Kristina* (1980). Way spent nine months on his classical album, *Concerto For Electric Violin And Synthesiser* (1978), which featured an orchestra synthesised by Monkman, and in 1982 released a solo single called 'Little Plum'. Monkman himself went on to help form Sky, recording two albums with them before leaving to record a solo album, *Dweller On The Threshold* (1982). Of all the musicians associated with Curved Air, Stewart Copeland has found the greatest success, going on to worldwide acclaim with the Police.

Although the various incarnations of Curved Air were active for almost seven years, it is for 'Back Street Luv' that they are best remembered. Perhaps it is fitting that a group who produced some of the most unusual music of the early Seventies should be best-known for one of the decade's most inspired and powerful singles.   ALAN KINSMAN

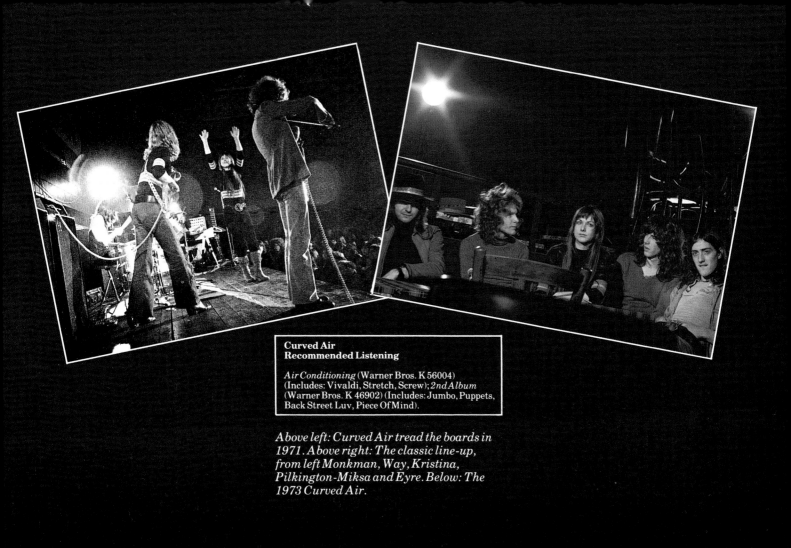

**Curved Air
Recommended Listening**

Air Conditioning (Warner Bros. K 56004)
(Includes: Vivaldi, Stretch, Screw); *2nd Album*
(Warner Bros. K 46902) (Includes: Jumbo, Puppets,
Back Street Luv, Piece Of Mind).

*Above left: Curved Air tread the boards in
1971. Above right: The classic line-up,
from left Monkman, Way, Kristina,
Pilkington-Miksa and Eyre. Below: The
1973 Curved Air.*

SOFT MACHINE

Thinking-man's rock with a jazzy flavour

THE PRE-1966 UNDERGROUND scene in the UK was a strange entity, full of poets, satirists, bomb-banners, jazzers and a sprinkling of genuine eccentrics, like the Alberts. Some of it – like the Alberts' Evenings of British Rubbish – was wholly English; but much of it was inherited from the Americans, notably the Beats.

It was from this kind of cultural heritage that the Soft Machine emerged in 1966. More than any other British band of the era, they represented all the elements of the 'old' underground. Their story starts several years earlier at the Simon Langton School in Canterbury, whose pupils at the time included Robert Wyatt, Mike Ratledge and Hugh Hopper – all of varying ages, but sharing a common interest in jazz, especially avant-garde jazz. Much has been made, over the years, of the idyllic and liberal atmosphere of the school and its influence on a Canterbury supposedly

on the brink of turning into a kind of English Haight-Ashbury. But Robert Wyatt has since dispelled the myth by saying: 'It was an extremely dull grammar school and I can't remember a single stimulating thing about Canterbury.'

Around this time Wyatt and Hopper met a genial Australian by the name of Daevid Allen. Aged 21, Allen was a fully-fledged beatnik – he knew and had worked with William Burroughs and the then-unknown Terry Riley in Paris; he had taken LSD and had long hair. With Hopper playing bass and Wyatt learning the drums, the three of them performed occasionally as an avant-garde trio but spent much time in Paris, on Allen's houseboat, working on tape-loops and experimenting with all manner of new delights.

Ayers' style

By 1964, with the Beatles and Stones sweeping all before them, Canterbury was developing its own healthy music scene. At the centre was a group called the Wilde Flowers, the initial line-up of which comprised Hugh Hopper, his brother Brian on saxes, Robert Wyatt, Richard Sinclair on guitar and Kevin Ayers – who had been recommended because he was the only other long-hair in Kent – on vocals. The Wilde Flowers played a strange mixture of R&B, soul and experimental jazz.

The band continued in various incarnations until mid 1966, when Ayers and Allen took off to Majorca for the summer. On their return, they discovered that Ratledge – a brilliant keyboard-player,

The Soft Machine (below) came to convey a serious, 'arty' image (inset opposite), a far cry from the flower-power freakiness of *their first line-up (above) – from left Robert Wyatt, Daevid Allen, Kevin Ayers and Mike Ratledge.*

heavily into contemporary classical music – had left Oxford University and wanted to form a new band. Wilde Flowers then split two ways. One half went on to become Caravan in 1968. Ayers, Wyatt and Allen joined up with Ratledge and eventually became the Soft Machine. The name was Allen's idea, coming from the title of a William Burroughs novel; he actually phoned Burroughs for permission to use it.

Initially the new band's repertoire wasn't vastly different from that of the Wilde Flowers, but they soon became totally original, performing Ayers' and Wyatt's own compositions. Ayers' were prototypes for the quirky but oddly philosophical songs for which he later became known; Wyatt was already writing about the minutiae of his daily life. Both were singing, in their different ways, in very English accents, proving that it *was* possible to sing in a rock band without affecting a mid-Atlantic drawl. Apart from the songs, they were developing an interest in improvisation, largely through Ratledge. By the end of 1966 their music was, in both style and execution, way beyond most of their British contemporaries.

The timing was perfect – through Allen and his connections with the international freak set, the band were able to find gigs in the newly-emerging underground. They played on the same bill as Pink Floyd at the *International Times* launch party in October 1966 and went on to become regulars at UFO. For these early gigs they were supplemented by an American guitarist, Larry Nolan, a mysterious character who was, apparently, the veteran of various Californian bluegrass bands alongside Jackson Browne sideman David Lindley.

Alien Allen

Like many of the more adventurous bands of the period, the Soft Machine suffered from audience incomprehension and hostility almost every time they played out of London or at a non-underground gig. As a result, shortly after their memorable performance at 'The 14 Hour Technicolor Dream' at the Alexandra Palace in April 1967, they shifted their base of operations to the South of France, their popularity in Europe dating from this period. On their return at the end of the summer, Allen was refused entry as an undesirable alien, the band continuing as a three-piece. However, they had already recorded a single entitled 'Love Makes Sweet Music', on which Allen played. At the end of the year the Soft Machine embarked on a gruelling six-month tour of the States with Jimi Hendrix, and after this they recorded their first album, *Soft Machine*.

Although everything was completed in one take, it was a stunning album, containing charmingly silly Wyatt songs and slightly more disarming numbers by Ayers, linked by pieces of improvisation. Despite its quality, it remained unreleased in the UK until the mid Seventies. The tour virtually killed off the band, however; Ayers disappeared, but Ratledge and

Wyatt recruited Hugh Hopper, who had roadied for them, to play bass – and a new band came together in July 1968 to rehearse for a second album.

Ratledge had felt that the original band was too 'poppy'; although adventurous and bizarre, the new line-up was to be considerably more serious. Nevertheless, the two 'aspects' coexisted for a while, as is demonstrated by the second album, *Volume Two* (1969). Despite more technical problems, it was another classic album, this time with the added dimension of Hopper's roaring fuzz bass. By the end of the year, the limitations of a three-piece led to the addition of a four-piece brass front-line. On a good night they were amazing, but the sheer originality of the first line-up had virtually disappeared; they were moving towards a jazz-rock norm. Unable to sustain such a large unit, they dropped back to a four-piece, only Elton Dean on alto sax remaining from the big band. This line-up produced *Third* (1970), in many ways their most polished album – though, with the exception of Wyatt's 'Moon In June', most of the humour and what the French saw as 'Dadaist' qualities had gone.

Shortly after the release of *Third*, the band played at the Promenade Concerts, much to the chagrin of the dinner-jacketed audience. It wasn't a good gig, but it was significant in that it showed that the band had become the 'intellectuals' of the rock set and were being taken up by the establishment. Ratledge, in particular, was starting to concentrate more and more on 'technical expertise'. Wyatt's contributions, especially the vocals, were being cut back virtually to nothing. He left the band, returning briefly to drum on *Fourth* (1971), a rather flaccid version of *Third*. With Wyatt gone, the charm of the original band had disappeared completely. Even new recruit Elton Dean left; an improviser by choice, he found little room to move in Ratledge's increasingly tight compositions. The next line-up, with John Marshall on drums and Karl Jenkins on saxes, recorded *Fifth* (1972) and *Six* (1973), both cold jazz-rock albums.

The Softs in the early Seventies; from left Karl Jenkins, Mike Ratledge, John Marshall and Hugh Hopper.

Name dropping

By May 1973 Hopper had left and been replaced by another jazz-rocker, Roy Babbington. At this point Ratledge should seriously have considered dropping the name Soft Machine but, undaunted, the band went on to make *Seven* (1973) and *Bundles* (1975). Even the addition of a guitarist, Allan Holdsworth, had made little difference to the sound. Ratledge himself quit in January 1976, but Jenkins and Marshall held on to the name and, with various additional musicians, made the albums *Softs* (1976), *Alive And Well In Paris* (1978) and, after a gap when everyone thought that the name had gone for good, *Land Of Cockayne* (1981).

For most of the Seventies, the band bearing the name Soft Machine bore little relation to the original. Aspects of the original ideas lived on in the work of ex-members, notably in Gong, the anarchic – if self-indulgent – band led by Daevid Allen. Throughout the late Sixties and early Seventies, Kevin Ayers tottered on the brink of success with a string of solo albums, but seemed happier sunning himself in Majorca. Wyatt formed Matching Mole, a sort of radical version of Soft Machine. Following an accident in which he fell from a window, causing him to be paralysed from the waist down, he was unable to drum any more, but such releases as *Rock Bottom* (1974) and a series of singles on the Rough Trade label in the Eighties have shown that his distinctive vocal style, once so important in the Soft Machine, remained unimpaired.

JOHN PLATT

Soul Satisfaction

Slickness and sentimentality characterised a new decade of black pop

THE PRESTIGE BLACK music enjoyed by 1970 owed much to the success of Berry Gordy's Motown organisation, which had sold soul to a worldwide and predominantly white audience from the early Sixties onwards. By the Seventies, the company was keen to extend its operations into the lucrative areas of cinema and international cabaret.

Soul substitutes

But while Motown had sought to expand the horizons of soul, it had unwittingly created a new series of stereotypes. The success of Philadelphia International, masterminded by Leon Huff and Kenny Gamble, had many interesting parallels to Motown, while the artist roster checked name for name with the Motor City favourites of yesteryear. The O'Jays allied a searing Four Tops lead/harmony trade-off with a touch of Whitfield-like social comment in songs like 'For The Love Of Money', 'Love Train' and 1974's *Ship Ahoy* album; the Three Degrees provided ersatz Supreme sex appeal with a little of the Vandellas' bluesiness, while the lazy, sensual delivery of Billy Paul evoked Marvin Gaye at his most laid-back.

The 'production line' techniques of Gordy at Motown and the Gamble-Huff team in Philly left little room for those who sought to free themselves from the attentions of house writing, arrangement and production teams. Stevie Wonder renegotiated his contract and achieved a degree of artistic freedom within Motown thanks to his attorney Johannan Vigoda – yet still had problems, notably in connection with Motown's insistence that his song 'Superstition' be released as a single (Wonder had promised the number to Jeff Beck). If one of the world's finest singer-songwriters had trouble gaining artistic freedom at Motown, the chances were slim, to say the least, for a group such as the Jackson Five whose career had been plotted by others to the extent that they didn't even own the rights to their own name. Their move to CBS/Epic in 1975 paralleled that of the Isley Brothers six years earlier in that both acts revealed hitherto unsuspected songwriting and production talents that ensured their continued success while many Motown acts foundered during a general decline in the company's fortunes in the mid Seventies.

Sounds familiar

One of the most talented refugees from Motown was Gladys Knight, who had spent her time with the company in the Supremes' shadow. Following her departure to the Buddah label, she began to record the work of white songwriters, such as Jim Weatherly; the result was an equal measure of classic soul ('Midnight Train To Georgia') and embarrassingly sentimental slush ('Best Thing That Ever Happened To Me'). With scant pop success to her name at

that point, she could change her musical style in ways that the Supremes without Diana Ross (who became Motown's only multi-media superstar) could not. Other new stars that helped break Motown's hold on black pop music were Barry White, who cashed in on Isaac Hayes' musical style, and the Stylistics, who were little more than soundalike imitators of Smokey Robinson and the Miracles.

If the Sixties had seen an expansion of soul music on several fronts, the Seventies represented something of a retrenchment. Significant developments in black music occurred out of the commercial spotlight with the acceptance of reggae by rock audiences and the first musical ventures of Parliament and Funkadelic. Soul had become part of the showbiz establishment; it was to take the late Seventies disco boom, headed by bands such as Trammps, Chic and the Commodores, to present a significant new challenge to a music that had become increasingly smug and slick.

MICHAEL HEATLEY

Gladys Knight sacrificed her earlier gutsy delivery for a smooth, supper-club soulfulness when she left Motown for pastures new in 1972 – but, in so doing, she reached a new, lucrative audience.

YOUNG, GIFTED AND BLACK

The rise and rise of the Jackson Five

THE LIST OF TALENT that Berry Gordy, founder and owner of Motown Record Corporation, has been able to secure over the years has been quite extensive and impressive. Marvin Gaye, Stevie Wonder, Diana Ross, the Supremes and the Commodores immediately spring to mind as acts that have reached international status. To these must be added the Jackson Five, a group of brothers whose vibrant young black sound was nurtured by the Motown machinery to produce million-selling records.

The Jackson Five initially comprised five young brothers from Gary, Indiana; they were Michael (born 29 August 1959), Jermaine (born 11 December 1954), Sigmund Esco – known as 'Jackie' (born 4 May 1951), Marlon (born 12 March 1958) and Toriano Adaryll – known as 'Tito' (born 15 October 1953). Their younger brother, Randy (born 29 October 1962) joined them later, and they also had three sisters – Maureen, Latoya and Janet.

Their motivation came initially from their father, Joe Jackson, a crane operator who played in a local R&B band named the Falcons. He turned his own musical ambitions towards his children and encouraged them to learn to play instruments, putting them through daily rehearsals and grooming them for talent contests. Their mother, Katherine, was a blues and country singer. The brothers soon became a tight, polished and assured line-up with smooth dance routines, doing cover versions of Temptations, Sly Stone and Smokey Robinson numbers.

Lucky break

The group's first date was at a local club, Mr Lucky's, where they made five dollars from the audience pitching coins onto the floor. Joe Jackson booked his sons as a regular attraction on the club circuit where, during the school holidays, they supported such bands as Gladys Knight and the Pips and their heroes, the Temptations. He also secured a six-month recording contract with a local label, Steel Town, on which the brothers released one single in 1968 – 'I'm A Big Boy Now', produced by Gordon Keith. Two other early songs – 'Some Girls Want Me For Their Love' and 'You Don't Have To Be Over 21 To Fall In Love' – appeared on Dynamo in 1971 to capitalise on the brothers' success.

The Motown version of the Jacksons' success story plays on their 'discovery' by Diana Ross, promoting them through her by calling their first LP *Diana Ross Presents The Jackson Five* (1970). Admittedly, it was Ross who tipped Berry Gordy off about the family band when she was persuaded to see their show during her visit to Gary in 1968. At that time, Motown desperately needed another group to succeed commercially, as their Sixties acts the Temptations, the Four Tops and the Miracles ran out of steam.

The famous Five (above) were renowned for their colourful stage shows. From left: Tito, Marlon, Jackie, Michael and Jermaine. Opposite: The Jacksons, with Randy (left) replacing Jermaine.

The Jackson Five injected a fresh appeal to the Motown sound and brought them a new market of teenies and pre-teenies who could identify with the 10-year-old Michael. They were nice, clean-living, polite, good-looking boys who displayed energy and style and proved to be more than a mere bubblegum group. Their well-packaged image was backed up with a fair degree of musical talent – not just collectively, but in their solo careers, too.

The band's output included both poppy soul numbers and melodic, emotive ballads. The success of their fresh approach can be demonstrated by the hits they had with Bill Withers' 'Ain't No Sunshine' (by Michael Jackson) and Jackson Browne's 'Doctor My Eyes', the UK chart success of which eclipsed the original in both cases.

Motown signed up the Jackson Five early in 1969 and released their debut single, 'I Want You Back' (written by a collection of the company's top composers and producers known as the Corporation), in October. It was an international big-seller, making Number 2 in the UK charts, Number 1 in the States, and was arguably the best single the Jackson Five made. It had a tight Sly-influenced soul arrangement of bass, drums, piano and guitar, behind the unbroken voice of Michael, stretched to its bubbly heights. Follow-up singles achieved similar success – 'ABC', 'Mama's Pearl', 'The Love You Save', 'I'll Be There', 'Never Can Say Goodbye' and 'Doctor My Eyes'.

On stage the brothers wooed audiences with youthful energy, pulsating music and tightly-rehearsed dance routines, led by little Michael writhing around like a miniature James Brown. The Five were often augmented on stage by two cousins – Johnny Jackson on drums and Ronnie Rancifer on piano. They were to prove a model for the Osmonds, a young Mormon family unit who were later marketed as the Jackson Five's white counterparts.

Rockin' Michael

With fame came fortune, so the Jackson family moved to a 12-roomed mansion in the San Fernando Valley, California. The school-age brothers attended a nearby private school, with tutors accompanying them on tour. The group received unprecedented worldwide acclaim; the press reported their every move and word, a cartoon series devised around them was screened in America and England, and they hosted several American television specials.

Not content with the group's almost fairytale success, Motown decided to record certain brothers individually. Michael Jackson, being lead singer, was the first with the sweeping ballad 'Got To Be There' in October 1971, followed closely by an album of the same name. The album provided several million-selling singles such as 'Rockin' Robin' (a revival of Bobby Day's 1958 hit) and 'I Wanna Be Where You Are'. His solo chart run with Motown lasted, on and off, until 1981. Hot on Michael's heels was older brother, Jermaine, with 'That's The Way Love Goes' in August 1972, taken from his *Jermaine* album released four months later. Michael had little difficulty in securing chart hits;

Jermaine, on the other hand, found it hard going outside America.

Touring took up much of the group's time and energy, but it was a necessary part of their life which they both loved and hated. They attracted mass hysteria and fan worship in every country they visited. Meanwhile, the conveyor-belt hit formula continued with the singles 'Sugar Daddy' in November 1971 and 'Little Bitty Pretty One' (a cover of Bobby Day's 1957 hit) in April 1972. A change of musical style – an almost mature sound – arrived with 'Lookin' Through The Windows' in June 1972. That same month Michael Jackson's biggest-selling solo single, the title song from the movie *Ben*, was issued, with Jermaine's million-selling 'Daddy's Home' following in November. The group's next single, 'Corner Of The Sky', was more adventurous in style, with the chirpy 'Hallelujah Day' following early in 1973. Jackie was the third brother to embark on a solo career within the group with his first album, titled after himself, being issued in January 1974.

Farewell to Motown

It had become evident that the group's bubblegum soul sound was very much a part of their past. No longer was Motown assured of chart-topping albums and singles, and discontent grew within the group as the company's interest waned. This, combined with the ongoing argument caused by Berry Gordy's refusal to let the brothers expand as writers and producers, saw the Jackson Five join the exodus from Motown in 1975. Other big names on the move had included Mary Wells, Martha Reeves and Gladys Knight, and these departures inevitably led to legal battles over rights and contracts.

Motown retained the name Jackson Five and one of the brothers, Jermaine, whose marriage to Gordy's daughter, Hazel, in 1973 had been a much-publicised event, costing 200,000 dollars and featuring 175 doves and Smokey Robinson performing a specially-written song. Jermaine continued in his solo career and acted as Motown's talent scout; the other brothers signed a multi-million dollar deal with CBS/Epic as the Jacksons. The group formed two publishing companies – Peacock Music and Stone Gold Music – and obtained total control of all their recordings, while Randy took Jermaine's place in the ranks.

The brothers' stay at Motown had produced six platinum singles and 10 gold albums, with estimated worldwide sales of 100 million units. After their departure from the label, Motown continued to release their material in various re-packages backed up by special campaigns, their biggest coup being the UK chart-topping

Slick mover Michael was the master of the dance routine (opposite), slipping into leather (left) for his 1983 video to sing that 'Billie Jean' was not his girl. Rumour hinted that Diana Ross (above left) was.

success in 1981 of Michael Jackson's 'One Day In Your Life', which had originally been issued in 1975.

The first Epic album, *The Jacksons*, was produced by Philadelphia's Kenny Gamble and Leon Huff and reached gold status. The brothers had wanted to work with the duo while at Motown, but Gordy had insisted on keeping recordings in-house. During 1977 the single 'Show Me The Way To Go' reached Number 1 in the UK. Motown were quick to cash in by issuing a three-track single containing 'Skywriter', 'I Want You Back' and 'The Love You Save'. *Goin' Places* was the second Epic album, again written and produced by Gamble and Huff, and the title track was lifted for single release at the close of 1977. Compared to the first release, this was uninspiring; it seemed the Jacksons/Philadelphia marriage was heading for the rocks. The group's initial CBS success was nowhere near that achieved in the heady days at Motown.

By 1979 Michael Jackson's interest had turned towards the film industry and he decided to take up an offer to appear in *The Wiz*, sharing top billing with Diana Ross. The film provided the uneventful single 'You Can't Win', produced by Quincy Jones (who was responsible for writing the musical score) in 1979. Later that year, with no new group material due, Michael went back into the studios with Jones to record his debut solo Epic album, *Off The Wall*. The LP, which featured session players the Brothers Johnson and songwriter Rod Temperton (of Heatwave), covered a wide spectrum of music and excelled on dance numbers as well as ballads like 'She's Out Of My Life'. 'Don't Stop Till You Get Enough' was the first of four singles taken from the album, all of which were Top Ten entrants on both sides of the Atlantic.

The album itself reached double platinum status and sold over four million copies. This astounding worldwide selling power affected Michael badly – he became rather reclusive and eccentric, unable to handle his daily life. As a solo artist he had reached massive heights, far beyond that previously enjoyed with the group. One offshoot of this success was that many artists sought to secure his writing and producing talents. Again Motown cashed in by releasing the Jackson Five's *20 Golden Greats* album which spanned material from 1969 to 1974.

The Jacksons' next LP was *Destiny* (1978), the title track being issued to coincide with a UK tour that formed part of a worldwide trek. The album was the first to be written and produced by the brothers, and this policy was to continue with future releases. By 1980 Michael had produced sister Latoya for Polydor, worked with a handful of other artists, and in 1981 won the R&B Grammy Award for the Best Male Vocal Performance, on 'Don't Stop Till You Get Enough'. That success wasn't allowed to pass by – Motown issued *The Best Of Michael Jackson* in its mid-priced album series. That wasn't the only time the two crossed, as the Jackson family paid Motown 100,000 dollars in settlement of the company's lawsuit against the group and CBS. The settlement, among other things, provided full usage by Motown of all Jackson Five and Michael Jackson product recorded during their Motown days.

Rumours of romance

October 1980 saw the release of *Triumph*, an album critics claimed was just that. This dance-oriented set was light on ballads, with 'Time Waits For No-One' being the most commercial. 'Lovely One' was the first single to be lifted, but 'Can You Feel It' was to prove the biggest-selling track. Michael hit the headlines at this time for his association with Diana Ross. He appeared on her 'Diana' television special and the romance on screen was said to be flourishing off-stage as well. Whatever the relationship, it did lead to him writing and producing Ross's 1982 hit single 'Muscles'.

The Jacksons as a group continued to go from strength to strength, and with the success came elusiveness. Interviews with the press, on radio or television became practically non-existent, and their closeness with their audiences was lost as they chose videos, rather than live performance, to promote their songs. Jermaine, meanwhile, had achieved a UK Top Ten hit single with Stevie Wonder's 'Let's Get Serious' in 1980.

In September 1982 Michael Jackson and ex-Beatle Paul McCartney collaborated to release 'The Girl Is Mine', a mediocre track that appeared on Jackson's second solo album, *Thriller* (1982). Jackson worked on the album with Quincy Jones, while Marlon produced tracks for Betty Wright. Meanwhile, the Jacksons released *The Jacksons Live* (1981), a double set recorded during an American tour.

Thriller provided Michael Jackson with the hit single 'Billie Jean' which was accompanied by a slick and imaginative video produced by Steve Barron, showing a rather more sophisticated and self-conscious Michael injecting an almost sobbing emotion into his vocals. The album may not have matched the brilliance of *Off The Wall*, but it nevertheless wasted no time soaring to the top of the album charts in both the UK and the States. 'Billie Jean' hurtled to Number 1 in the singles charts on both sides of the Atlantic, and 'Beat It', another track from the album, followed it into the US and UK Top Ten.

Though the Jacksons did not work together again after 1984's *Victory* album and tour, Michael's success story continued. SHARON DAVIS

**Michael Jackson and the Jackson Five
Recommended Listening**

Anthology (Motown TMSP 6004) (Includes: I Want You Back, ABC, Lookin' Through The Windows, Ben, Ain't No Sunshine, Rockin' Robin, Dancing Machine); *Off The Wall* (Epic EPC 83468) (Includes: Rock With You, Don't Stop Till You Get Enough, Girlfriend, Off The Wall, Burn This Disco Out, She's Out Of My Life).

GLADYS KNIGHT AND THE PIPS

Soul veterans who struck gold

WITH A CAREER spanning some three decades, Gladys Knight and the Pips can justifiably claim to have achieved every goal that popular music has to offer. They have won Grammy Awards, received gold and platinum discs by the score, appeared on virtually every stage around the world, performed for royalty and heads of state – yet they have continued to perform and record, their enthusiasm undiminished.

First Knights

Gladys (born 28 May 1944) began singing almost as soon as she could talk. She joined the choir of her local church and her natural talent prompted her mother to put Gladys's name on the list of competitors on the radio show 'Ted Mack's Amateur Hour' by the time she was eight. Gladys won three heats before walking off with the first prize of 2000 dollars at Madison Square Garden for her rendition of 'Too Young'. After spending a year on the road with Ted Mack, Gladys headed home to Atlanta, Georgia.

A birthday celebration for Gladys's elder brother Merald led to an impromptu singing session with Gladys, Merald, sister Brenda and cousins William and Elenor Guest. The family group kept together, rehearsing during the week and performing together at church, with two more cousins involved – Edward Patten as singer and James Wood as manager. James's nickname was 'Pip', and when the question of a group name came up it was he who suggested the Pips.

The Pips made their first record in 1957 for Brunswick, 'Whistle My Love', which failed to sell and led to both Brenda and Elenor leaving the group. By 1961, however, the remaining Pips had secured a residency at the Builders' Club in Atlanta. After a show one night, the owner, Clifford Hunter, asked the Pips to try out some primitive recording equipment he had recently purchased. One of the songs the group performed, Johnny Otis's 'Every Beat Of My Heart', sounded good enough to release as a single. Hunter and his partner Tommy Brown set up the Huntom label, and put out 'Every Beat Of My Heart' to good local reaction.

Bobby Robinson, owner of the Fire and Fury labels based in New York, heard about the single and sent word down to Atlanta that if the Pips were prepared to come to New York he would record them. The Pips sold whatever personal items they had to raise the fare and, on arriving in New York, went into the studio to re-cut 'Every Beat Of My Heart' with 'Room In My Heart' as the flipside. However, after a further two singles for Fury things began to go wrong for the Pips. Langston George, who had joined the Pips in 1957, departed – as did Gladys herself, in order to start a family. The three remaining Pips continued to record for a while, making a

couple of singles for Fire/Fury before the company folded.

It was with some relief for all concerned that Gladys decided to rejoin the group towards the end of 1963, and a new recording deal with Maxx Records, founded by Larry Maxwell, soon followed. He put them in the hands of Van McCoy, who produced a hit first time out with 'Giving Up'. The success that the Maxx single achieved prompted both Vee-Jay and Bobby Robinson's new label Enjoy to delve into their back catalogues for material by the group. Yet after a couple of further hits, and with barely a year of their Maxx contract expired, Larry Maxwell went bankrupt; Gladys Knight and the Pips were out in the cold again. Fortunately, thanks to the Pips' growing reputation for live performance, it wasn't long before Motown Records signed them.

In the clear

In retrospect, it has to be said that their Motown stay promised much but delivered little. Only rarely were the Pips given the best material with which to work. They started off working with Norman Whitfield, who gave them hits in 1967 with 'Take Me In Your Arms And Love Me', 'Everybody Needs Love' and 'I Heard It Through The Grapevine', which made Number 2 in the US.

However, writer/producer Whitfield's policy of milking every song for all it was worth quickly saw Marvin Gaye hit Number 1 on both sides of the Atlantic with the same song. In later years, whenever the Pips performed it they would be unfairly slated for covering 'Marvin's song'. Another number that was originally a hit in 1968 for the Pips was 'It Should Have Been Me'; the song became an even more successful record for Yvonne Fair some eight years later.

Gladys Knight and the Pips: from the Motown shadows (above) to the Seventies spotlight (top and opposite).

Despite having further hit singles, Gladys Knight and the Pips were keen to leave Motown. In March 1972 they signed to Buddah, ironically while they were at the Number 1 spot in the US with 'Neither One Of Us'. Jim Weatherly, the composer of that song, became as sought-after as Gladys Knight and the Pips, and Buddah were quick to secure his signature as well. This decision was to pay dividends – further Weatherly numbers such as 'Best Thing That Ever Happened To Me' and 'Midnight Train To Georgia' became international hits. In addition, the Pips were awarded two Grammys in 1973, one for the Best R&B Vocal Performance for 'Midnight Train To Georgia' and the other for the Best Pop Vocal Performance for 'Neither One Of Us'.

Buddah continued to keep Gladys Knight and the Pips in the forefront of soul music for some seven years, mainly by ensuring that they were given the best pro-

ducers to work with. Van McCoy returned in 1977 to give them another international hit with 'Baby Don't Change Your Mind'; Curtis Mayfield worked with them on the soundtrack LP to the film *Claudine* (1974); Tony Camillo produced the hit 'Perfect Love', while Ralph Moss helped supply the group with their hit record 'Try To Remember – The Way We Were'.

Gladys Knight made her acting debut in *Pipe Dreams* (1976), while the Pips, having made their solo debut with 'Street Brother', finally recorded their own albums for Casablanca, *At Last . . . The Pips* and *Callin'* (both 1978). Gladys herself cut a solo album for Buddah, *Miss Gladys Knight* (1979), which prompted rumours of a rift in the family group. Those rumours were scotched a year later, however, when Gladys Knight and the Pips signed with CBS. Nickolas Ashford and Valerie Simpson, who produced many of the Pips' Motown sides, returned to give them further hits with 'Bourgie Bourgie' and 'Taste Of Bitter Love'.

Sadly for Knight, her spell at CBS was to sour and 1988 found her and the Pips at MCA. She'd meanwhile hit the top of the US charts in 1985 in the company of Dionne Warwick, Stevie Wonder and Elton John on the AIDS-relief single 'That's What Friends Are For'. The friendship theme was more than appropriate as she and her faithful Pips enjoyed their fourth decade together.

GRAHAM BETTS

Gladys Knight and the Pips Recommended Listening

Spotlight On Gladys Knight And The Pips (Buddah SPOT 1006) (Includes: Midnight Train To Georgia, Part Time Love, Come Back And Finish What You Started, It's A Better Than Good Time, So Sad The Song).

WHITE
UNLIMITED

The wide-ranging talents of Barry White

THE CAREER OF Barry White has often been likened to that of Isaac Hayes – a comparison made all-too-frequently to White's detriment. True, both were gravel-voiced singers who stretched slabs of symphonic soul over singles and albums alike; and both were unlikely sex symbols – Hayes with his shaven head and outlandish stage gear, the portly White in his ill-fitting lounge suits. Yet although Hayes was undeniably first in the field, his rival's commercial success in the Seventies as a writer, producer and arranger had equal impact.

Barry White was born in Galveston, Texas on 12 September 1944 and moved with his family to the East Side of Los Angeles in 1957. His teen years were spent in the tough environs of Reese High School, running with the local gangs. Church was his salvation, because there he was encouraged to play organ and arrange for the choir.

His first involvement with secular music came in 1960 when he joined an R&B group, the Uptights. The following year he studied production under Jack Stern at Rampart Records and made his singing debut as Lee Barry on the Downey label. By now he was married and struggling to keep wife and family from the breadline. He played keyboards for Bob and Earl on 'Harlem Shuffle' which made the US Top Fifty on the Marc label in 1963. When Earl Nelson dissolved the partnership to record 'The Duck' as Jackie Lee, it was White who was waiting in the wings to act as road manager. The disc was one of Mirwood's biggest hits, making Number 14 nationally by January 1966.

Bronco bustin'
The same year White became head of A&R with Bob Keene's Mustang-Bronco Records and cut his first side under his own name – unfortunately, when 'All In The Run Of A Day' appeared on Bronco, it dropped from sight. His work as writer and producer for others was much more rewarding. Deep soul balladeering, such as Viola Wills' 'Lost Without The Love Of My Guy', vied for attention alongside the frothy confections of Felice Taylor. With arranger Gene Page, White composed and produced 'I Feel Love Coming On' for her and had the satisfaction of seeing it reach Number 11 in the UK charts during November 1967.

When Mustang-Bronco folded in 1968, White devoted himself to developing Love Unlimited. Glodean and Linda James were local girls, born in Long Beach and raised in San Pedro; the third member, Diane Taylor, hailed from Buffalo in New York State but was resident in Compton, California. They met White when they were doing session work and within two years he had arranged for them to be signed to Uni Records. Their first single 'Walkin' In The Rain With The One I Love', written by Bob Relf (of Bob and Earl) and arranged by the ubiquitous Page, came out in February 1972 and by May was Number 14 in the Hot Hundred, reaching the same slot in Britain a month later. With its lush keyboards, overwhelming orchestration and soap-opera sincerity from a breathless Glodean, it was very much the shape of things to come.

Inevitably Barry White was persuaded to venture on wax himself. In March 1973 he ploughed familiar ground with 'I'm Gonna Love You Just A Little Bit More Baby', disguising the limitations of his vocals in a rich layer of sound and proffering a calculated eroticism. 'Oh what a groove! You have no idea how it feels,' he moaned, working himself up to add 'My hands just won't keep still!' And although his growling monologues and mumbled asides were hardly equal to Isaac Hayes'

Opposite: At the controls – Barry White, singer, producer and soul superstar. Above: The master with Love Unlimited.

steamy raps, they were undoubtedly more focused. Chocolate-box soul triumphed when it climbed to Number 3 in May 1973 and reached Number 23 in the UK. Released that same year, his debut album for 20th Century was modestly titled *I've Got So Much To Give* and was a harbinger of things to come. The sleeve revealed corpulent Barry White playing King Kong, four women in his hands, a gross troubadour painfully intent on returning women to their pedestal. Not for him the doubtful values of R&B. 'My music ain't no shake-your-butt stuff' he remarked with startling moral rectitude. The same year he separated from the wife who had given him four children and rebuilt his life with Love Unlimited lead singer Glodean James.

Over the next six years he recorded prolifically. Some 16 albums resulted in an even greater number of generally successful singles. Learning from Hayes' example, he was careful to provide long album tracks that could be edited without much difficulty to cover two sides of a single. And if the albums efficiently created that mellow mood for sexual foreplay, then the singles were culled with due regard for their impact on the dance floor.

With Hayes' career in disarray at Stax, the way was clear for White to clean up. Successes included the double-tracked pillow talk of 'Never Never Gonna Give Ya Up', 'Can't Get Enough Of Your Love, Babe' (a US Number 1 in August 1974), the especially infectious 'You're The First, The Last, My Everything' (a UK Number 1 in November 1974) and 'You See The Trouble With Me' (a UK Number 2 in March 1976).

White's lack of discrimination has seen him too easily dismissed in the face of an eloquent track record. Occasional gems like 'It's Ecstasy When You Lay Down Next To Me' showed what could be achieved when he lightened his voice and allowed it flexibility in the manner of more accomplished singers like Marvin Gaye. As an arranger he has stunned audiences with shimmering renditions of other people's material. The Holland-Dozier-Holland classic 'Standing In The Shadows Of Love', included on his first album, provided early evidence of his skill. This, rather than Barry White the singer, has led to albums like *Stone Gon'* (1973), *Can't Get Enough* (1974) and *Barry White Sings For Someone You Love* (1977) topping the US R&B charts. In Britain his albums made three assaults on the Top Twenty; *Can't Get Enough* peaked at Number 4 in November 1974. Seven complementary albums from his Love Unlimited Orchestra also registered strongly under the master's baton.

White gold
When his association with 20th Century ended in 1979, White set up Unlimited Gold for distribution through Columbia. *Change*, his third album on the label, sold quite well in 1982. He later signed to A&M's Breakout label for 1987's *The Right Night And Barry White*.

Like his idol Ray Charles, White has placed great emphasis on financial security. The wider the market place the better; music must not be confined to the ghetto. Already a millionaire, Barry White seems likely to remain a fixture in the industry.   CLIVE ANDERSON

Barry White
Recommended Listening

Greatest Hits (20th Century T-493) (Includes: You're The First, The Last, My Everything, Love Serenade, I'm Gonna Love You Just A Little More Baby, I've Got So Much To Give, Standing In The Shadows Of Love).

■DIANA

How Motown's superstar spread her wings

BERRY GORDY JR has been a shrewd decision-maker many times in his life, but never more so than when he planned the departure of Diana Ross from the Supremes. He knew then, in the late Sixties, that Motown Records would evolve into the multi-media entertainment complex of his ambitions only if it had a multi-media superstar – one who could capture the public imagination, and its disposable income, through sheer intensity of talent, personality and style.

He wanted Ross to be that superstar. He wanted her to join that 'rarified constellation of first-name acceptance alongside Barbra, Billie, Ella and Judy'. Indeed, that quote itself – from one of Motown's 1970 trade press advertisements – revealed Gordy's interest in the performer through whom he hoped Ross could secure 'first-name acceptance': Billie Holiday. So it was no surprise when, twelve months later, Motown announced that the former Supreme would make her motion-picture debut in a biography of the late jazz singer entitled *Lady Sings The Blues* (1972).

Truth is no stranger
In fact, much of Ross's own career in the Seventies might have been scripted for a movie: the challenge of her first solo appearances ('Welcome to the can-Diana-Ross-make-it-on-her-own show', the singer said on opening night); the intimate relationship, professional and personal, with Berry Gordy; and her subsequent controversial marriage to a white man. Her music, too, reinforced the Hollywood connection. Recordings like 'Reach Out And Touch', 'Ain't No Mountain High Enough', 'Touch Me In The Morning' and 'Love Hangover' were passionate, big-production adventures in the sonic equivalent of CinemaScope.

As one of Berry Gordy's executives said in 1973: 'The record artists of Motown have built great public identification, which is almost exactly like the old Hollywood "star quality".' He might have said 'star system', because Gordy appeared to be pursuing his new goals with all the arrogance and autocracy of the old-time movie moguls. When Paramount Pictures, with whom Motown made *Lady Sings The Blues*, baulked at some aspects of the production, Gordy paid the studio two million dollars for creative control of the finished film. On a later occasion, when Tony Richardson, the director of *Mahogany* (1975), disagreed with Gordy over certain creative elements of that movie, the Motown boss fired him and became the director himself.

Ross didn't always go along with the game plan of her mentor. Gordy, for example, didn't want to release 'Reach Out And Touch' as her first solo single in 1970, because it was a waltz and totally unlike the music that her fans were used to hearing. But the singer felt strongly about the song's message, particularly in the light of the social alienation of the times brought about by the Vietnam War.

The give-and-take between Gordy and Ross was probably at the heart of her rise to superstardom in the Seventies. The first couple of solo years were concerned with the media by which she had previously established her popularity: records, concerts and television. Her live appearances collected good reviews, especially at New York's Waldorf Astoria and Hollywood's Coconut Grove, and if tickets were beyond the financial means of most Supremes fans, Diana's discs provided an acceptable substitute. Her first and third albums, released in 1970 and 1971 respectively, *Diana Ross* and *Surrender* (entitled *I'm Still Waiting* in Britain), were among her best.

Much of the material was written and produced by Nick Ashford and Valerie Simpson, who recognised that the singer's finest – and most commercial – music came from a carefully crafted combination of melodrama and vulnerability. Those qualities were evident in 'Ain't No Mountain High Enough', which swept to the top of the US charts in September 1970, and in 'Remember Me', which followed it into the Top Twenty four months later. 'I'm Still Waiting', poignantly penned and produced by Deke Richards, reached the summit in Britain during August 1971, Diana's only UK chart-topper of the decade.

Diana's mid-Seventies image of feline sensuality and million-dollar sophistication was both beguiling and exclusive.

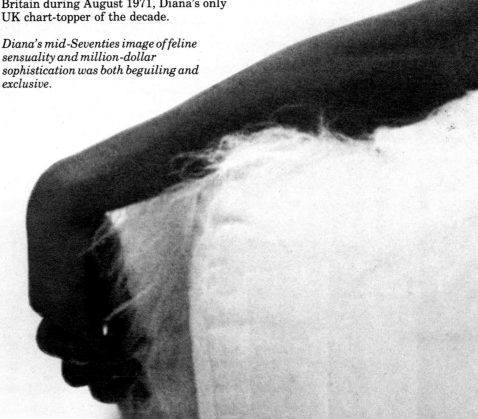

In 1972, Gordy's plans for Hollywood stardom for Ross began to take shape when she began filming *Lady Sings The Blues*. It was a consuming experience, by all accounts. She plunged herself into the role, researching and absorbing every aspect, every detail of Billie Holiday's tempestuous, tragic life and death. 'I read anything anyone had written about her,' said Ross. 'I went to the library, read newspaper clippings, the backs of album covers. I got pictures from her personal collection and studied them, everything from her red fingernails to the knick-knacks on the table. And as I went to sleep at night, I'd try to imagine how Billie Holiday would feel going to sleep after a hard day's work.'

The finished movie reflected both Diana's commitment to the role and her innate acting ability – much to the surprise of critics who, while castigating the script's misrepresentations of Holiday's life, acknowledged that Ross had captured the singer's spirit, her essence. For once, a publicity catchphrase ('Diana Ross *is* Billie Holiday') was not merely movie-makers' hype.

Lady Sings The Blues was a hit, generating close to 20 million dollars at the box-office in North America alone, as well as a Number 1 soundtrack package of such Holiday classics as 'God Bless The Child', 'Good Morning Heartache' (also a Top Forty single in the US in 1973) and 'T'ain't Nobody's Bizness If I Do'. Recognition for Diana personally came in the form of an Oscar nomination for best actress. She didn't win, but later observed, graciously, 'It showed any little black girl living in Detroit's Brewster project who watched TV that night that she, too, can be up there one day.'

On the sentimental side

For all that she had given to Gordy and to *Lady Sings The Blues*, Ross took care of some personal business during 1971-72. She married publicist Bob Silberstein, and gave birth to daughters Rhonda and Tracee (a third child, Chudney, was born a couple of years later). It was surprising not for the fact of black marrying white, but that Ross should marry anyone but Berry Gordy. Their intimacy throughout the Supremes' heyday was well-publicised, to the point where Gordy once admitted that he had 'tried to marry her a couple of times'. Then he said, 'Why should she marry me when she's got me already?'

But if Diana Ross was achieving goals in acting and in her personal affairs, her music was becoming less than satisfying. 'Touch Me In The Morning', a dramatic ballad, was a major hit, but the subsequent album of the same name, released in 1973, carried that song's underlying sentimentality too far, featuring cloying covers of songs such as the Carpenters' 'I Won't Last A Day Without You' and John Lennon's 'Imagine'. The decline was only partially arrested by *Diana And Marvin* (1974), a comfortable (and occasionally seductive) union with Motown's premier male singer, Marvin Gaye. It yielded several hits, despite the fact that it was rumoured that the two singers were never in the recording studio at the same time.

These and other LPs exemplified the problems of Diana on disc between 1973 and 1978. She allowed herself to be recorded by any number of producers – Michael Masser, Tom Baird, Michael Randall, Mel Larson and Jerry Marcellino, Hal Davis, Ron Miller, Bob Gaudio – so that each album became a patchwork quilt of different moods and styles, often lacking conviction. What had been tolerable in the singles-oriented Sixties was no longer the case, especially after the satisfying nature of Ross' initial solo work with Ashford and Simpson. The Richard Perry-produced *Baby It's Me* in 1977 was an attempt to correct this situation that was, sadly, a creative disappointment.

By contrast, Diana Ross in concert was almost always confident and convincing. Her shows were extravaganzas – theatrical and showbiz-heavy, featuring Broadway tunes and Tin Pan Alley standards – but never dull. Her 1976 world tour, staged as 'An Evening With Diana Ross' and subsequently issued as a live album in 1977, exhibited her enthusiasm and inter-reaction with her audience. Many of the songs seemed like personal statements, even the somewhat earnest tribute to 'the working girls' (Billie Holiday, Josephine Baker, Ethel Waters, Bessie Smith). And if Ross rather rushed through the Supremes segment, most fans forgave her in face of the show's sheer spectacle.

For Diana's second movie, Berry Gordy chose a more conventional vehicle than *Lady Sings The Blues*. *Mahogany* was originally to have been a musical scored by B. B. Merrill, the composer of Streisand's *Funny Girl*, but it came out as straight drama, the tale of a jetsetting model's progress through the world of international

KODAK SAFETY FILM 5077   KODAK SAFETY FIL

1A   → 32   → 32A   → 33   33A

fashion. Cinematic clichés abounded, including the slogan coined by Gordy for the picture's publicity campaign: 'Success is nothing without someone you love to share it with.'

Mahogany was poorly received by the critics upon release in 1975, but generated more than 14 million dollars' worth of ticket sales. Diana Ross's performance of the title tune, a squishy ballad from the pens of Michael Masser and Gerry Goffin, topped the US charts and made Number 5 in the UK.

Commercial good fortune did not attend Diana's third movie, a mega-budget version of *The Wiz*, the Broadway hit musical based on *The Wizard Of Oz* to which Motown acquired rights in 1976. Universal Pictures was said to have spent more than 30 million dollars on producing the film – which also starred Richard Pryor, Lena Horne and Michael Jackson – only to watch it disappear into box-office oblivion. 1976 also saw her divorce – on account of 'irreconcilable differences' – from Robert Silberstein.

Out on her own

And so it was that Diana returned to records. She worked again with Nick Ashford and Valerie Simpson on *The Boss* (1979), an album of good songs and slick production, performed with panache and self-confidence. It was followed by an inspired union with Chic's Nile Rodgers and Bernard Edwards, whose street-smart, stripped-down songwriting and production techniques were then at the cutting edge of contemporary black music. *Diana* (1980) became her biggest-selling LP in eight years, spending a full 52 weeks on the *Billboard* charts and yielding the hit singles 'Upside Down', 'I'm Coming Out' and, in the UK, 'My Old Piano'.

Diana Ross left Motown early in 1981, just before her swansong for the label, 'Endless Love' with Lionel Richie, turned

Three facets of Diana Ross's towering performing talent – the smiling public relations woman (above left), the accomplished actress of Lady Sings The Blues *(above) and the entertainer (below).*

into an international smash. The departure was 'a business decision', she said at the time, emphasising that there were no 'problems' or disputes with the company or people who had helped her reach and retain superstardom. 'Motown is my family,' she stated. 'They always will be.'

The early Eighties saw Ross enjoying new freedom and control over her future. Her recording deal with RCA (for North America) and EMI (for the rest of the world) allowed her to produce her own albums, *Why Do Fools Fall In Love* (1981)

and *Silk Electric* (1982), for the first time; she also began to write more of her own material.

Her solo career continued to flounder with just one US Top Ten pop hit since 1982. Then, in 1988, it was reported that she had re-signed to Motown—ironically just at the time Berry Gordy had sold the label to MCA. Further developments were awaited.

ADAM WHITE

Diana Ross
Recommended Listening

Diana (Motown STMA8033) (Includes: I'm Coming Out, Upside Down, My Old Piano, Friend To Friend, Give Up); *Why Do Fools Fall In Love* (Capitol EST 26733) (Includes: Mirror Mirror, Why Do Fools Fall In Love, Endless Love, Work That Body, Never Too Late).

Sweet Soul Music

Saccharine harmonies from the Stylistics

THE STYLISTICS represented the sweet-soul side of the Seventies Philadelphia scene. The five-piece vocal group achieved consistent success in the singles charts on both sides of the Atlantic, aided in no small measure by the retirement from the music scene of Motown's William 'Smokey' Robinson in 1972, while a compilation of their best-sellers, *Best Of The Stylistics* (1975), became one of the top-selling albums ever in the UK – it was estimated two years later that one person in 50 owned a copy. Although their music had little message or substance, it was this candy-floss consistency that was the key to its enormous popularity.

Three members of the ice-cool quintet were natives of Philadelphia. Airrion Love was the oldest; he was born on 8 August 1949, followed by James Dunn on 4 February 1950, and Russell Thompkins Jr on 21 March 1951. Although resident in the city since the age of 12, James Smith actually came from Harlem, New York City, where he was born on 16 June 1950. Herbie Murrell, the oldest in the group, was a Southerner and hailed from Lane, South Carolina, where he was born on 27 April 1949.

Thompkins, Love and Smith began their career singing locally with the Monarchs, while Dunn and Murrell worked the same territory with the Percussions. Three years later, in 1968, the five came together as the Stylistics and toured with a backing quintet called Slim and the Boys. In 1969 guitarist Robert Douglas and road-manager Marty Bryant wrote 'You're A Big Girl Now' and the group cut it for Bill Perry's Sebring Records. The single was something of an anachronism except in the North-eastern states where the doowop tradition still endured. When Avco took over distribution the record received the exposure it deserved and, although it reached only a humble position in the Hot Hundred, it became an uncertified million-seller.

Ringing the Bell
When Avco secured the group's contract, they brought in Thom Bell as producer. He had an impeccable pedigree where doowop and soft-soul balladry were concerned, having recently worked with Gamble and Huff and the Delfonics. The first official Avco release 'Stop, Look, Listen To Your Heart' made Number 39 and became the group's first official million-selling disc. This composition was the first of many collaborations by Bell with Linda Creed over the next three years.

In November 1971 'You Are Everything' hit Number 9 in the Hot Hundred, thereby establishing itself as a popular standard.

Above: The Stylistics, from left Airrion Love, James Smith, James Dunn, Herbie Murrell and Russell Thompkins Jr. Left: The group in the late Seventies following Dunn's departure.

Joe Simon recorded it in 1972 and it was subsequently covered by Roberta Flack in 1979 and Eloise Laws in 1981.

February 1972 brought the definitive Stylistics recording in 'Betcha By Golly Wow', the apotheosis of the Philly sound and a perfect vehicle for the coolly insinuating tenor of Russell Thompkins Jr. Twisting, turning and caressing against a cunningly restrained, yet ultimately rich background, he was supported by slick harmonies entirely in keeping with the group's name. In March it lodged at Number 3 in the US pop chart and was Number 13 in the UK by June. Other artists approached it at their peril, although Phyllis Hyman cut a passable version with Norman Connors in 1977.

Along with 'People Make The World Go Round' from May 1972, and the original Sebring side, these tunes were all to be found on *The Stylistics*, their first album with Thom Bell, issued in December 1971. In September 1972 another stunning ballad, 'I'm Stone In Love With You', heralded their *Round Two* LP. By November this silky single was oozing ghetto chic at Number 10 across America and Number 9 in the UK. The same album contained the melancholy 'Make Up To Break Up' which proved even more popular, slotting in the Hot Hundred at Number 5 in March 1973.

The Stylistics took a calculated risk with 'Rockin' Roll Baby'. A fine rhythm item, with an atypical country guitar break and cute lyrics, it marked a move away from the soul mainstream and in September 1973, three months after release, it reached Number 14 in the US Hot Hundred. By January 1974 it was Number 6 in Britain. The album of the same name was Bell's swan-song for the group. Issued in November 1973, it yielded a fine ballad in 'You Make Me Feel Brand New', which, with Airrion Love sharing lead with Thompkins, made Number 2 on both sides of the Atlantic that summer.

Stuck in the middle

Thom Bell had honoured the doowop heritage, using top Philly session men like Norman Harris, Earl Young, Ronnie Baker, Bobby Eli and Ron Kersey to underpin achingly pure vocals with a rhythmic pulse of considerable ingenuity. And no matter how romantic the song, lyrical nuance and vocal inflection remained unmistakably R&B, always keeping it at a subtle remove from the blandishments of Tin Pan Alley.

When Hugo and Luigi assumed ownership of Avco they changed the Stylistics' direction, steering the group towards the lucrative easy-listening market. With George David Weiss they busied themselves writing hackneyed songs with obvious melodies. Veteran arranger Van McCoy was recruited to keep the mix sweet, adding French horns, yet more lavish string arrangements and unnecessary backing singers. Where Thom Bell had held Russell Thompkins Jr in check, the singer's falsetto flights became a tiresome affectation.

Hugo and Luigi's 'brave new world' was ushered in with the unexceptional *Let's*

Put It All Together in February 1974, an event rendered ironic by the inclusion of one good track in 'You Make Me Feel Brand New', commandeered from Bell's final set. The malaise deepened with *Heavy* (entitled *From The Mountain* in the UK) in October 1974. It supplied singles like the appalling 'Star On A TV Show' which went to Number 12 in the UK in January 1975. Showbiz cliché had finally ousted soul. The whitening process was an easy one and it secured the group a slice of the growing European market. When their *Best Of The Stylistics* package was released in February 1975 it was heavily promoted by Phonogram on British TV and radio. The result was a golden chart-topper in the UK and reputedly the highest sales ever achieved by a black vocal group.

Thank You Baby finally scuppered their credibility as soul singers. The title track, coupled with the obnoxious 'Sing Baby Sing', oozed out in March 1975. By the time the album was issued in May, 'Sing Baby Sing' was at Number 3 in the UK charts. There seemed little point in resisting public demand. In July the bland 'Can't Give You Anything (But My Love)' topped the UK chart, despite facile harmonies and cornball horn embellishments. Of the singles culled from the album, only 'Na Na Is The Saddest Word' suggested former glories and reached Number 5 in the UK in November 1975.

May 1976 brought a galloping version of Presley's 'Can't Help Falling In Love', the first release on Hugo and Luigi's H&L label. It tickled British fancies, charting at Number 4. Other pop offerings followed suit in the UK, notably 'Sixteen Bars' (Number 7, August 1976), Dionne Warwick's 'You'll Never Get To Heaven' (an EP at Number 7 in November) and '7000 Dollars And You' (Number 24, March 1977).

In 1978 James Dunn quit because of ill-health and the remaining quartet signed with Mercury where, despite expert guidance from Teddy Randazzo, they failed to register in the charts. In June 1979 they tried The Sound Of Philadelphia with Dexter Wansel as producer. Two sleek albums cut at Sigma Sound in 1980 and 1981 attracted some attention, and an internal switch to Philadelphia International Records resulted in the beautifully crafted *1982*.

From 1970 to 1973 the Stylistics were in the first division, comparable with the Delfonics, the Manhattans and Blue Magic. The demise of Philadelphia International Records in 1983 left the group without a recording contract, and with little immediate prospect of regaining their former status.   CLIVE ANDERSON

TSOP
THE SOUND OF PHILADELPHIA

Philly soul-brothers Gamble and Huff

AS A RESULT of the size and geography of the USA, numerous conurbations across the nation have tended to develop quite recognisable and distinctive musical styles. This is particularly so in the world of black music and in its various facets – jazz, blues, and the more 'popular' end of the spectrum which has developed into soul.

The Philadelphia sound grew from the relatively limited resources employed by the Cameo-Parkway label to sustain the impact of nebulous teenage dance crazes that came and went during the early Sixties. When Cameo folded, the rather stark simplicity of their characteristic sound was superseded by the swirling, hyperactive orchestrated productions of Kenny Gamble and Leon Huff on the Philadelphia International label.

Business gambles
Gamble and Huff share a musical pedigree dating back to the early Sixties. The duo first met in 1964 when Leon Huff played keyboards on Candy and the Kisses' 'The 81', a hit for Cameo which was written by Kenny Gamble. Huff had been working as a session musician in New York with Jerry Leiber and Mike Stoller, but had moved back to his native Philadelphia to replace the departing Thom Bell in Gamble's group, the Romeos. The duo began to produce sessions on a freelance basis, using facilities at Joe Tarsia's Sigma Sound Studio, and in 1966 launched their own Excel label, soon restyled Gamble Records, to market product by local vocal group the Intruders. In July, the group scored a crossover pop/R&B hit with 'United' and a succession of hits ensued during the late Sixties, keeping the Intruders in both the Hot Hundred and the R&B charts.

The duo now saw the opportunity to broaden their horizons and in 1969 they set up Neptune Records, struck a distribution deal with Chess, and expanded their artist roster to sign the O'Jays, the Vibrations, Linda Jones, Billy Paul, Bunny Sigler and the Three Degrees. Misfortune struck, however, with the death of Leonard Chess; his company was sold off to the GRT conglomerate, which terminated the distribution deal. But wise investment of their finances now bore fruit for Gamble and Huff, who promptly bounced back by establishing Philadelphia International Records.

They negotiated a distribution deal with Columbia, maintained their Neptune roster and made the most of a cordial relationship with Jimmy Bishop, a renowned local DJ/entrepreneur who was employed

Left: Thom Bell, one of Philadelphia's most talented arrangers, whose orchestral scores graced many hits. Top right: Leon Huff (left) and Kenny Gamble – soul brothers and father figures of the Philadelphia International label.

in a promotional capacity by Columbia. Though Columbia at that time were probably unaware of the eventual potential of Philadelphia International, almost certainly considering the deal as a means to expand their interests in the dependable, if restricted, rhythm and blues market, the combination of Gamble and Huff's musical ability and business acumen – plus Bishop's exploitative abilities – was to yield remarkable results.

Teddy's tearjerkers

Philadelphia International issued a steady flow of discs during 1971, the company's first year of operation, but managed only local success with artists like Johnny Williams, the Ebonys, Billy Paul and Bunny Sigler. The Intruders, still on the Gamble label, kept the company finances in a healthy state with hits while the industry and the public gradually caught on to the new Philly sound.

The new year brought a notable upturn in fortunes, beginning with the signing of Harold Melvin and the Blue Notes, a soulful vocal group who had spent some years label-hopping in the hope of rekindling the flame of success ignited back in 1960 with their doowop hit 'My Hero'. Led by the searing baritone of Teddy Pendergrass, the Blue Notes found immediate success on PIR with 'I Miss You', an intense soul ballad spread over both sides of a 45 which crossed over from the R&B charts to make Number 58 in the Hot Hundred that summer. Their feat was soon surpassed by the O'Jays' brisk, wry, lyrical 'Back Stabbers', which reached Number 3 in September. Then, in December, Billy Paul's storyline saga of 'Me And Mrs Jones' gave the label its first US Number 1.

A major contributory factor in the early success of Philadelphia International and Gamble and Huff was the skill and professionalism of Sigma Sound Studio's session

The Three Degrees on stage (right) and smiling at Seventies success (below).

The Three Degrees

THE THREE DEGREES' story has taken them from their native Philadelphia to the cabaret stages of the world. Fayette Pickney, Linda Turner and Shirley Porter were the protégées of former Valentines baritone Richard Barrett, who turned writer, producer and manager to place the group with Swan Records. Their 1965 debut single was 'Gee Baby (I'm Sorry)', a gritty period piece which made the Hot Hundred. By the time of their next hit, 'Look In My Eyes', a year later, Barrett was aiming the group upmarket. Turner and Porter left and were replaced by Sheila Ferguson and Valerie Thompson. After the demise of Swan Records, the group spent brief and unsuccessful spells on Warners (1968) and Metromedia (1969)

before signing to Roulette in 1970.

The Three Degrees promptly charted with their soulful revival of the Chantels' 'Maybe', which reached the national Top Thirty. 'I Do Take You', 'You're The One' and an appearance in *The French Connection* (1971) maintained their hit status, so that the group were already in the public eye when Philadelphia International was launched. They had already cut one single with Gamble and Huff – on Neptune just prior to their Roulette contract – and signed to Philadelphia in 1973.

'Dirty Ol' Man', with its hustling beat, was a moderate chart success, but it was 1974's 'When Will I See You Again' that really took off, reaching Number 2 in the US pop charts and

Number 1 in the UK. Indeed, while they remained moderately successful in the US, they were to find their biggest audience in the UK, where 'Take Good Care Of Yourself' made Number 9 in 1975. As CBS recognised that the group's appeal was shifting away from R&B to the commercial mainstream, they transferred them from Philadelphia to Epic, where they recorded the stunning torch ballad 'What I Did For Love'.

As the group leant heavily towards the emergent disco boom, Barrett signed them to Ariola, where they had a string of UK hits: 'Givin' Up Givin' In' (1978), 'Woman In Love' and 'My Simple Heart' (both 1979). The early Eighties saw them the toast of royalty, in constant demand on the international cabaret and variety circuit.

CLIVE RICHARDSON

musicians who were collectively known as MFSB (popularly expanded to Mother-Father-Sister-Brother, but perhaps derived from a colloquial black expletive). Drummer Earl Young, bassist Ronnie Baker and guitarists Norman Harris, Roland Chambers and Bobby Eli were among the regular members of the MFSB team, while violinist Don Renaldo headed a string section and sax player Leno 'Zack' Zachery took charge of the horns. Arrangements were usually the work of Philly 'family' members Thom Bell, Norman Harris, Ronnie Baker and Bobby Martin, while Kenny Gamble and Leon Huff produced along with Gene McFadden and John Whitehead.

Right: McFadden and Whitehead, producers-turned-singers, in 1979.

1973 saw the PIR team building on the success of the previous year through hits with the Blue Notes' 'The Love I Lost' and the O'Jays' 'Love Train', which reached Number 1 in March. Bunny Sigler, equally talented as writer, producer and singer, scored briefly with his beaty update of Bobby Lewis' R&B classic 'Tossin' And Turnin'', and the Ebonys (David Beasley, James Tuten, Clarence Vaughn and Jenny Holmes) carried their eclectic deep soul into the soul charts with the searing baritone-led 'It's Forever'.

Blue Philly
Then towards the end of the year, the Three Degrees charted, albeit quite low, with 'Dirty Ol' Man'. This clipped, rhythmic number dressed in swirling strings with a catchy unison chorus was sung with

Harold Melvin (below) led his Blue Notes (right) through a series of line-up changes to a run of successful singles.

Harold Melvin and the Blue Notes

THE BLUE NOTES started their career as a doowop outfit with the single 'If You Love Me' on the Josie label in 1956. They had a hit in 1960 when 'My Hero', a tender ballad incorporating a Johann Strauss melody, entered the pop and R&B charts. With John Atkins as lead, supported by Lawrence Brown, Harold Melvin and Bernard Wilson, the Blue Notes switched labels throughout the Sixties: 'Get Out' appeared on Landa (1962), 'Go Away' on Arctic (1967) and 'Goodbye My Lover' on Checker (1968).

Sessions for the Glades label in Miami yielded 'This Time Will Be Different', which was subsequently leased to Uni. The Blue Notes' line-up was fluid at this time, with Atkins leaving, Lloyd Parkes joining and drummer Teddy Pendergrass taking over as lead vocalist.

In 1972 the group signed to Philadelphia International. Their intense, emotional ballad 'I Miss You', featuring Teddy Pendergrass's throaty baritone, leapt into the R&B Top Ten before crossing over into the Billboard Hot Hundred. This success was followed up by the poignant 'If You Don't Know Me By Now', 'The Love I Lost', 'Satisfaction Guaranteed', 'Where Are All My Friends', 'Bad Luck' and 'Wake Up Everybody'.

The discrepancy between Harold Melvin's star billing and Teddy Pendergrass's lead vocals led to tension within the group; Harold Melvin took the Blue Notes to ABC, recruiting new vocalist David Ebo (Sharon Paige also guested on 1975's 'Hope That We Can Be Together Soon'). Teddy Pendergrass stayed on Philadelphia, where he en-

joyed a highly successful solo career.

The Blue Notes, who now consisted of Jerry Cummings, Dwight J. Johnson and Bill Spratley alongside Ebo and Melvin, began to flounder. 'Reaching For The World' did reasonably well on ABC, but Ebo could not match Pendergrass as a charismatic frontman. As their second ABC LP hit the streets in 1977, Glades issued an LP featuring an alternative Blue Notes line-up: Bernie Wilson, John Atkins, Lloyd Parkes and Larry Brown. Neither record sold well, and the ABC contract lapsed. Harold and his group were then signed to the MCA-backed Source label, but the label folded after they had released one single. The early Eighties saw the Blue Notes still active on the concert circuit but without a recording contract.

CLIVE RICHARDSON

The late Seventies saw Teddy Pendergrass carrying the Philly torch in the Hot Hundred. A car crash in 1982, however, curtailed his live appearances.

appeal – if not intense passion – by the trio of Fayette Pickney, Sheila Ferguson and Valerie Thompson. A synthesis of the danceable, floating Philly sound with the Miami-based TK label's rhythm-machine style, it provided a foretaste of the disco boom of the next few years.

With PIR's success came expansion. In 1974 Gamble, Huff and Thom Bell set up sister-label TSOP (The Sound Of Philadelphia), and it was on this eye-catching blue label (in contrast to the plain green of PIR) that house-band MFSB reached the top of the US charts with 'TSOP', a number that perfectly captured the spirit, vitality and musical precision of the Philly sound.

For a while PIR could do no wrong, charting frequently with their three head-lining acts, the O'Jays, Blue Notes and Three Degrees, while TSOP showed well as an outlet for some more left-field product and new signings like Archie Bell and the Drells and People's Choice, who arrived in 1975 with the thumping, atypical funk of 'Do It Any Way You Wanna'. The song was built around an insistent bass riff that has been frequently imitated ever since, while Frankie Brunson's throaty baritone vocal displayed more immediate power than almost any other voice in the company. The song was a US Number 11 pop hit.

Solo soulsters

By 1976 PIR were looking to strengthen their roster and spread their wings outside the 'City of Brotherly Love' by signing a couple of established soul performers – Don Covay and Lou Rawls. Covay's rich writing talent and individual vocal style were moulded into a solitary LP, *Travelin' In Heavy Traffic* (1976), while Rawls drifted through the lilting 'You'll Never Find Another Love Like Mine' to reach Number 2 in the Hot Hundred the same year.

More changes were afoot as Harold Melvin felt the lure of corporate riches and took his Blue Notes from PIR to ABC; lead baritone Teddy Pendergrass decided to remain loyal to Gamble and Huff, who set about launching him as a solo singer. Two other classy solo performers also joined the fold – Jerry Butler, fresh from years of hit singles with Vee-Jay and Mercury, and Jean Carn. TSOP's roster was also strengthened when Kenny Gamble's wife Dee Dee Sharp (who had had big hits in 1962 with 'Mashed Potato Time' and 'Ride!') decided to return to recording.

While these acts all made artistically pleasing records, it was only Teddy Pendergrass who proved commercially successful. He developed a reputation as a ladykiller on stage through a dynamic combination of his vocal power and macho sexual charisma; on tour, his management would organise 'Ladies Night' concerts for female fans only, at which Teddy would often be bombarded with underwear from his adoring fans. Sadly, however, Pendergrass sustained spinal injuries in a car crash on 26 March 1982 and it seemed unlikely that he would ever be able to perform live again.

The O'Jays

IT WAS IN 1958 that Eddie Levert and Walter Williams teamed up with William Powell, Bobby Massey and Bill Isles in their hometown of Canton, Ohio to form the Triumphs, singing at local clubs and parties. Their talent eventually came to the notice of Syd Nathan, boss of King Records in nearby Cincinnati. Renamed the Mascots, the quintet had two singles on King in 1960, a dance ditty, 'Do The Wiggle', and the more melodramatic 'Lonely Rain'. Sales were minimal, however, and the group remained disillusioned until Cleveland DJ Eddie O'Jay began to take an interest in their activities.

Re-christening them with his own name, O'Jay arranged a disc deal through producer Don Davis. A single on the Dayco label was picked up by Apollo early in 1963; as a result, the O'Jays went to Los Angeles to record on H. B. Barnum's Little Star label, leading to a deal with Imperial which lasted three years and yielded pop/R&B hits like 'Lonely Drifter', 'Stand-In For Love' and 'Lipstick Traces'. Following the acquisition of Imperial by Liberty, the group were placed on the Minit R&B outlet in 1967, but 'Working On Your Case' flopped and a disgruntled Bill Isles quit.

A gig at New York's Apollo Theatre led to a contract with Bell, where the O'Jays recorded under the aegis of Richard Tee and George Kerr. 'I'll Be Sweeter Tomorrow' made Number 66 in the Hot Hundred in 1967, but they could not improve on this success and in 1969 the group signed with Kenny Gamble and Leon Huff's Neptune label. The storming 'One Night Affair' and 'Looky Looky' quickly became hits.

Neptune, however, was distributed by Chess Records, and the death of Leonard Chess saw the end of the deal and the demise of Neptune. After one single on Saru, the O'Jays signed with the emergent Philadelphia International label in 1972. They were reduced to a trio when Bobby Massey left, but led by the distinctive tenor of Eddie Levert, the group soon scored a series of hits like 'Back Stabbers' (a Number 3 in 1973), 'I Love Music' (Number 5, 1976) and 'Love Train' (a US chart-topper in 1973). All three were Top Twenty hits in the UK. William Powell left the O'Jays due to illness in 1975, and was replaced by Sammy Strain. They continued to enjoy fame and fortune into the Eighties, though the collapse of PIR in 1983 left them awaiting a new record deal. CLIVE RICHARDSON

Messrs Williams (left), Powell (centre) and Levert: collectively, the O'Jays.

Blind alley

Although the O'Jays remained consistent in the quantity and quality of their output, others have stepped into the spotlight from time to time to keep the PIR flag flying – most notably McFadden and Whitehead. Gene McFadden and John Whitehead were primarily writers and arrangers, yet they proved to be performers of note when 'Ain't No Stopping Us Now' emerged as a transatlantic smash hit in 1979 and something of an anthem for the label.

The Eighties, however, saw the future of PIR waning dramatically. Just as Motown had failed to keep pace with changing tastes towards the end of the Sixties, the Philadelphia sound had become somewhat dated by the end of the Seventies. During 1982, Gamble and Huff tried a further venture with the launch of Peace International, a label devoted to gospel music with a roster including the legendary Five Blind Boys. But all was far from well within the company and in February 1983 the distribution deal with Columbia was terminated, thus effectively ending the story of Philadelphia International Records. CLIVE RICHARDSON

Loud and Proud

US bands turned up the volume and found a new young audience

WHILE IT WAS the British blues-based trio Cream that laid the foundations of hard rock, it took the brash American opportunism of Grand Funk Railroad to strip the formula down to basics – repetitive, thudding bass riffs and mind-numbing guitar noise – and sell it to a mass audience. Whereas Cream had placed more emphasis on virtuosity than on musical content, Grand Funk were a triumph of volume over both.

Among the earliest examples of US heavy metal had been Iron Butterfly, whose success was based entirely on 'In-A-Gadda-Da-Vida', a repetitious number that lasted up to 50 minutes when performed live, and Blue Cheer, whose sound was dominated by the frantic and undisciplined guitar playing of Randy Holden. They proudly boasted of being the loudest group in the world; at one of their concerts in 1968, the volume killed a dog in the audience by perforating its eardrums. The Litter were

Former Amboy Duke Ted Nugent spent ten years on the road before his hard-rocking style brought him sustained commercial success. This emphasis on constant touring was common among US heavy-rock outfits, whose grass-roots following often outstripped record sales.

inspired by Cream to change their original garage pop into high-volume guitar improvisation; Ted Nugent of the Amboy Dukes (motto: 'If it's too loud, you're too old') would still be drawing excruciating feedback from his guitar a decade later; while Pineapple Filter guitarist Ronnie Komoritz attempted to outdo Hendrix by setting his instrument alight – while he was still playing it.

The success of these late-Sixties American heavy-rock bands proved limited, however; Iron Butterfly were unable to follow up *In-A-Gadda-Da-Vida* and Blue Cheer stagnated after their first two releases, while few of the other groups achieved more than local recognition. By 1970, older rock consumers were contenting themselves with the acoustic introspection of the singer-songwriters, but there was now a younger audience eager for high-volume rock.

Grand Funk Railroad, under the guidance of manager Terry Knight, surfaced at the Atlanta Pop Festival in 1969, picked up the mantle of American trash HM – 'loud white noise' – and, despite unanimous derision from hip rock critics, were soon selling records in extraordinary quantities. Mountain, meanwhile, served up equally deafening riffs. In comparison with Grand Funk and Mountain, other successful hard rock outfits of the era – the James Gang, Canada's Guess Who and Bachman-Turner Overdrive – seemed almost sophisticated, but they were still dominated by the sound of loud electric guitars and heavy riffs.

A bigger splash

The early Seventies also saw the rise of the Southern boogie pioneered by the Allman Brothers Band (whose guitarists Duane Allman and Dickie Betts depended more on crafty interplay than volume), Black Oak Arkansas (fronted by outrageous vocalist Jim Dandy who, on the million-selling 1972 LP *Keep The Faith*, was responsible for rock's only known urination solo), Cactus (featuring drummer Carmine Appice and bassist Tim Bogert, both formerly of Vanilla Fudge) and bearded Texan cowboys ZZ Top.

By the mid Seventies, hard rock had become a major part of FM radio's staple diet, and new bands had grown up to meet this demand – bands like Aerosmith, fronted by pretty-boy Steven Tyler, Kiss, with their sci-fi comic book image and HM thrash, and Foghat, British expatriates who were virtually unknown in their native country but whose LPs went gold in the States. American hard rock and heavy metal, with ever-increasing sales, had now become respectable, and by the end of the decade, the brutal approach of Blue Cheer, Grand Funk, Mountain and the rest had been replaced by polish and 'adult-oriented' blandness.

TOM HIBBERT

1601

Southern Fried Boogie

Triumph and tragedy came too fast for the Allmans

'TODAY THE ALLMAN BROTHERS Band are the biggest most successful rock band in the USA' reported Chris Charlesworth in *Melody Maker* in early 1974, and the evidence supported his assertion. The previous summer, the Allman Brothers Band headlined a bill in July 1973 that included the Grateful Dead and the Band at the Watkins Glen Grand Prix Circuit in upstate New York. The event attracted over 600,000 people, well in excess of Woodstock and perhaps the largest turnout ever for a single-day festival. The 1973 album *Brothers And Sisters* reached Number 1 in the American charts within two weeks of release and at that time became the biggest-selling album in the US since the Beatles' *Abbey Road*. Their 'Summer Campaign '74' tour of America broke attendance records all over the States, eclipsing the previous achievements of even Led Zeppelin and the Rolling Stones. All this, ironically, occurred over two years after the death of founding member Duane Allman.

Nashville cats

The brothers were born in Nashville, Tennessee – Duane on 20 November 1946, and Gregg on 8 December 1947. Their father died in 1949, and their mother, Geraldine Allman, brought them up in Nashville until 1958 when the family moved to Daytona, Florida. Gregg learned to play guitar after he was given one for Christmas, and taught Duane before taking up keyboards himself. Around 1960 the brothers joined a youth club band called the Y-Teens, and a couple of years later they were making 41 dollars a week in a group called the House Rockers.

In 1965 the Allmans formed a four-piece group called the Allman Joys; their first commercial release, a version of 'Spoonful' on the Dial label, sold well locally and the band moved to the West Coast. Despite a steadily-building reputation, the band split up in 1967 and the Allmans, now based in Los Angeles, went on to form a group called Hourglass. The band had a good live reputation, but their two 1968 albums on the Liberty label were disappointingly bland. Duane and Gregg considered the recordings substandard, and Hourglass split up, disillusioned.

Duane then built himself a formidable reputation as a session player at Muscle Shoals, Alabama. One of his earliest contributions was to Wilson Pickett's 'Hey Jude', the singer's biggest UK hit since 'In The Midnight Hour'. On the strength of this record, studio owner Rick Hall put Duane on a salary; in the ensuing period he backed Aretha Franklin, Clarence Carter,

Laura Nyro and Otis Rush. Duane maintained this side of his activities after the Allman Brothers Band became successful; an inveterate jammer, he loved hanging out with other musicians. Some of his most enduring work emerged from collaborations outside the Allman Brothers Band, notably on Boz Scaggs' 1969 debut LP and with Eric Clapton on Derek and the Dominos' *Layla* (1971).

Come again

1968 saw the beginnings of the Allman Brothers Band. Duane and Gregg played on an occasional basis in a band called the 31st of February, which featured percussionist Butch Trucks. (The 1972 album *Duane And Gregg* consisted mostly of demos the 31st of February had made in Miami in 1968.) Duane had begun recording a solo album, employing bassist Berry Oakley who, along with guitarist Dickie

Left: The Allmans on stage at the peak of their career. Right: Duane Allman was a successful session musician. Above right: Duane and Gregg's early band, Hourglass.

Betts, played in a group called the Second Coming.

Early in 1969, the mutual connections led to a jam session in a Jacksonville park between various members of the Second Coming and 31st of February. The musicians involved were Duane Allman, Dickie Betts (guitar), Berry Oakley (bass), Butch Trucks (drums/percussion) and Jai Johanny Johanson – later known as Jaimoe – (drums/percussion), and a unique band spirit was forged. Duane scrapped his solo album, called up Gregg and the Allman Brothers Band was formed.

The band secured the management services of Phil Walden, formerly Otis Redding's manager, who set up Capricorn Records as an outlet for the Allmans' recordings. The group moved to Macon, Georgia, where they rehearsed intensively during the spring of 1969 before going to Atlantic Recording Studios in New York City to record their first album.

The Allman Brothers Band was a powerful debut. The two drummers provided an urgent rhythmic backdrop to the melodic inventiveness of Betts and Duane Allman's twin guitars. Gregg Allman's vocals were raucous and soulful above his keyboard-playing. The majority of the songs were written by the two Allmans – and, while the material was firmly rooted in the blues, there were many inventive deviations from the traditional 12-bar format that gave the album freshness and vitality. Above all, the recording captured a raw intensity rare in their later work. After recording the album, the band embarked on a string of tours around America and built up a solid following.

Their second album, *Idlewild South*, was recorded in the summer of 1970 in Macon and reflected that sleepy Southern town in contrast to the rush of New York where the previous album had been cut. Named after

a farm where the band had been living, *Idlewild South* had a soft, country feel that disappointed many admirers of the first album. In place of raucous energy were poignant melodies, notably Betts' haunting instrumental 'In Memory Of Elizabeth Reed' and Gregg's 'Midnight Rider'.

Their third album was a double live set recorded on 12 and 13 March 1971 at the Fillmore East, New York. Consolidating their live reputation, the album captured extended workouts of blues standards ('Statesboro Blues', 'Stormy Monday'), Allman rockers (the 22-minute 'Whipping Post') and the newer melodic style ('In Memory Of Elizabeth Reed'). It went gold in America and confirmed the band as a top US attraction.

All six members of the band were busted for drug possession in Jackson, Alabama on 22 March 1971, but apart from such scrapes occasioned by their freewheeling lifestyle, the Allman Brothers Band were in good shape when they moved into Miami's Criteria studio to begin work on their *Eat A Peach* album in the autumn of 1971. They had recorded three tracks when Duane Allman went to visit Linda Oakley – Berry's wife – on her birthday, 29 October. Returning on his motorcycle, Allman swerved to avoid a lorry, lost control of the bike and was pinned underneath it as it skidded 50 feet along the road. He died four hours later in Macon Medical Centre, aged 24. Berry Oakley crashed his car the same evening but wasn't hurt.

Music minus one
The band closed ranks, and after a brief period of mourning renewed their activities despite the loss of their founding member. *Eat A Peach* was completed and released in February 1972. Another double album, it incorporated studio tracks recorded with and without Duane, and some live material left over from the *Fillmore East* recordings. Towards the autumn of 1972 they began preparations to record their fifth album, and it was decided to add pianist Chuck Leavell to the line-up. Two days before Leavell's recruitment was officially announced, tragedy again struck the group in a macabre re-run of previous events. On 11 November 1972, one year and 13 days after Duane's fatal accident, Berry Oakley drove his motorcycle into a Macon city bus. Despite refusing hospital treatment, remounting his bike and driving home, Oakley died from brain damage several hours later at the Medical Centre of Central Georgia. He was 24.

As after Duane's death, the band rallied round once more, determined to continue. Lamar Williams, a longtime friend of drummer Jaimoe, was drafted in as Oakley's replacement on bass, and with Chuck Leavell restoring them to a six-piece, they resumed work on the new album. With its more carefully structured approach and country influences, *Brothers And Sisters* – released late in 1973 – was the Allmans' most commercially successful album. Their road safety record, however, didn't

The death of Duane Allman in a motorcycle accident in 1971 left a gap in the ranks (right). Duane's brother Gregg (above) and guitarist Richard Betts (above left) steered the band through its subsequent career.

improve; on 25 August 1973, drummer Butch Trucks broke a leg in a car crash in Macon, causing *Melody Maker*'s Geoff Brown to dub the band the 'Uneasy Riders'.

Since the death of Duane Allman, much of the credit for the band's musical and commercial success had been due to Richard Betts. 'Duane always told people that Dickie Betts was as good as he was. And he meant it to be taken seriously,' commented manager Phil Walden. Not only did Betts step into the breach instrumentally, he also made valuable contributions as a composer; *Brothers And Sisters* yielded the Allmans' first hit single, the million-selling 'Rambling Man'. Betts wrote the song and, with his typical Southern charm, first introduced it to Gregg Allman as 'Just an old piece of work in case you're looking for something to round off the album.' 'Jessica', a Betts-penned instrumental, was another hit for the group.

Despite their enormous success in America, the Allman Brothers Band never repeated this in the UK. This was hardly surprising, since they rarely ever left the North American mainland. Their first venture to Europe took in one date in Holland and an appearance at the Knebworth Festival in the UK in July 1974.

After the staggering success of *Brothers And Sisters*, however, the group's energies began to dissipate. Gregg Allman released a solo LP in late 1973 entitled *Laid Back*, which was certified gold by early 1974. Richard Betts released his solo album *Highway Call* (1975), and this was followed by a Gregg Allman double live

album, *Gregg Allman Tour*, consisting of recordings culled from a spring 1974 solo tour. He had maintained a fairly low profile as lead singer with the Allmans, with his keyboards set to one side, but his 1974 tour incorporated 29 musicians onstage and saw Gregg the star of the show, with his Hammond organ stage centre, decked out with flowers and lighted candles.

When the Allman Brothers Band did get together again in 1975, it was to produce the musically lacklustre *Win Lose Or Draw* album. Subsequent releases included a retrospective compilation *The Road Goes On Forever*, a live album of recordings from 1972, *Wipe The Windows, Check The Oil, Dollar Gas*, and further reunion albums in *Enlightened Rogues* (1979) and *Reach For The Sky* (1980).

Levelling out

The band's family feeling was weakened still further when Gregg Allman testified in court against road manager Scooter Herring, who was up on a drugs charge. The rest of the band, particularly Betts, were dismayed at this turn of events, and the ensuing acrimonious feelings found their way into print. Herring got 75 years, while Allman continued his much-publicised romance with singer Cher.

Allman's career was, thenceforth, more gossipworthy than noteworthy. He married Cher in 1975, they separated after nine days but got back together again in an on-off relationship. He also recorded the solo albums *Playin' Up A Storm* and *Two The Hard Way* (both 1977). Richard Betts formed his own band Great Southern,

while Jaimoe, Leavell and Williams joined up with guitarist Jimmy Nalls to form Sea Level. None of them repeated the kind of fortune they enjoyed with the Allman Brothers Band, a group for whom success seemed equally balanced by tragedy. While the group was sustained by their strong family feeling, no amount of tragedy, it seemed, could daunt them. Once that spirit disappeared, no amount of success could rekindle the magic.

DAVID SINCLAIR

Allman Brothers Band
Recommended Listening

The Best Of The Allman Brothers Band (Capricorn Super 2429 198) (Includes: Ramblin' Man, Dreams I'll Never See, Midnight Rider, Melissa, Jessica, Statesboro' Blues, Little Martha).

MOUNTAIN CLIMBING

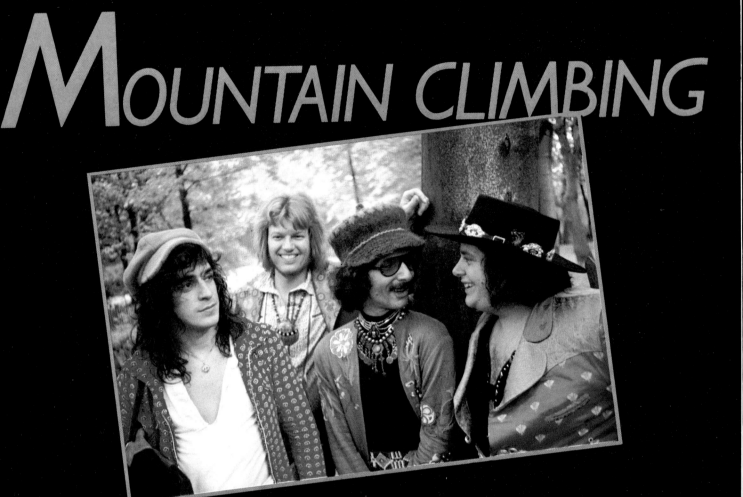

An abundance of decibels and never-ending improvisations were the essence of the heavy-rock sound that put Mountain on the landscape of the American music scene in the late Sixties and early Seventies. The band combined the talents of bassist Felix Pappalardi and guitarist Leslie West and inherited an audience that had mourned the demise of the earlier leading heavy rock trio, Cream.

Pappalardi was born in the Bronx district of New York in 1939. The son of a doctor, he received a comprehensive musical education, studying piano from the age of five at the Diller-Quaile School of Music, viola from 13 to 17 at the High School of Music and Art, and brass and strings at the University of Michigan Conservatory for Music. He wanted to become involved in conducting and choral work, but after dropping out of university and serving a spell in the army reserve during the latter half of 1962, the only employment he could find was as a door-to-door salesman selling encyclopedias and hi-fi equipment. Disillusioned, he drifted into the Greenwich Village area, hanging out with the musicians there, playing bass with Tim Hardin and grabbing any other work he could find.

Through doing studio arrangements and session work, he eventually became a producer, his first important job being the Youngbloods' debut album. But it was as

Leslie West took heavy rock to a new peak

producer for Cream, who recorded *Disraeli Gears* (1967) under his direction at Atlantic Studios in New York and subsequently retained his services for *Wheels Of Fire* (1968) and *Goodbye* (1969), that Pappalardi first achieved international recognition. As well as production, he also garnered some songwriting credits, most notably as co-author of Cream's 1967 hit 'Strange Brew'.

Enter the fat man
In 1968 Pappalardi was assigned by Atlantic Records to produce a single by a New York group called the Vagrants. Their guitarist was the gargantuan Leslie West. Born Leslie Weinstein on 22 October 1945 in Queens, New York, he had bought his first electric guitar with the proceeds from his barmitzvah and been inspired to form the Vagrants after seeing the Beatles in New York during their first American tour in 1964. In contrast to Pappalardi, he had received no formal musical training nor boasted any track record when the two met in 1968. Pappalardi thought the Vagrants were dreadful, but recognised the potential in West's guitar-playing. They began jamming together, and when

the Vagrants split up after two failed singles, Pappalardi produced and played on West's 1969 solo album *Leslie West – Mountain*.

West and Pappalardi then decided to form a band, taking their name from the album. Steve Knight, a keyboard-player with many previous credits including a spell with a Pappalardi-produced band, Devil's Anvil, was enlisted, and drummer Norman Smart, who played on the West album, completed the first line-up. They swiftly achieved wide recognition, their fourth gig being an appearance at Woodstock in August 1969. They recorded an album, *Mountain Climbing* (1970), which went gold, and provided a US Top Thirty single with a driving heavy rock number, 'Mississippi Queen'.

Smart was replaced in 1970 by drummer Corky Laing (born 28 January 1948 in Montreal), and the band's best-known line-up of West, Pappalardi, Knight and Laing recorded the 1971 album *Nantucket Sleighride*, the high-point of the band's career. The title track was so popular it was chosen as the centrepiece of two sub-

Above: Mountain's first, classic line-up, from left Corky Laing, Steve Knight, Felix Pappalardi and Leslie West. Opposite: West extracts the maximum from his Gibson Flying V.

sequent live albums, filling one side of Mountain Live (The Road Goes Ever On) in 1972 and more than two whole sides of a double live set, Twin Peaks (1974) – a fair illustration of their heavyweight live approach. The format of long, improvised workouts had been one of Cream's most distinctive calling-cards, and Mountain took the idea to ever greater extremes.

The frail Pappalardi, weighing just over 126 pounds, contributed a thick, cranked-up Gibson bass sound. Mountain were often referred to as one of the loudest bands in the world at that time, and it is said that Pappalardi's hearing was impaired during his years with the group. Opposite stood the 294-pound Leslie West – a mass of uncontained flab and multiple chins – who was actually a player of remarkable grace and melodic flair. He could whack out the power chords when required, but his playing often reflected a poignant lyricism.

West and Pappalardi shared the vocals, providing further contrast within the format. A microphone to West was like a red rag to a bull; he sang in a huge barrel-house bawl, a thick phlegmy roar, rampaging through lyrics and melody. Pappalardi, with his more conventional nasal whine, was usually assigned the more 'sensitive' and 'meaningful' songs. These often featured embarrassing lyrics, written in conjunction with his wife Gail Collins, about canoodling swans or hippie whale quests, providing a soft-focus relief from the raucous intensity of West's rant'n'roll.

Brightest hope

Flowers Of Evil, the second 1971 album, was notable for a crushing live version of 'Mississippi Queen'. After a visit to the UK in May 1971 when they supported Pink Floyd and the Small Faces at Crystal Palace, Mountain were voted Brightest Hope in the international section of the Melody Maker readers' poll. (Grand Funk Railroad were not far behind, while in the British section all eyes were fixed on newcomers Black Sabbath.)

Hopes for Mountain were not realised in Britain, however. In 1972 the band split for the first time; Pappalardi quit to do more work in the studio and Knight disappeared, while West and Laing joined forces with former Cream bassist Jack Bruce to form West, Bruce and Laing, a short-lived and derivative 'supergroup' that put out two albums, Why Doncha (1972) and What Ever Turns You On (1973), before Bruce left in the summer of 1973. A live album in 1974 entitled Live And Kickin', appeared posthumously. West and Laing worked briefly as Leslie West's Wild West Show before reforming Mountain in January 1974 with Pappalardi and rhythm guitarist David Perry. The reunited band recorded one LP, Avalanche (1974), before splitting up again in 1975.

West retained the services of Laing and produced two disappointing solo albums, The Great Fatsby and The Leslie West

Band (both 1975). His solo career was subsequently blighted by drug problems, while in 1978 he was declared bankrupt. Corky Laing released his own solo offering, *Makin' It On The Street*, in 1977.

Pappalardi departed to live in Japan, where he produced and played with heavy-metal group Creation; the collaboration yielded the album *Felix Pappalardi And Creation* (1976). In April 1983, Pappalardi was shot dead in his Manhattan apartment. His wife Gail Collins was charged with his murder, and remanded for

Always in their element on stage (above), Mountain cut a brace of live albums to prove the point. Drummer Laing and guitarist West later joined ex-Cream bassist Jack Bruce in West, Bruce and Laing (below).

psychiatric tests. The couple, it seemed, had a long history of domestic strife.

Despite their imaginative shortcomings and their often tediously over-long improvisations, Mountain nevertheless managed to steamroller to the forefront of the heavy-rock scene in the US, although this

success was never repeated in the UK. Their forte was undoubtedly live performance; the sheer power of their sound did not translate so well onto record.

DAVID SINCLAIR

Mountain
Recommended Listening

Nantucket Sleighride (Island ILPS 9148) (Includes: Taunta (Sammy's Tune), Nantucket Sleighride, Tired Angels (To J.M.H.), The Animal Trainer And The Toad, Travellin' In The Dark (To E.M.P.), The Great Train Robbery).

We're an American Band

IF THERE WAS any group that polarised rock opinion, it was the blunt, effective power trio Grand Funk Railroad. Bypassing the ruling elite of 'progressive' rock's taste-makers and scene-dwellers, they took their music directly to the concert stages of all 50 United States, making enemies of hip critics but friends of a mass teenage audience. In the course of two years, they moved from an unpaid opening slot at the 1969 Atlanta Pop Festival, where they received a standing ovation, to headlining New York's Shea Stadium. The Beatles had taken six weeks to sell out that massive venue; Grand Funk Railroad accomplished the same feat in 72 hours.

Ultimate accolade

Mark Farner, Grand Funk's lead singer and guitarist, saluted the 55,000-strong crowd that night in July 1971, the beams of Shea turned on full after a triumphal rendition of 'Inside Looking Out'. 'Y'know,'

Flying the flag with Grand Funk Railroad

he began, tossing back his long hair and trying to catch his breath. 'We've just come back from Europe . . . we're going to Tokyo, Japan, to play the Olympic Stadium there . . . I know I said this at Madison Square Garden . . . I've said this before, but when it's the truth you can't help but say it again. You're the best rockin' audience in the world!'

The crowd roared predictably in response and Terry Knight, sitting behind the mixing console, probably permitted himself a secret smile. For it had been he, more than anyone, who had masterminded this version of the American dream.

Knight (born 9 April 1943) was a disc

Above: Mark Farner lets rip over Don Brewer's steady drum rhythms.

jockey in the Detroit area at the age of 20 and in 1964 became singer in his own band, Terry Knight and the Pack. Classic garage-rockers of the time, they had attracted a modest amount of national attention through one minor hit, 'I (Who Have Nothing)', which reached Number 46 late in 1966. Don Brewer (born 3 September 1948) was his drummer and Mark Farner (born 29 September 1948) often deputised as bass-player.

By February 1969 the group had become the Fabulous Pack; Knight had left, Mel Schacher (born 8 April 1951) had joined on bass and Farner had switched to guitar. Finding themselves stranded in the midst of a New England winter, the band were on the verge of selling their instruments to get home when Knight offered to take over their management if they agreed, unconditionally, to follow his complete instructions. With no other prospects, the soon-to-be Grand Funk Railroad signed on.

Laying it on the line

Knight's *modus operandi* was simple. He realised that his young intended audience cared little for subtlety and precise displays of virtuosity; they were interested in volume and live impact. The band's first Capitol album, *On Time* (1969), offered simple blues-based rock that emphasised guitar and drums. It was promptly written off by the press as 'one-dimensional' – but Knight realised the last thing that would matter about Grand Funk Railroad would be the shortcomings of their music.

Instead, he concentrated on building their image, setting them as a direct response to contemporary rock trends. Grand Funk rejected rock's upward mobility of the post-Woodstock era, preferring to cut their music to the bone. Farner, bare-chested, arm-band glistening with sweat, would drop to his knees to wrench another ounce of noise from his guitar, straddling the Schacher-Brewer rhythm section like a primitive jockey. It was an unmistakable image, and Knight exploited it to the hilt.

As Grand Funk embarked on a lengthy series of tours and released further albums of basic noise – *Grand Funk* and *Closer To Home* (both 1970) – the rock press reacted with venom and derision. But the ferocity of the (over)reaction only served to solidify Grand Funk's identification with their fans and increase their grass-roots popularity. Everything about the group was gauged to be colossal, from the Times Square billboard Knight rented to show the world their glory to the unending stream of press releases recounting album sales and concert attendances.

For both Terry Knight and the group, the Shea Stadium gig was a pinnacle of achievement. Throughout, Knight never lost his touch, orchestrating a media event composed of equal parts phenomenon and braggadocio. Two weeks before, full-page ads ran in most of the New York entertainment sections, announcements of the impending occasion with big 'Sold Out' banners gleefully plastered over the date. Within five minutes of each new develop-

ment, it was announced that fans had camped by the box office days before their scheduled openings, or that ticket sellers had 'never seen anything like it' in all their years of working the stadium.

The *coup de grace* was a press conference called in late May to announce the historic date, to which only six media representatives came. Though Knight neglected to mention that most of the invitations had never reached the mail-box, he was still able to moan, to the *Wall Street Journal* of all publications, that 'It's the grossest case of nonrecognition in the history of the business.'

Phoenix funk

But things were never the same for Grand Funk and Terry Knight after Shea. While Knight had his private plane and oil fields, Grand Funk now wanted their independence. Tired of seeing themselves described as non-musical puppets, aware of the trust and loyalty of their fans, they sued for divorce in March 1972. 'I knew there was going to be trouble when Mark came to me and said he didn't want to fall down on his knees during the show any more,' said Knight. Though their former manager bombarded the group with a blizzard of lawsuits, injunctions and equipment confiscations, Grand Funk persevered.

Their initial album without Knight, *Phoenix* (1973), was a haphazard affair, easing in new organist Craig Frost while testing the borders of their hard-won independence. Later in the year, Todd Rundgren was brought in to produce their next album, *We're An American Band*, and it was an instant success. The title song,

written by Don Brewer, laid out the red, white and blue Grand Funk creed in all its star-spangled splendour, celebrating rock 'n'roll road life in a series of vignettes, from staying up all night 'playing cards with Freddy King' to meeting the infamous 'sweet sweet Connie' from Little Rock. In September, 'We're An American Band' went to the top of the singles charts.

The following year Rundgren gave them another single with a grotesquely heavy version of 'The Locomotion' and in 1975 they turned to power-pop producer Jimmy

Opposite: Muscles tensed, face contorted and hair flying in the wind, Mark Farner (left) was the archetypal guitar hero. Above, from left: Farner, keyboard player Craig Frost, drummer Don Brewer and bassist Mel Schacher. Below: Grand Funk live.

Ienner, whose credits included the Raspberries, among others. Ienner smoothed out the sound and provided further hits with the slick harmonies of 'Bad Time (To Be In Love)', which reached Number 4, and the relentless rhythmatics of 'Some Kind Of Wonderful' (Number 3). But with the dilution of their basic, grating sound came the dilution of the Grand Funk image: they became just another malleable rock band. They were no longer hated by hip rock critics – they were just ignored – and they were no longer loved by teenagers.

Farner's farewell

Following an unsuccessful collaboration with producer Frank Zappa for the inaptly-titled *Good Singin' Good Playin'* (1976), Grand Funk disbanded. Farner made a pair of comeback solo albums in the late Seventies but he had outgrown his old followers and was unkindly booed off stage.

In the early Eighties, Grand Funk reformed to produce a couple of albums of well-crafted hard rock – *Grand Funk Lives* and *What's Funk* – but these were generally ignored. It had become obvious that Grand Funk would never recapture the spirit of '71 when, at full throttle, churning out their simplistic heavy metal at enormous volume and bawling triumphantly, Farner, Brewer and Schacher had held Shea Stadium in the palms of their hands.

LENNY KAYE

Grand Funk Railroad Recommended Listening

Live (Capitol EST DW1/2) (Includes: Inside Looking Out, Paranoid, In Need, Mark Says Alright, Heartbreaker, Words Of Wisdom, Into The Sun).

ROCK 'N' ROLL OUTLAWS

Who rode the trail with the James Gang?

BASED ON THE CLASSIC heavy rock combination of guitar, bass and drums, capable of recording strong records and performing well on stage, the James Gang once seemed destined to be a major, long-lasting influence on rock. This never happened, however, and the band is now mainly remembered for fostering the career of its star, guitarist Joe Walsh.

The group was formed by drummer Jimmy Fox, who grew up in Cleveland, Ohio. At the age of eight, he began taking classical piano lessons and, while still a youngster, became interested in jazz. He taught himself to play a wide variety of instruments, including drums. By 1966, along with the rest of teenage America, he had been converted to the 'British' sound. He teamed up with bass-player Tom Kriss and guitarist Glenn Schwartz to perform Beatles, Rolling Stones and Yardbirds covers at high-school dances, abetted by various acquaintances. One year later, after Cream had proved that there was a viable musical alternative to the usual four-man unit, the newly-named James Gang settled down as a trio.

Guitar heroics
The band played the Ohio area throughout 1968 and 1969, refusing to join the migration of musicians to California despite the loss of Schwartz, who left for the West Coast and joined Pacific Gas and Electric Co. Fox picked up a part-time college student, Joe Walsh, to fill in on guitar. Walsh (born 20 November 1947) had attended Kent State University for a year and had become totally involved with the guitar, although he continued to attend classes in electronics, acoustics, wiring and welding. Inspired by his hero, Eric Clapton, he was determined to learn about every aspect of the electric guitar and investigate its musical possibilities by rewiring pick-ups, removing or changing condensers and capacitors and adjusting the bridge and neck. When Walsh joined the James Gang, his technical knowledge enabled him to create a distinctive and unique guitar sound. He also took the bulk of the lead vocals.

Guitarist Joe Walsh (left and inset far left) took fellow James Gang members Jimmy Fox (inset centre) and Tom Kriss (inset right) to the brink of stardom.

Walsh's growing reputation attracted the interest of Bill Szymczyk, then a fledgling producer with ABC Records. The company agreed to take a chance on signing the band and Szymczyk quickly produced its first LP, *Yer' Album*, which was released in mid 1969. By the Eighties the record had come to sound somewhat dated, owing to the inexperience of both band and producer. Particularly annoying were the superfluous intros and studio raps which were considered so stylish at the time. The album was redeemed, however, by touches of whimsical humour, such as the choice of a washed-out lithograph of Jesse James and the original James Gang for the sleeve, and by Walsh's stirring guitar-playing, which varied between crashing chords, wailing blues and jazzy soloing. Szymczyk kept within bounds Fox's eclectic musical influences and Walsh's tendency to become over-concerned with technical effects; the result was an accessible LP that balanced hard rock with identifiable tunes (including Buffalo Springfield's 'Bluebird', the Yardbirds' 'Lost Woman' and Jerry Ragavoy's 'Stop'). By the autumn of 1969, *Yer' Album* had made the upper half of *Billboard*'s album chart; it remained there for six weeks.

Shortly afterwards, bassist Tom Kriss decided to leave the rock business and Jim Fox brought in Dale Peters, an old acquaintance he had previously played alongside in several garage bands. This new trio began a series of US national tours to critical and popular acclaim. Walsh responded to being the centre of attention by writing several strong numbers. June 1970 saw the release of *The James Gang Rides Again*, which promptly became a US top-selling album.

In addition to the balance and control now closely identified with Walsh's guitar-playing was a strong rhythmic base, provided by Fox and Peters. The material ranged from the power of 'The Bomber' to the delicacy of 'Ashes The Rain And I'. Original pressings of the album became overnight collectors' items because Walsh had included a few bars of Ravel's 'Bolero' in 'Cast Your Fate To The Wind'; these were edited from subsequent pressings owing to copyright problems.

Major success seemed guaranteed when the band joined the Who for their UK/Europe tour in late 1970, but record sales failed to reflect the favourable audience reaction they encountered. The band returned to the States to begin work on a new album, appropriately called *Thirds*. Released in March 1971, it seemed at the time a natural progression for the band. The material was often as good as that on *The James Gang Rides Again*, although it tended to feature a more acoustic sound. With hindsight, however, the record was more self-conscious than its predecessors and failed to achieve a balance between hard rock and the band's more mellow musical influences.

Initial sales of *Thirds* were not spectacular and the band was discouraged by its failure to win a wider audience than the hard-rock fans they had previously catered for. This section of the public got just what it wanted, however, barely five months later, with *The James Gang Live At Carnegie Hall* (1971), which featured lengthy versions of the loudest tracks from the first three albums. The result was a 'greatest hits' package of LP cuts that hardly merited re-recording. The band seemed to have hit a creative trough. This was further deepened by the departure of Walsh in November 1971 to pursue a solo career that would draw on various musical influences as well as heavy rock. He formed his own group, Barnstorm, before joining the Eagles in 1975.

Gang warfare
The loss of Walsh, the band's major song-writer and the author of its distinctive sound, was disastrous. To make matters worse, the group began a series of lawsuits with ABC, each side accusing the other of breach of contract. Instead of formally breaking up the James Gang, Fox and Peters brought in two Canadians as replacements for Walsh, Dom Troiano (guitar) and Roy Kenner (vocals). *Straight Shooter* appeared in February 1972, probably before the public even knew that Walsh had quit. The record's weak sound and abysmal songs soon ensured everyone was informed, however; August's *Passin' Thru* did nothing to remedy matters.

The James Gang eventually found a guitarist who was almost as good as Walsh in Tommy Bolin. December 1973 saw the release of *Bang* on a new label, Atco/Atlantic. Bolin provided the group with a revitalised sound; he also co-wrote all but one track of the whole album. But by now rock was beginning to split into clear-cut categories and a band such as the James Gang, who were still playing in a combination of styles, attracted no-one. Both *Bang* and its follow-up *Miami* (released in August 1974) were completely ignored and the group broke up.

Never appreciated in the UK and never as successful as expected in the US, by the Eighties the James Gang seemed easy to dismiss. However their work with Joe Walsh represents the height of an era when a rock album was expected to provide genuinely new musical avenues for exploration and to reach a wide audience in the process. The band's first three albums reveal a variety of exciting possibilities that still make them significant for anyone interested in rock music.   ED HANEL

SPIRIT OF CALIFORNIA

A potent brew of psychedelic rock

WHILE IT WOULD BE impossible to claim that any of the better music created in Los Angeles during the mid to late Sixties was in any way mainstream – the energy and breadth of myriad styles indicate otherwise – the innovations of the group Spirit were certainly more offbeat than most of their contemporaries. The techniques and musical freedom they employed would later become commonplace as players grew in accomplishment and ambition, yet the variety of different contexts the band worked in produced results that were not only innovatory at the time, but have remained as fresh and inspired as when first created.

Rebellious spirits

The backgrounds of the five musicians who constituted Spirit were initially responsible for this spontaneous expertise. Drummer Ed Cassidy was in his early forties when the band formed in 1967. He had emerged from a formal jazz-training, having played with Gerry Mulligan, Art Pepper, Thelonious Monk and Cannonball Adderley as a sideman. He brought with him an ability to experiment with rhythm that was far removed from those drummers weaned in the garage bands and R&B-derived combos of the period.

Pianist John Locke was similarly gifted, a former member of the New World Jazz Company and a musician equally at home with avant-garde keyboards and straighter melodic structures. Vocalist Jay Ferguson and bassist Mark Andes came from poppier backgrounds; Andes had the dubious distinction of having been a session man with Bobby 'Boris' Pickett (he appeared on 1962's US chart-topping 'Monster Mash') and also played with blues outfit Canned Heat for a while.

Spirit's instrumental finesse was completed by the excellence of their youthful guitarist Randy California – a mere 16 years of age when the group came together – who was fortunate enough to have met up with Jimi Hendrix, then simply Jimmy James, when the latter was playing a residency at New York's Cafe Wha in 1966. California was converted from acoustic to electric guitar by Hendrix and joined his Blue Flames at the Cafe to play four sets a night for four months. When Chas Chandler came to New York to hear Hendrix play and persuaded him to come to England, Randy California returned to

Los Angeles and formed Spirits Rebellious, named after a Kahil Gilbran novel, with Cassidy, his stepfather.

The band gigged locally for several months, abbreviating their name simply to Spirit, before entrepreneur and Ode Records boss Lou Adler auditioned them at the Whiskey A Go Go on Sunset Strip. The group's substantial experience stood them in good stead on their debut album, *Spirit*, released in 1968. This was a sophisticated entry into the recording world, combining the jazzier finesse of the rhythm section with pertinent lyrics reflecting the social climate of the time. 'Mechanical World' and 'Fresh Garbage' put over the message, with Ferguson's clear, tuneful vocal and California's refined and tasteful guitar-playing to the fore.

It was not an elaborately psychedelic album – Spirit preferred a mood of 'understatement'. The atmosphere that characterised their work was assisted by sympathetic production from Adler himself and by the string and horn arrangements of Marty Paich, a big-band veteran of the Fifties.

Model movie stars

Spirit continued to develop their empathy and graceful melodies throughout a fine second set, entitled *The Family That Plays Together*, released later in 1968. It was from here that they gained their first and only substantial single hit with California's 'I Got A Line On You', which reached Number 25 the following year. This demonstration of their poppier side proved that the group couldn't be categorised in any particular style, a quality that in the end was to undermine their chances of sustaining commercial success. Although their first two albums each sold in excess of 200,000 copies, Spirit never attained the heights of popularity their music merited, despite being respected by peers and critics alike.

A third album – *Clear*, also released in 1969 – was their most experimental recording yet. One song from it, 'Ice', was used in the same year to open a rather self-conscious film called *The Model Shop*, directed by Jacques Demy and starring Anouk Aimée. Spirit also appeared live in a club scene, but the obscure nature of the movie did nothing to further their career.

Lack of financial reward and a souring of their relationship with Adler, who had secured for himself the majority of the band's publishing rights, led to internal wranglings within the group. California

and Ferguson had differing ideas on which way their music should develop. Their final album as a five-piece was recorded in acrimonious and bizarre circumstances, but in retrospect was their most overtly

Above: Spirit vintage '68, from left Locke, Andes, Cassidy, Ferguson and California. Left and below: California kept the band rocking into the Seventies.

commercial work. Indeed, *The Twelve Dreams Of Dr Sardonicus*, released in 1970, has since been hailed as Spirit's masterpiece, with its hallucinogenic tone reflected by David Briggs' production.

The band broke up during the album's completion, leaving Randy California to mix the tracks. The line-up played their final concert at Bill Graham's Fillmore East on New Year's Eve.

Although this was the end of Spirit proper (Jay Ferguson and Mark Andes left to form mainstream rockers Jo Jo Gunne and gain a US and UK Top Thirty hit in 1972 with 'Run, Run, Run'), a version of the band continued to function with new members Al and John Christian Staehely, assisted by Locke and Cassidy. This rather bogus outfit recorded one album together, *Feedback*; released in 1971, it was a collection with little to redeem it and none of the magic of the earlier work.

California earthquake

California suffered the further traumas of an increasing drug problem and a failed marriage, his state of mind being reflected in a much heavier and depressing venture – his 1972 album, *Kaptain Kopter and The Fabulous Twirlybirds*. The Kopter band undertook a European tour in 1973, including a successful date at London's Rainbow Theatre. Shortly afterwards the guitarist attempted suicide by jumping off London Bridge.

California's mental upheaval hadn't been helped by the Columbia label's rejection of a project called *Journey Through Potatoland*, for which he'd enlisted the aid of Cassidy and bassist Larry Knight. One song in particular, '1984', angered Columbia executives sensitive to its political connotations. It was released as a single, but hurriedly withdrawn. In retrospect *Potatoland* was a mild allegory, a mixture of George Orwell and Lewis Carroll. It was aired on BBC radio and its popularity among Spirit fans led to California finally remixing the songs and releasing them on Beggar's Banquet in 1981.

The close bond between California and Cassidy has seen them continue to function as Spirit, augmented by a variety of different bassists. Several fine albums emerged during the Seventies, including the double *Spirit Of '76* (1975) and a full band reunion, minus Jay Ferguson, called *Farther Along* in 1976.

Randy California has enjoyed more popularity in Europe than in America, with two live records being made in England and Germany. Perhaps his most extreme venture to date has been the *Future Games* set in 1977, where images from 'Star Trek' and 'The Muppets' were integrated into a seamless collection of weird and wonderful nonsense.

A reunion in 1984 resulted in *Spirit Of '84/The Thirteenth Dream,* an album of re-recordings and new material that showed some of the old magic as the band's earlier material was released.

MAX BELL

Spirit
Recommended Listening

Spirit (CBS 63278) (Includes: Fresh Garbage, Uncle Jack, Mechanical World, Straight Arrow, Topango Windows, The Great Canyon Fire In General); *Twelve Dreams Of Dr. Sardonicus* (Epic 64191) (Includes: Nature's Way, Mr. Skin, Animal Zoo, Street Worm, Love Has Found A Way, Soldier, When I Touch You).

THE GUESS WHO

Canadian rockers at home and abroad

It is hard to place the Guess Who in a particular niche of the rock'n'roll pantheon. They were a singles band who placed only two singles in the UK Top Fifty. Their five US Top Ten singles were hits when serious rock fans ignored AM radio and paid no attention to the singles charts. They were Canadian and flaunted it at a time when Neil Young, Joni Mitchell and everyone else Canadian looked, talked and acted as American as possible. The Eighties success of Australian rock has sanctified the cult status of mid-Sixties Australian hit-makers the Easybeats, but the growth of Canada's rock music has done nothing to enhance the Guess Who's reputation. Power-pop revivals have made old Kinks and Raspberries albums collectors' items, but many Guess Who LPs sell for less than their original cover price. The Guess Who certainly deserve better.

Their leader, Randy Bachman, was born in 1946 and raised near Winnipeg, Manitoba. His parents encouraged him to study classical music and his first instrument was the violin. Bachman once told *Guitar Player* magazine: 'The violin turned into a sore spot in my life. When I was 10 or 11, all my friends were going out to play football or going to the movies, while I was up in my room practising violin. And when I was bad, instead of saying, "Go to your room; you can't have dinner", my parents would say, "Go to your room and practise your violin." This thing was supposed to be a pleasure – they made it a punishment.'

Bachman gave up music totally for three years. In 1959, however, he saw Elvis Presley perform on TV and became interested in the guitar; since then, his playing has showed a flair for country and jazz. Besides the obvious influence of Elvis' guitar-player, James Burton, he was also devoted to the country-pop of Chet Atkins. He had been introduced to this style by watching Lenny Breau on one of his tours. This influence led to him joining up with a friend, Chad Allen, in a rockabilly outfit called Al and the Silvertones that took its name from Bachman's first guitar.

Just a Canadian band?

With Allen on vocals, and Bachman developing quickly on guitar, the duo began jamming with some of Winnipeg's better musicians. Drummer Garry Peterson was professional enough to have played with the Winnipeg Symphony Orchestra despite his youth, and was eager to move into rock. James Kale was likewise an excellent craftsman on bass and had been playing in local bands for several years. The next obvious step was to move the group to the US and look for a record contract. The only problem was that Randy had become a full-time student at Manitoba Instutite of Technology. While all the later public emphasis on being proudly Canadian was sincere, the simple truth was the band was in no position to move south while their leader pursued his college education.

Just when the name Guess Who came about is hard to settle, but its origins probably stemmed from an admiration for Pete

Townshend's outfit across the Atlantic. Bachman admits he saw the Who play at the Marquee on an early visit to the UK in the mid Sixties, and it was about this time that his band began calling themselves the Guess Who. The Guess Who also incorporated 'My Generation' into their stage act and, like Townshend and Moon, began smashing up their equipment as a finale.

This direction didn't please Allen, and he left to be replaced in 1965 by Burton Cummings. By the end of 1966, the year in which Bachman graduated, the Guess Who no longer needed to mimic the Who and their stage show won them a weekly Canadian TV programme, 'Where It's At'. Through most of 1967, the band used TV to introduce a variety of songs written by Bachman and/or Cummings, such as 'And She's Mine', 'Clock On The Wall', 'Of A Dropping Pin' and 'Laughing'. Altogether, almost 20 singles had been released in Canada by 1968, with virtually no reaction in the States. Minuscule ads of two or three lines appeared in the back pages of *Billboard* for various releases, but the only Americans who seemed to know anything about the band lived along the border where they could pick up a Canadian radio station. The only exception to this general neglect had occurred in May 1965, when the band's version of Johnny Kidd and the Pirates' 'Shakin' All Over' managed to reach Number 22 in the *Billboard* chart.

This failure to crack the United States market only hardened the group's resistance to move south. The signs, logos and names of American institutions, businesses, products and personalities that can be seen throughout Canada often give the impression that the country is in some way subservient to its neighbour. The resentment this has fostered reinforced the Guess Who's frustration at failing to make it in the US as a Canadian band.

Crossing the border
In late 1968, another Bachman/Cummings original, 'These Eyes', resulted in a further Canadian Top Twenty hit. Independent producer Jack Richardson (soon to work with Alice Cooper) heard the song, felt it was a potential US hit and approached RCA, who signed the band in January 1969. Within the next few months, 'These Eyes' sold a million copies and got to Number 6 in the US Top Twenty.

The next 18 months saw the Guess Who at their most successful. They had five singles in the Top Ten, another in the Top Twenty (a seventh hit was a B-side that charted at Number 22 in its own right), and three top-selling albums – *Wheatfield Soul* (1969), *American Woman* (1970) and *Share The Land* (1970). Meanwhile, the Guess Who's live performances were

Left: The Guess Who's most successful line-up; from left bassist James Kale, drummer Garry Peterson, singer-guitarist Burton Cummings, lead guitarist Randy Bachman. Right: The band promote 'American Woman' on UK television, 1970.

masterpieces of melodic hard rock; audience reaction was strong, and the band seemed set for stardom. The fact that the rock press totally ignored them didn't really seem to matter. At the height of this period, the Guess Who released 'American Woman', their chilling warning about American domination and unconscious neglect of Canada, with its lyrics '. . . stay away from me American Woman, momma let me be . . .'. The single reached Number 1 in the US charts.

The key to the band's sound lay in the interplay between Cummings' vocals and Bachman's guitar. But Bachman was growing disenchanted with the sound. His Mormon background also conflicted with the more hedonistic attitudes of the rest of the band. In any event, when Bachman decided he no longer wanted to lead his group, the magic disappeared.

Bachman left in 1970 to produce a solo LP, *Axe*, and was then invited to join Keith Emerson's new unnamed band – later Emerson, Lake and Palmer – but instead began producing an album for former cohort Chad Allen, eventually forming Brave Belt with him. Two albums later, Bachman and bass-player Fred Turner reorganised the line-up and entered the growing heavy-metal market as Bachman-Turner Overdrive, charting worldwide in

1974 with the *Not Fragile* LP and a single, 'You Ain't Seen Nothin' Yet'.

Cummings replaced Bachman and took over control of the Guess Who, but despite a few good singles, the band had lost inspiration. Nine albums and several personnel changes later, the band finally gave up in 1975 when Cummings began a solo career. He had some success, notably with 'Stand Tall', a US Top Ten single in 1976. Long-serving bass-player Jim Kale continued recording and touring under the group name, but until the band reformed for a Canadian TV special in the mid-Eighties, it seemed pointless.

The Guess Who never really had a rock image, and so could never slot into a convenient category. But at their best, they created a special sound with enough hooks to grab everybody's attention. Unfortunately, good music isn't always enough to succeed in the rock business. The Guess Who seemed doomed to suffer from that fact even at the peak of their success.

ED HANEL

Guess Who
Recommended Listening

Best Of The Guess Who (RCA AFLI 2594) (Includes: American Woman, These Eyes, Undun, Laughing, Share The Land, Bus Rider, Hang On To Your Life).

BEAT IT

The changing shape of the rock drum kit

DURING THE SEVENTIES, the most clearly visible development in the rock drum kit was its dramatic increase in size; the modest jazz-derived kits that had carried rock drummers through the Sixties were replaced by vast multi-drum kits. The twin bass-drum had become standard for most heavy-rock drummers and this move was followed by a new enthusiasm for row upon row of tom-toms, to the extent that there could be as many as 20 drums in a single set-up. Parts of such kits were virtually unplayable and literally made long arms a vital attribute of the rock drummer.

The drums themselves also underwent considerable change. A wider variety of types became available to the general customer, though the general trend was for drum shells to have more depth to provide greater acoustic volume and better sound projection. However, the main way of increasing volume – and gaining greater control over the overall sound – has remained miking up the kit; during the Seventies, it became common practice to festoon the kit with a multitude of microphones for both live and studio work. Side-by-side with this development was the introduction of single-headed tom-toms which, besides being another means of projecting the sound, also allowed the microphone to be placed directly inside the drum shell.

This growing interest in drum technology included the widespread introduction of new materials. The traditional plywood shells were supplemented by synthetic designs that were lighter and stronger and could be manufactured in a variety of finishes – including transparent – that proved popular for more flamboyant drummers who considered visual display as important as tonal quality. The coated plastic head that had replaced the old animal-skin heads was joined by other man-made materials, including Kevlar, Fiberskyn and Banana skin, which provided the drummer with greater tonal variety as well as a different response. A major development was the Remo CS (controlled sound) or black spot, which consisted of an ordinary transparent head overlaid with a black circular plastic head to deaden the sound. There was also the Evans oil-filled head – two layers of plastic with a film of oil between them to give a dead, 'thudding' sound.

High and dry
Besides new materials improving existing drums, the Seventies saw the widespread introduction of new drum types. The rototom was much in vogue in the late Seventies; without any shell, this drum consisted of a plastic skin stretched over a metal

Above left: The kit of ex-Vanilla Fudge and Rod Stewart sticksman Carmine Appice features double bass drums cut away for easy microphone access. The twin single-headed tom-toms, mounted to his left, are also close-miked. Above: One-time Yes drummer Alan White has a set of roto-toms to his left, with two sound-projector tom-toms mounted forward. Four bells hang below his left hand, while behind him are ranged crotales or tuned finger-cymbals.

frame which, by simple rotation, allowed the drum to be tuned to a variety of pitches. In contrast was the Tama octoban, a drum with a small-diameter head but long shell which provided a dry, high-pitched sound. Taking up little space, the octoban is typically used in conjunction with other octobans which, when tuned at different levels, provide a whole range of high tones that can supplement the deeper tones of the tom-toms.

Rock drummers had traditionally shown little interest in cymbals, but with the development of progressive rock this began to change. The Swiss firm Paiste produced a 602 series specially designed for the rock drummer, and they were soon joined by the other major companies who began to manufacture high-quality rock cymbals. The most important cymbals for rock were the hi-hat (for time-keeping) and powerful crash/ride cymbals, though the Chinese cymbal also became common through the influence of jazz-rock.

The increase in size and number of drums forming the typical rock kit called

for a corresponding improvement in stands and fittings. The lightweight equipment designed for the jazz and dance-band drummer was clearly unsuitable for the brutal pounding the kit received night after night from the heavy-rock drummer of the Seventies. The extra number of drums also called for more complex fittings which developed into heavy, robust interlocking 'systems'. The conventional upright cymbal stand was complemented by the boom-stand, enabling the cymbal to be positioned over the extended kit and within the drummer's reach. As the multiplicity of drums developed into something of a nightmare for roadies having to set up a kit in precise positions every night, the memrilock system was introduced. In this, each fitting could be pre-set to the desired position on a regular basis.

In the Eighties, the major developments reflected a move away from the acoustic sphere to electronics. One of the most revolutionary developments was the introduction of the Simmons SDS V electronic drum kit. Each drum has a touch-sensitive perspex playing surface that is directly sensitive to the level of force supplied by the drummer's stick. The variety of sounds obtainable from such a kit are considerable; each drum contains four memories, so that the six-drum kit marketed by the company can produce 24 drum sounds. Manufactured in hexagonal shapes, the drums can be set up as a conventional kit (with a standard bass pedal for the bass drum), or replace any specific part of the old kit.

The other major development in electronics has been the rapid growth of the drum machine, which allows an unlimited variety of rhythmic patterns to be programmed into the machine and will reproduce them with metronomic efficiency. The drum machine is simple to use and, as no knowledge of drum technique is necessary, the drummer can even be dispensed with altogether. More positively, drummers can now incorporate pre-set drum programmes against which they can play during live performance. The range of effects that were once the preserve of the guitarist, including echo-delay units, can be used to give the drummer a virtual over-dubbing facility. While the acoustic kit seems virtually to have reached its fullest development, the most exciting developments in drum technology may well be found in the field of electronic percussion.

It is instructive to compare the sound of the snare drum on Bill Haley's 'Rock Around The Clock' – all echo and resonance – with the heavy, dull sound of the drums that feature on the disco singles of the late Seventies. Each represents an extreme of rock drumming. The sound of drums became flatter and less resonant for a variety of reasons. Partly, it was because it made the kit easier to manage in a studio, in that each drum could be miked separately without its sound spilling over into other mikes. It was also because the sound of rock groups themselves changed in the late Sixties as the guitars, both bass and lead, or keyboards played most of the sustained sounds necessary, and the drums had no need for sounds other than the most distinctive initial impact.

In terms of influence, the greatest rock drummers of the mid Sixties – Keith Moon or Mitch Mitchell for example – were not necessarily the most important. But the sound of the drums that Stevie Wonder used (and often played) on his LPs were very influential, as were the musical effects achieved by the Beatles on *Sgt Pepper* (1967) and *Abbey Road* (1969) or by Aynsley Dunbar or Frank Zappa's *Hot Rats* (1970). Recognisable tunes were now being played around the kit.

Then, in the late Sixties and early Seventies, the great names of jazz-rock – Billy Cobham, Lenny White, Michael Walden – began showing how new, technically difficult effects could be obtained, and they too used a much deader sound than had previously been in vogue.

Sticks tricks

The peaks of jazz-rock coincided with a general raising of the technical level of rock drumming. Suddenly, many extremely competent musicians found that there was an enormous amount to be gained from exploring the basic rhythmic material of rock – patterns of semi-quavers played across the kit, various independent exercises between bass drum and snare drum – in a way hitherto unknown.

The result was that, by the mid Seventies, there were expert drummers working in all fields and at all levels. There were the showmen, Carl Palmer and John Bon-

Above right: The futuristically-shaped Simmons electronic kit. Right: This drum machine is triggered by touch-sensitive pads. Below: Billy Cobham proudly displays his collection of octobans.

ham, for example, who supplemented their technical proficiency with light-shows or tricks like Jon Hiseman's stream of drumsticks flying through the air. Then there were the thoughtful musicians like Bill Bruford or Henry Cow's Chris Cutler, and the speed kings – Billy Cobham, Alphonse Mouzon, Lenny White – at whom a stupefied audience gazed in awe. And there were the kings of reggae drumming – Winston Grennan, Leroy 'Horsemouth' Wallace – who were developing a feel that was completely distinctive.

By this period, rock had taken over drumming. The drum companies produced kits for would-be rock stars, not for use in night-clubs or by jazz groups. The sound of the drum kit in disco came from the technical developments mentioned earlier; the use of drum machines and a very flat-sounding drum kit.

Given the increased range of possibilities available by the late Seventies, it is perhaps surprising that the punk revolution and its aftermath failed to produce any exciting developments in the world of drumming. New masters developed an eclectic musical mix of reggae rhythms, funk and hard rock – and skilful use of the studio and electronics provided the interest.   ADRIAN GILBERT

Ringing the Changes

**The trendsetting style
of David Bowie**

DAVID BOWIE HAS ALWAYS excited violently opposing passions. For many, he was one of the most consistently stimulating and innovative musicians of the Seventies; for many more, he represented all that was worst in the era of painted poseurs, charlatans and punks. This controversy remains at the heart of his music and his image; Bowie personifies the conflict within rock in the Seventies.

Although Bowie is a contemporary of many of the famous musicians of the Sixties (he was born in 1947, only one year after his early idol Syd Barrett), he spent that turbulent decade in obscurity, first as an R&B singer in the London clubs and later as a 'cult' songwriter and author of one notable hit single, 'Space Oddity', in 1969. By the time Ziggy Stardust burst upon the public in 1972, the rock world had changed. Gone were the optimism and the certainties of the Sixties, and no rock performer was capable of unifying the public the way the Beatles had done. Gone, too – or severely dented at least – was the idea of emotional authenticity that the hippies derived from the blues. In the place of sweaty, denim-clad musicians 'telling it how it is' were pretty, canny showbiz entertainers like Marc Bolan, David Cassidy and the Osmonds.

Old ideas die hard, however, and although the likes of Little Jimmy Osmond could be safely ignored by 'serious' rock fans, Bolan – and later Bowie himself – posed more of a threat. For they were serious artists who had apparently committed an act of betrayal by embracing the demon showbiz. Bolan had been part of the hippie underground before he slapped on his make-up and strapped on an electric guitar; DJ John Peel (who had plugged Bolan's group from their earliest days) was so offended by the transformation that he vowed never to play Bolan's records again.

Ziggy played guitar

When Bowie dyed his hair orange, climbed into a revealing bodystocking and went down on Mick Ronson's guitar, the shock waves were even greater. Rock journalist Dave Laing expressed that shock in *Let It Rock* magazine in 1973: 'He has compromised with showbiz, with the whole manipulative process of image and stardom . . . take away Bowie's image, and there's nothing left.'

In tune with Bowie's gleeful use of all the suspect trappings of showbiz was another, perhaps even more unforgivable transgression – the distance and irony he applied to everything he did. 'The actor' was what he called himself on the sleeve of *Hunky Dory* (1971) – and if the phrase referred to Bowie's theatrical training, it also indicated how he perceived himself. But rock stars in the early Seventies weren't supposed to be actors . . . rock stars were meant to be for real, like Janis Joplin or Neil Young. 'He's too knowing,' Laing complained. 'He knows everything that's been said and every lick that made a Top Ten hit, but ends up communicating nothing.'

Bowie cheerfully confessed guilt to both charges. 'I'm not an innovator, I'm just a photostat machine,' he said in 1973. And, on another occasion: 'I have no message whatsoever. I really have nothing to say . . .' Both statements were more mischievous than serious, but they show how aware Bowie was of the effect he was

having, and how it angered the rock establishment. As *New Musical Express* rock critic Charles Shaar Murray has pointed out, Bowie didn't so much 'strip rock of its innocence as attack the idea that it ever had a degree of innocence in the first place'.

Aside from the spectacle and sheer *fun* of the whole Ziggy Stardust pantomime, this ironic detachment was what made Bowie such a breath of fresh air on the music scene. His cool irony made nonsense of the pretensions of the progressive rockers. Their carefully faded jeans, deliberately unkempt hair and 'spontaneous' macho guitar heroics were no more innocent than Bowie's lurex, orange dye and guitar-licking; paradoxically, it was Bowie who was more honest in that he didn't aim to hide the pretence.

Hazy cosmic jive

As an observer of the hippie dream and its aftermath, Bowie was second to none. It's a theme that runs through his work from 'The Cygnet Committee' on the *Space Oddity* album in 1969 to the punk fallout of 'Teenage Wildlife' on 1980's *Scary Monsters (And Super Creeps)*. Bowie believed the hippie idea that people fulfil only a fraction of their potential: 'I'm . . . just a mortal with potential of a superman,' he sang on *Hunky Dory*'s 'Quicksand' – but he was also aware of the dangers of such beliefs, and the song is a chilling and unsettling one. 'Oh You Pretty Things', on the same album, put forward the frightening proposition that 'The earth is a bitch/We've finished our news/Homo Sapiens have outgrown their use'.

In the light of such statements, Bowie's later, ill-judged comments about fascism seemed all the more regrettable. To make glib predictions that Britain was 'ready for another Hitler' is not the same as saying that that would be a good thing, but the distinction was lost on British neo-Nazi groups and their potential supporters among the impressionable young. Disturbingly, this interpretation was lent credence by the sinister public persona he had evolved by 1976.

From being the joker of rock, he had come – around the time of *Diamond Dogs* (1974) – to take himself very seriously indeed. *The Rise And Fall Of Ziggy Stardust And The Spiders From Mars* (1972) and *Aladdin Sane* (1973) had both been concept albums with apocalyptic scenarios of a world on the brink of disaster, but they were shot through with deflating humour and camp theatricality. *Diamond Dogs* – for all the fine music it contained – took itself in deadly earnest. And the new character Bowie developed, drawing on his role as the alien in the film *The Man Who Fell To Earth* (1976), was a reserved aristocrat called the Thin White Duke – the embodiment of icy control. The name occurs in the title track of *Station To Station* (1976), and it is no coincidence that the song also contains the line, 'It's not the side effects of the cocaine . . .', for Bowie was displaying the emotional and intellectual insensitivity and delusions of grandeur typical of cocaine addiction.

To Bowie's credit, he realised what he was becoming and pulled himself together. 'I've stopped trying to adapt. No more characters,' he later explained: 'The Thin White Duke was a

Identity parade: Eighties musicians owing an obvious debt to Bowie included (clockwise, from top) Steve Strange, the Eurythmics' Annie Lennox, Gary Numan and David Sylvian.

very nasty character indeed . . . an isolationist, with no commitment to any society.'

It is a truism that one generation's rebels become the next's establishment. In the early Seventies, Bowie's use of image, irony and distance was a healthy corrective to the smug self-indulgence of much music of the day. His ideas revitalised the careers of Mott the Hoople, Iggy Pop and Lou Reed, and helped pave the way for bands like Roxy Music.

Bowie retained his enormous influence through the punk years, inspiring groups like Japan and the Human League and founding a whole new school of male vocalists. But, by the time punk was subsiding, Bowie's example was being misinterpreted by many. The use of showbiz tactics, in Bowie's hands a contrast to rock's solemnity, was itself taken in deadly, obsessive earnest; as Bowie himself put it, 'I hold myself responsible for a whole new school of pretension.' 'Guitarist with image wanted' became a cliché of the rock press small-ads pages; cult band Bauhaus had a Top Twenty hit with a carbon copy of 'Ziggy Stardust', while Hazel O'Connor employed Bowie's producer and sleeve designer for her album *Cover Plus* (1981). Left-wing rock groups talked complacently of 'embracing the contradictions of the music industry' (this usually meant it was acceptable to enjoy champagne breakfasts after all), while new romantics aped Bowie's aristocratic pose.

Bowie's blueprint was also used as an excuse to exclude positive emotions like humour, compassion and warmth from music, in favour of arrogance and self-pity, by those who had little else to offer. The irony of this is that Bowie's own catalogue is full of warm, humane songs: 'God Knows I'm Good', the little vignette of an old lady caught shoplifting; 'Kooks', about the joys of parenthood; '"Heroes"', with its lovers' meeting under the Berlin Wall; 'Repetition', an angry, compassionate song about wife-beating, and many more. Sadly, all these seem to have been eclipsed by the shadow of the Thin White Duke as far as the likes of Gary Numan or Ultravox are concerned. When fashion-leader Steve Strange named his nightclub Helden (German for 'heroes'), after Bowie's 1977 album *'Heroes'*, he omitted the inverted commas Bowie had placed around the word to indicate the irony behind the idea.

Put on your red shoes . . .
The release of the *Let's Dance* LP in 1983 saw Bowie expressing his concern at this state of affairs: 'I think there's a strange, nihilistic quality to music that seems to be overshadowing everything at the moment – style over content.' Bowie went against the tide with a dance record that had a sunnier, more optimistic feel than any of his previous work. The following year's LP, *Tonight*, continued this trend with a collection of good time rock'n'roll. Bowie was also at pains to clean up his public image, performing charity concerts and extolling the joys of fatherhood in interviews. Whether this was a deeply felt change of heart or simply an astute career move is hard to tell. Whatever the truth, many Bowie fans must have secretly longed for him to rip aside the mask of compassion and reveal that he really was Dracula all the time.   CHRIS SCHÜLER

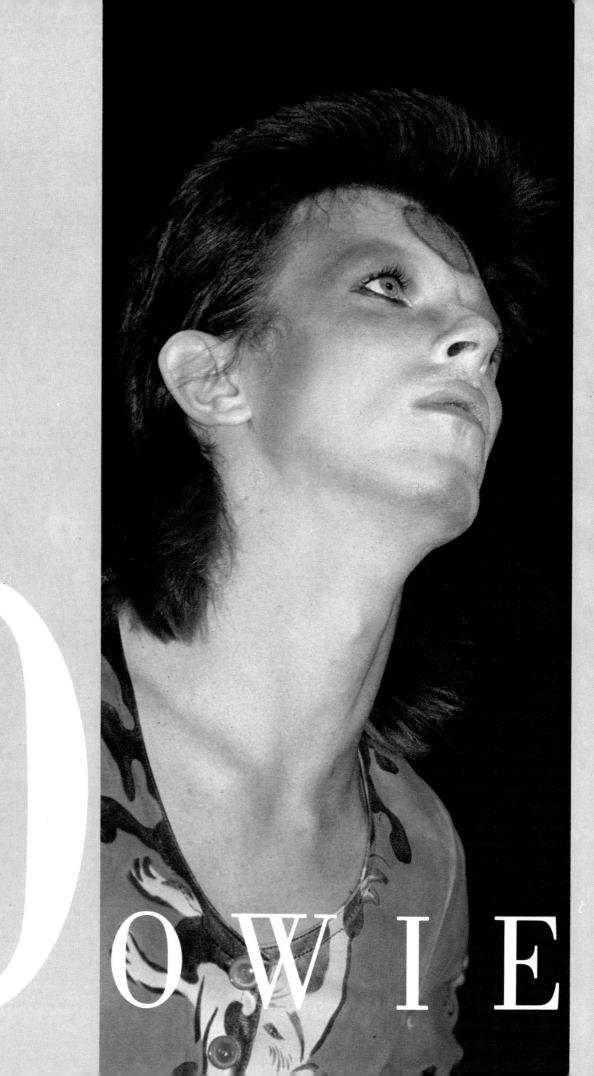

b

10

OWIE

Image and inspiration from the rock chameleon

ROCK WAS READY for Ziggy Stardust. Swishing and staggering in the spotlight, Bowie's outrageous alter-ego was camp, glamorous, fiendishly entertaining and – above all – the antithesis of everything rock had become since the emergence of the virtuoso instrumentalist in the mid Sixties. Perhaps it was all a con trick, an extension of the showbiz maxim that the greater the ostentation, the greater the reward; but it was the most exciting thing to happen to rock for many a year.

David Bowie changed things and carried on changing, re-inventing himself in different musical and visual guises throughout the next decade. Ultimately, David Bowie turned out to be much more than a mere hype. He is rock's greatest chameleon, an artist who has refused to trade on a proven formula.

On the road

Although Ziggy Stardust burst on the world in 1972, his creator had worked unsuccessfully in rock for years. Born David Robert Jones on 8 January 1947, he was raised in the poor South London area of Brixton until the age of eight. After two years on his uncle's farm in Yorkshire, the family moved back to London, this time to the suburb of Bromley.

Influenced by his jazz-loving half-brother Terry, who introduced him to Jack Kerouac's famous 'Beat' novel *On The Road*, David took saxophone lessons from the age of 13, and two years later performed with a school group, George and the Dragons. During his last year at school, his eye was injured in a fight, leaving the pupillary muscles paralysed. As a result, he has one blue eye and one grey, with the right pupil considerably larger than the left. It was at this time that Terry was committed to a mental institution.

Leaving school in 1963, graduating in just art and woodwork, David soon got a job as a commercial artist, hated the experience and left after six months. He then formed a group called the King Bees and started playing R&B on the London circuit; signed by Decca, they released two singles in 1964, 'Liza Jane' and 'You're Holding Me Down', before splitting up. Between 1965 and 1969, under the management of Ken Pitt, David went through a series of bands (the Manish Boys, Lower Third, David Bowie and the Buzz) and record labels without achieving any success or developing a distinctive musical style. He became David Bowie—having previously recorded as David Jones – in 1966 to avoid confusion with Davy Jones of the Monkees, and recorded his first solo single, 'Rubber Band', for Deram in 1967. A further single, 'Laughing Gnome' and an LP, *Love You Till Tuesday* followed, but with little success. (The compilation LP *The World Of David Bowie* contains substantially the same material.)

Above: Bowie plays the blues with the King Bees. Below: The family man with his wife Angie and child Zowie. Opposite: Ziggy Stardust contemplates his future as a rock'n'roll star.

At that time, Bowie's greatest vocal influence was cabaret singer Anthony Newley; although Bowie was to develop his own highly distinctive style in years to come, Newley's influence remained in Bowie's cabaret leanings and his 'Bewlay Brothers' cockney accent. Other influences on this period of Bowie's career included rhythm and blues, Buddhism, Bob Dylan (*Hunky Dory* contains an affectionate tribute, 'Song For Bob Dylan') and mime artist Lindsay Kemp, with whom Bowie studied in 1968. He befriended Marc Bolan and record producer Tony Visconti, won song festivals in Italy and Malta, worked as a model and a film extra (including a bit part in *Virgin Soldiers*), formed an arts lab at the Three Tuns public house in Beckenham and performed occasional concerts at London's Marquee Club and on a Scottish tour with Humble Pie.

Major Tom lifts off

None of David Bowie's records made any headway, however, until 'Space Oddity' was released on Philips to coincide with the American moon landing in September 1969. The tale of doomed astronaut Major Tom was underscored by Gus Dudgeon's dramatic production. A minor classic of British pop, the song reached Number 5 in the charts. (Six years later it was to hit Number 1 when re-released.)

Bowie was unable to consolidate this success, however, and retired to his Beckenham arts lab, marrying American design student Angela Barnett in March 1970. It was Angie who had got David his Deram contract through her connections, and her designs were to have a great influence on his visual image. Bowie became disenchanted with the old-style showbiz preconceptions of his manager, who wanted to mould Bowie into an all-round entertainer, while the album released to capitalise upon the success of 'Space Oddity' was all but ignored, despite its wealth of (disorganised) good ideas.

It was not until the release of *The Man Who Sold The World* 18 months later that his ideas began to take shape and Bowie emerged as a cult figure for modernists to whom hippiedom was no longer acceptable. He was pictured on the sleeve wearing a dress – 'a man's dress', he declared – while the lyrics, chanted over relentless hard rock, explored visions of a world edging closer and closer to some unthinkable catastrophe: subject-matter that was to recur on future Bowie records.

After the release of *The Man Who Sold The World*, Bowie undertook a promotional visit to America, where he befriended Andy Warhol (the subject of another *Hunky Dory* song), picking up a host of visual ideas at pop artist Andy Warhol's studio, the Factory. After encountering a sharp entrepreneur called Tony De Fries, Bowie extricated himself from Ken Pitt's management; De Fries was to be his manager for the next five years.

From this moment in late 1971, things happened with alarming rapidity. De Fries signed Bowie to RCA for a handsome advance (quite an achievement in view of Bowie's previous failures) and convinced anyone who would listen that his new client was a superstar 'potentially as big as Presley'.

Bowie, meanwhile, had recorded *Hunky Dory*; a far more coherent album than its predecessors, it contrasted the sunny optimism of 'Kooks' with the sombre reflections of 'The Bewlay Brothers'. The album's acoustic arrangements and whimsical humour gave it an intimacy reminiscent of the singer-songwriter school. Bowie also invested in a wardrobe of extraordinary clothes: futuristic, camp, colourful and quite unlike anything worn by rock singers before him. Adopting the Warhol ideology that all that is necessary to be a star is to act like one, Bowie looked into the mirror and perceived himself a winner; the actual winning was just a matter of time – and a short time at that.

Pretty thing

The event that really set the wheels in motion was a cover story and interview with *Melody Maker* in January of 1972, a month after *Hunky Dory* was released. 'David's present image,' wrote Michael Watts, 'is to come on like a swishy queen, a gorgeously effeminate boy. He's as camp as a row of tents with his limp hand and trolling vocabulary. "I'm gay," he says, "and always have been, even when I was David Jones".' True or not, the disclosure was the first example·of Bowie's growing flair for exploiting the media to his own advantage.

With *Hunky Dory* chalking up respectable sales, Bowie took to the road and delivered the goods in style. The concerts were a razzamatazz of colour and cacophony, *events* in the fullest sense of the word. Bowie used a three-piece band

(later augmented by keyboards), led by guitarist Mick Ronson. Their clothes, hair and make-up were skilfully designed to complement – but never overshadow – the outrageous aestheticism of Bowie himself. The highpoint in the show was when Bowie would kneel before Ronson and lick his guitar.

The music itself was the typical hard rock of the era, but spiced with the occasional fine melody like 'Changes', 'Life On Mars?', 'Starman' and 'Space Oddity' – all delivered in a carefree spirit that poked two fingers at the intensity of the rock virtuosi of the day.

The Rise And Fall Of Ziggy Stardust And The Spiders From Mars, the album that typifies this phase of Bowie's career, was released in June 1972. A concept album, it chronicled the arrival of a space age Messiah ('Moonage Daydream') on a dying world ('Five Years'), offering the hope of salvation through rock'n'roll ('Starman', 'Ziggy Stardust') before cracking up under the strain ('Rock'n'Roll Suicide'). Aside from having a powerful storyline and showcasing some of Bowie's best material, from infectious boogie numbers like 'Suffragette City' to bittersweet melodies like 'Lady Stardust', it was also calculated to raise Bowie himself to star-

dom. The concerts, the clothes, the performances – both on and off stage – became even more intoxicating, a show within a show: Bowie *was* Ziggy and the band were the Spiders.

As a much-publicised sideline, Bowie produced records by Lou Reed, Mott the Hoople and Iggy Pop, and in all three cases his intervention realised commercial rewards. Mott scored a UK Number 3 hit with a Bowie song, 'All The Young Dudes', while Reed's 'Walk On The Wild Side', produced by Bowie, also made the Top Ten. 'Starman' from the *Ziggy Stardust* album became Bowie's first hit single since 'Space Oddity', the first in an unbroken line of eight UK Top Twenty singles that would continue until 1974.

A world tour, undertaken during the first three months of 1973 by road, sea and rail because Bowie refused to fly, sealed his international reputation. *Aladdin Sane*, a patchy follow-up to *Ziggy Stardust*, went to

The outrageous antics of Bowie's Ziggy Stardust persona hit the headlines in 1972.

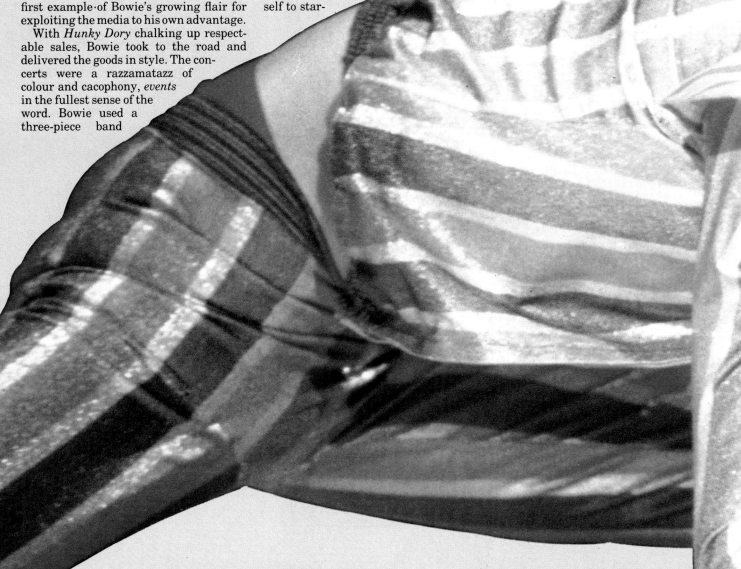

Number 1 in April, and a badly organised concert at London's Earls Court arena before 18,000 fans ended in chaos. The runaway juggernaut had to stop somewhere and Bowie chose to bury Ziggy on stage at the Hammersmith Odeon on 4 July, the last date on a UK tour that had played to 150,000 fans and visited 40 venues from Aberdeen to Torquay. At the end of the show, to the anguish of a packed house, Bowie announced the impending disbandment of the Spiders and his own temporary retirement.

Diamond doghouse

Partially released from the burden of celebrity, Bowie retreated to Paris to record *Pinups* – an undistinguished album of cover versions. He then sacked the Spiders and employed session men to assist him on *Diamond Dogs*, an album initially intended as a musical based on George Orwell's book *1984*. Though Bowie was unable to obtain the rights from Orwell's estate and had to re-think the project, the record nevertheless takes a similar theme to the Orwell classic: the dehumanisation of society. But the songs were pure rock 'n'roll – especially the title track and 'Rebel Rebel', both singles – and the sleeve designed by *Rock Dreams* illustrator Guy Peellaert was sensational.

The 1974 Diamond Dogs Review was Bowie's most ambitious tour ever. It crossed America and Canada in June and July, but was abandoned for logistical reasons long before it could reach Europe. Nor was this surprising, for it incorporated an enormous set with a city-scape backdrop and mobiles that elevated the performer to breathtaking heights and angles. Unfortunately, the music became secondary to the spectacle, a fault brought home with considerable force on the inglorious *David Live* album, which was taped at the Tower Theatre in Philadelphia and released in October.

The tour continued without the props, and the music shifted direction towards the soul style that was to dominate *Young Americans* (1975), an album recorded largely at Sigma Sound in Philadelphia with a cast of illustrious American players that included bassist Willie Weeks and drummer Andy Newmark. It also marked the arrival of rhythm guitarist Carlos Alomar, who would become an important musical ally in years to come. Further sessions for *Young Americans* took place in New York in early 1975, and it was here that John Lennon stopped by to assist in the recording of his own 'Across The Universe', as well as the disco riff based 'Fame' that was to give Bowie his first Number 1 in the US Hot Hundred later in the year.

Bowie's relationship with Lennon was fruitful in other areas too. A veteran of contractual lawsuits, the former Beatle had come to the conclusion that his affairs would be better in his own hands. Bowie, who by this time no longer saw eye to eye with Tony De Fries, took Lennon's advice and commenced legal proceedings against his own manager. The relationship with De Fries was duly severed but Bowie's former manager retained a percentage of earnings from matters negotiated by him, including the contract with RCA Records which had a further six years to run.

Before the 1976 tour, Bowie accepted the offer of a starring role in Nicolas Roeg's film *The Man Who Fell To Earth*. The part seemed tailor-made for the character Bowie had adopted as a rock performer, but the result was disappointing. As Thomas Jerome Newton, an alien who lands in America seeking aid for his barren planet, Bowie seemed uncomfortably wooden, lacking in warmth and unconsciously trading on his popular image to carry the role. Not until Bowie's title role in the touring and Broadway production of *The Elephant Man* in 1980 would his talents as an actor be realised.

For most of 1975 Bowie lived in California, where he recorded *Station To Station* and where the indigenous rock jet-set subverted his lifestyle with drink, drugs and sycophantic hero-worship. It was not a happy period – 'Actually I was zonked out of my mind,' he said later – and his marriage to Angie became a casualty. At the same time he showed a lack of political acumen by appearing to uphold fascist views in interviews – advocating 'an extreme right front' to 'sweep everything off its feet and tidy everything up'. Despite his subsequent qualifications and denials of these remarks, it seems likely that they were provoked by the lure of controversy, although they did little to further his career. Bowie's next character, the Thin White Duke of *Station To Station*, was as distasteful as the indescretion itself.

New career, new town

Station To Station (1976) was a transitional album that wrapped up the past four years and opened the doors to the next three. The music was harsh but accessible, often cold but densely produced, a stepping-stone to the electronic music that would follow. On tour, Bowie was at his most professional with a slick band, a slick all-white light show and an even slicker programme that reached back to satisfy fans from every phase of his career.

When the tour reached London, Bowie encountered Brian Eno, former keyboard-player with Roxy Music and latterly an avant-garde composer and keen exponent of electronic minimalism. The pair hit it off immediately and Bowie persuaded Eno to work with him in Berlin on a cycle of experimental albums.

Low and *'Heroes'*, released in January and October of 1977 respectively, saw Bowie deliberately distancing himself from the pop mainstream. 'I knew I had to

David Bowie seemed equally at ease amid the Diamond Dogs *city-scape (above right), in Sigma Sound studios with Luther Vandross, 1975 (right) and back in the spotlight three years later (opposite).*

get to an environment which was totally different to Los Angeles, so I thought of the most arduous city I could and it was West Berlin,' said Bowie. The music was austere, experimental and largely instrumental, with Bowie's synthesiser work dominating the thick layers of processed sound. It was sombre music, much of it created through the experiments with chance that had long fascinated Eno. Of the two albums, *'Heroes'* was the more accessible: its title track, among the strongest melodies Bowie has ever written, became a minor hit and was to influence a score of young British groups over the next two years.

The main business of 1978 was a world tour that blended material from *Low* and *'Heroes'* with a retrospective journey through the past that included selections from *Ziggy Stardust* and that provided the material for *Stage*, the second double live album of Bowie's career. Though a vast improvement on *David Live*, *Stage* was by no means an unqualified success and it was later revealed that its release was a business move to discharge contractual obligations to RCA. Nevertheless, the album demonstrated that Bowie was capable of reproducing his studio material with considerable finesse in a live setting, especially the instrumental passages from his more recent work. Of less aesthetic value was his role in the film *Just A Gigolo* the same year. 'All my 32 Elvis Presley movies rolled into one,' was Bowie's description of a movie which was taken off the circuit almost immediately after release.

Lodger, released in 1979, was the third, and the least successful, collaboration with Brian Eno. Although it saw a

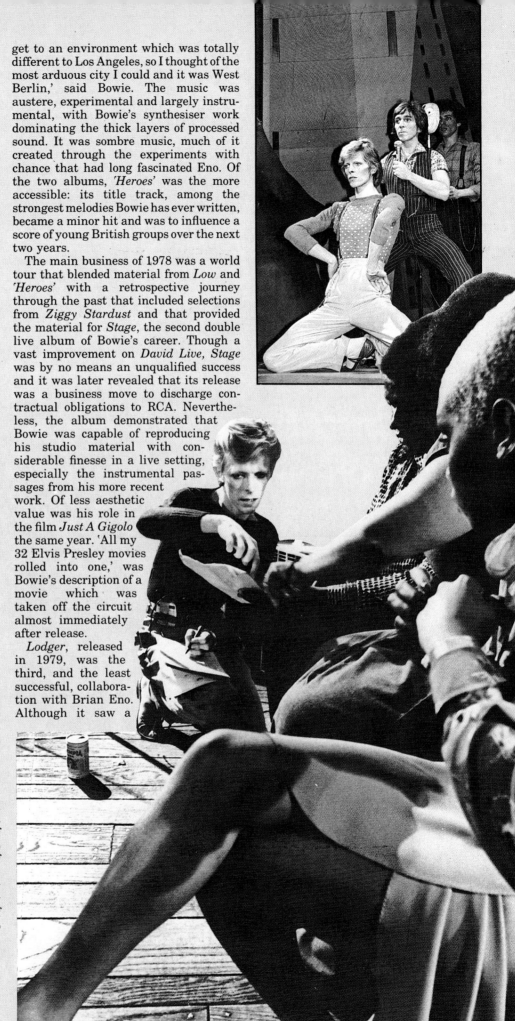

return to Bowie's narrative style of composition, the music was patchy and only 'Boys Keep Swinging', a minor hit single, saw him at anything like top form. Bowie seemed to be losing interest in the Berlin cycle, just as he had previously tired of alienation, Ziggy, soul and overt theatrics. His search now bypassed musical expression and alighted on 'The Elephant Man', the stage play that finally fulfilled his aspirations as an actor.

In the title role of John Merrick, the hideously deformed wretch who became a favourite of Victorian society, Bowie was a triumph. The performance brought laudatory reviews from theatre critics. John Corry of the *New York Times* wrote: 'When it was announced that David Bowie would play the title role in 'The Elephant Man' it was not unnatural to think he had been cast simply for the use of his name. Dismiss that thought now . . . as John Merrick, the Elephant Man, he is splendid.'

'The Elephant Man' run was a gruelling schedule for Bowie – eight shows a week including two afternoon performances – and his physical control in maintaining the illusion of Merrick's deformity (without using make-up) was quite

a remarkable achievement.

Bowie's next album of original material was released in 1980 during *The Elephant Man*'s Chicago run. *Scary Monsters (And Super Creeps)* was a triumphant comeback to the record market, both artistically and commercially. The music was harsh, modernist electro-pop, all bubbling synthesisers, heaving funk bass and distorted electric guitar courtesy of Robert Fripp. If the Berlin trilogy had been predominantly introspective, *Scary Monsters* showed Bowie looking outwards at society, not liking what he saw: the lyrics portrayed a cutthroat world of street violence, corruption and personal loneliness.

It was followed by a three year silence, broken only by the EP of music from 'Baal', a Brecht play in which Bowie appeared on UK television, 'Under Pressure', a single recorded with Queen, and 'Cat People (Putting Out Fire)', a movie theme song

Businessman Bowie contemplates his future after signing with EMI America in 1983.

that was released as a single.

1982 saw Bowie take acting roles in two feature films, *The Hunger* and *Merry Christmas Mr Lawrence*. His contract with RCA expired, and his first LP of original music in three years, *Let's Dance*, appeared on EMI America in 1983 on the back of a massive publicity campaign. Produced in collaboration with Nile Rodgers of Chic, its summery, funky feel showed Bowie in a new, optimistic mood, and the title track shot to Number 1 in the UK, reaching the Top Ten in the US. The follow-up LP *Tonight* (1984), an agreeable if lightweight collection, was followed three years later by the similar *Never Let Me Down,* which reached Number 6 in the UK.

David Bowie has been accused – with some justification – of dilettantism and even plagiarism. Certainly, he has flitted from one style to the next with carefree abandon, shamelessly adopting musical forms and then discarding them as the fancy takes him. But his ability to change and experiment have enabled him to survive the inherent fickleness of pop.

CHRIS CHARLESWORTH

DAVID BOWIE: Discography to 1984

Singles

As Davie Jones and the King Bees: Liza Jane/Louie Louie Go Home (Vocalion-Pop V9221, 1964). As the Manish Boys: I Pity The Fool/Take My Tip (Parlophone R5250, 1965). As Davy Jones and the Lower Third: You've Got A Habit Of Leaving/Baby Loves That Way (Parlophone R5315, 1965); Can't Help Thinking About Me/And I Say To Myself (Pye 7N17020, 1966).

As David Bowie
Do Anything You Say/Good Morning Girl (Pye 7N17079, 1966); I Dig Everything/I'm Not Losing Sleep (Pye 7N17157, 1966); Rubber Band/London Boys (Deram DM 107, 1966); The Laughing Gnome/The Gospel According To Tony Day (Deram DM 123, 1967); Love You Till Tuesday/Did You Ever Have A Dream (Deram DM 135, 1967); Space Oddity/Wild Eyed Boy From Freecloud (Philips BF 1801, 1969); The Prettiest Star/Conversation Piece (Mercury MF 1135, 1970); Memory Of A Free Festival Part I/Memory Of A Free Festival Part II (Mercury 6052 026, 1970); Holy Holy/Black Country Rock (Mercury 6052 049, 1971); Changes/Andy Warhol (RCA 2160, 1972); Starman/Suffragette City (RCA 2199, 1972); John, I'm Only Dancing/Hang On To Yourself (RCA 2263, 1972); The Jean Genie/Ziggy Stardust (RCA 2302, 1972); Drive-In Saturday/Around And Around (RCA 2352, 1973); Life On Mars/The Man Who Sold The World (RCA 2316, 1973); Sorrow/Amsterdam (RCA 2424, 1973); Rebel Rebel/Queen Bitch (RCA LPBO 5009, 1974); Rock'n'Roll Suicide/Quicksand (RCA LPBO 5021, 1974); Diamond Dogs/Holy Holy (RCA APBO 0293, 1974); Knock On Wood/Panic In Detroit (RCA 2466, 1974); Young Americans/Suffragette City (RCA 2523, 1975); Fame/Right (RCA 2597, 1975); Space Oddity/Changes/Velvet Goldmine (RCA 2593, 1975); Golden Years/Can You Hear Me (RCA 2640, 1975); TVC 15/We Are The Dead (RCA 2682, 1976); Suffragette City/Stay (RCA 2726, 1976); Sound And Vision/A New Career In A New Town (RCA PB 0905, 1977); Be My Wife/Speed Of Life (RCA PB 1017, 1977); 'Heroes'/V2 Schneider (RCA PB 1121, 1977); Beauty And The Beast/Sense Of Doubt (RCA PB 1190, 1978); Breaking Glass/Art Decade/Ziggy Stardust (RCA BOW 1, 1978); Boys Keep Swinging/Fantastic Voyage (RCA BOW 2, 1979); DJ/Repetition (RCA BOW 3, 1979); John, I'm Only Dancing (Again)/John, I'm Only Dancing (RCA BOW 4, 1979); Alabama Song/Space Oddity (RCA BOW 5, 1980); Ashes To Ashes/Move On (RCA BOW 6, 1980); Fashion/Scream Like A Baby (RCA BOW 7, 1980); Scary Monsters (And Super Creeps)/Because You're Young (RCA BOW 8, 1981); Up The Hill Backwards/Crystal Japan (RCA BOW 9, 1981); Cat People (Putting Out Fire)/Paul's Theme (MCA 770, 1982); Baal's Hymn/Remembering Marie A/Ballad Of The Adventurers/The Drowned Girl/The Dirty Song (RCA BOW 11, 1982); Let's Dance/Cat People (Putting Out Fire) (EMI America 152, 1983); China Girl/Shake It (EMI America EA 157, 1983); Modern Love/Modern Love (live version) (EMI America EA 158, 1983); Blue Jean/Dancing With The Big Boys (EMI America EA 181, 1984); Tonight/Tumble And Twirl (EMI America EA 187, 1984); Loving The Alien/Don't Look Down (EMI America EA 195, 1985).

Albums

David Bowie (Deram DML 1007, 1967); *David Bowie* (Philips SBL 7912, 1969); *The World Of David Bowie* (Decca SPA 58, 1970); *The Man Who Sold The World* (Mercury 6338041, 1971); *Hunky Dory* (RCA SF 8244, 1971); *The Rise And Fall Of Ziggy Stardust And The Spiders From Mars* (RCA SF 8287, 1972); *Aladdin Sane* (RCA RS 1001, 1973); *Pinups* (RCA RS 1003, 1973); *Diamond Dogs* (RCA APL 1.0576, 1974); *David Live* (RCA APL 2.0771, 1974); *Young Americans* (RCA RS 1006, 1975); *Images* (Deram DPA 3107/3108, 1975); *Station To Station* (RCA APL1-1327, 1976); *Changesonebowie* (RCA RS 1055, 1976); *Low* (RCA PL 12030, 1977); *'Heroes'* (RCA PL 12522, 1977); *Peter And The Wolf* (RCA Red Seal RL-12743, 1978); *Stage* (RCA PL 02913-2, 1978); *Lodger* (RCA BOW LP 1, 1979); *Scary Monsters (And Super Creeps)* (RCA BOW LP 2, 1980); *Changestwobowie* (RCA S BOW LP 3, 1981); *Christiane F Wir Kinder Vom Banhof Zoo* (soundtrack) (RCA BL 43606, 1981); *Bowie Rare* (RCA PL 45406, 1982); *Let's Dance* (EMI America AML 3029, 1983); *Ziggy Stardust – The Motion Picture* (RCA PL 84862(2), 1984); *Tonight* (EMI America EL 2402271, 1984).

Who lent Bowie his musical muscle?

A MAJOR REASON for David Bowie's creative longevity must be his ability, as an individual performer, to change the musicians he works with whenever it suits him. After 15 years and as many albums, most bands would long since have exhausted the creative potential of their own particular combination of talents and end up recycling the same ideas. Like Dylan – and unlike the Rolling Stones – Bowie has been able to refresh his songwriting at regular intervals by working with a different set of musicians, from the collective talents of the Spiders from Mars through to Nile Rodgers of the Chic Organisation.

Bowie's first musical collaborator, however, was one with whom he retained an association into the Eighties. Session player and producer Tony Visconti was an old friend who had lived in a flat in the same Victorian building in Beckenham. Visconti produced the 1969 album *David Bowie*, with the exception of the single 'Space Oddity', which became the title track when the album was re-released in 1972. The single had already been heavily orchestrated by Paul Buckmaster and pro-

Above: American producer Tony Visconti, whose association with Bowie continued to the Eighties. His one-time wife Mary Hopkin (background) sang on Low. *Below: David takes a back seat to Iggy Pop.*

duced by Gus Dudgeon who went on to work with Elton John. Visconti was sympathetic to Bowie's music, and together they arranged all the remaining tracks on the album. The flutes and recorders – some of which Visconti played himself – lent a romantic, pastoral quality to this slightly faded snapshot of Bowie's hippie phase.

Although Bowie has been credited as co-producer on many of his own albums, and has produced records for Iggy Pop and Lou Reed, he has always valued the critical objectivity that another producer could bring to his work. After producing *The Man Who Sold The World* (1971), for which he and Mick Ronson devised much of the music, Visconti fell out with Bowie and was replaced by Ken Scott. They were re-united in 1974 when Bowie called on Visconti to mix *Diamond Dogs*; they continued to work together through to the 1980 album *Scary Monsters (And Super Creeps)*. Only once did Bowie himself assume total responsibility for production; this was on *Diamond Dogs*, on which he also played most of the instruments (with the exception of the rhythm section). He later commented: 'It was frightening trying to make an album with no support . . . I never want to be in that position again.'

BOYS KEEP SWINGING

Rats and Spiders

Visconti produced *The Man Who Sold The World* (1971) and played guitar, bass and piano on the album. Also featured were Mick Ronson and Mick 'Woody' Woodmansey on drums, both former members of a Hull band, the Rats. Joined by Trevor Bolder (bass) on the subsequent album *Hunky Dory* (1971), they formed the nearest thing Bowie has ever had to a regular band: the Spiders from Mars, as they were known from *Ziggy Stardust* (1972) onwards.

A riff-based power trio, they condensed the free-form jamming of progressive bands like Cream into short, accessible pop songs like 'Star' or 'Suffragette City'. Their identification with the mythical band on the record won them a special place in the hearts of Bowie's fans. Ronson's input was considerable; apart from his heavy but melodic guitar-playing, he is credited as co-arranger with Bowie on all the LPs on which the Spiders played. These included *Aladdin Sane* and *Pinups* (both 1973), after which the band split; Ronson embarked on a comparatively unsuccessful solo career.

Bowie often worked with other established musicians. Marc Bolan had been an early friend and inspiration, and the duo recorded a single, 'The Prettiest Star'/ 'Conversation Piece', in 1971 under the name the Hype. The A-side resurfaced, without Bolan, on *Aladdin Sane*. Bowie was to appear with Marc on the latter's TV show, recorded in 1977 shortly before his death in a road accident.

Other well-known artists with whom Bowie worked include Rick Wakeman, who played keyboards on *Space Oddity* and *Hunky Dory*; jazz pianist Mike Garson, whose discordant, splintered-glass solo graced the title track on *Aladdin Sane* and who also played on *Diamond Dogs, Young Americans* (1975) and *Station To Station* (1976); Jeff Beck, who jammed with the Spiders on stage; Marianne Faithfull, who donned a nun's habit to duet with Bowie in Sonny and Cher's 'I Got You Babe' on an American TV special in 1973; Lulu, whose 1974 cover of 'The Man Who Sold The World' was produced and arranged by Bowie and Mick Ronson with Bowie on saxophone; and former King Crimson guitarist Robert Fripp, whose manic, eccentric playing appeared on *'Heroes'* and *Scary Monsters*.

Other stars to have contributed vignettes to Bowie albums include John Lennon, who sang and played guitar on *Young Americans*, and Pete Townshend, who played guitar on the *Scary Monsters* track, 'Because You're Young'. In 1981 Bowie teamed up with Queen to make the hit single 'Under Pressure', and the following year Bowie appeared in the charts with the unlikely duet, 'Little Drummer Boy', with Bing Crosby, recorded on the latter's Christmas Show in 1977.

Young Americans saw Bowie working with black session singer Luther Vandross, who co-wrote 'Fascination' and was

Above: The team behind 1983's Let's Dance *album comprised, from left Bowie, guitarist Stevie Ray Vaughn and co-producer Nile Rodgers. Left: Bowie makes a rare television appearance with Marc Bolan.*

jointly responsible with Bowie for the vocal arrangements. The playing of bassist Herbie Flowers and guitarist Carlos Alomar (who had played on the *Diamond Dogs* tour) contributed greatly to the disco-funk feel of the LP, and Alomar, who co-wrote 'Fame' with Bowie and John Lennon, was to become one of Bowie's regular musicians. He conducted the band on the 1978 tour and played on all Bowie's subsequent LPs, co-writing 'The Secret Life Of Arabia' on *'Heroes'* (1977) and 'Red Money' on *Lodger* (1979).

After the transitional LP *Station To Station*, Bowie's career changed direction; a major influence in that change was former Roxy Music keyboard-player Brian Eno. Moving away from the conventionally structured songs that had previously occupied him, Bowie turned to Eno's misty instrumental tone-poems as inspiration for *Low* (1977) and *'Heroes'*. Eno's slow, painstaking craftsmanship perfectly complemented Bowie's frenetic bursts of

activity. His working methods also included experiments with random selection: 'He laid down 430 finger clicks on a clean tape,' Bowie recalled. 'Then we put them all out as dots on a piece of paper and numbered them all off, and I picked sections of dots and he picked sections, quite arbitrarily. Then he went back into the studio and played chords, and changed the chord as he hit that number. Then we took the clicks out.' The resulting composition was 'Warszawa', on side two of *Low*.

Whatever the actual musical value of such experiments – on *Lodger*, Bowie's third album with Eno, they extended to utilising tapes of old Bowie songs played backwards – they had a liberating effect on Bowie's creativity, opening up whole new areas of sound. 'Boys Keep Swinging' saw the band exchange instruments: Carlos Alomar played drums, while drummer Dennis Davis played bass. This gave the song a ragged, almost garage-band feel that was quite appealing. 'What was extraordinary,' Bowie commented, 'was the enthusiasm that came from musicians who weren't playing their usual instrument. They became kids discovering rock'n'roll for the first time again.'

Bowie's critics would maintain that he has exploited the talents of others to revitalise his career, pointing out the strong similarities between side two of *'Heroes'* and Eno's ambient music, or 'Let's Dance' and Nile Rodgers' own 'In The Land Of The Good Groove'. But there is no doubt that, in remaining open to other musicians' ideas, Bowie has been able to approach each new phase of his career with freshness and enthusiasm, and has rarely failed to communicate that enthusiasm. CHRIS SCHÜLER

1633

GROWING UP IN PUBLIC

Lou Reed's revealing quest for maturity

Lou Reed has never courted conventional approval. Much of his best work has concerned his attempts to transcend good and evil, but he is more often associated with the latter. Like William Burroughs, Reed has dispassionately charted the lives of drug addicts, heavy drinkers and transsexuals without condemning or glorifying them. He sings with such precision and authority that the characters seem to come from real life. And often, as in 'Walk On The Wild Side', they do: Holly, who 'shaved her legs and then he was a she' in the first verse, was a well-known New York transvestite, who, like 'Little Joe' Dallesandro several verses later, was also part of the Andy Warhol junkie set.

Perfect transformation

Warhol, who had first brought the Velvet Underground to an unsuspecting (and largely uncomprehending) public back in 1966, was a mentor of Reed's, with his cold-blooded synthesis of glamour, pornography and boredom. In 1974, when Lou Reed was at his most jaded, he admitted: 'I would have given my right arm to be part of Andy's scene.' And it is hard to separate Reed from New York – even at his trashiest he reflects with painful accuracy the world around him.

Following his departure from the Velvets in mid 1970, Reed went into hibernation at his parents' house in Long Island.

However, the success of *Loaded*, the album that the band was recording when he left, meant that Lou Reed was suddenly in demand. RCA Records tracked him down, signed him up and brought him to England to record his first solo album in late 1971.

Lou Reed, released in May 1972, was something of a disappointment, however. The British session men – including Rick Wakeman, Steve Howe and Caleb Quaye – failed to invoke the demons that Reed's music needed to bring it to life; the album was short on atmosphere, with songs like 'Love Makes You Feel Ten Feet Tall' and 'I Love You' sounding particularly unconvincing. The production was particularly poor, and Reed was quick to disclaim the album, explaining to *Melody Maker*: 'Everybody was on dandy form, but something was missing'.

By 1972, the hippie look had lost its appeal, and 'glam-rock', in the hands of David Bowie, Roxy Music and others, had erupted onto the scene. The emphasis was

Lou Reed – man of many masks. Above left: The glam-rocker of the early Seventies. Above centre: The godfather of punk? Above right: Loaded . . . Reed sports a sneer and a six-gun.

now on tinsel and make-up, garish colours and dyed hair, the artificial light of subways and all-night parties, with a hint of bisexuality for good measure. Drug use changed too: any substances that created a mellow feeling were replaced with 'action packs'. Above all, it was an urban movement—and it set the scene perfectly for Lou Reed.

Bowie had long been an admirer of Reed, and his calculated transition to theatrical rock – *Ziggy Stardust* – owed a great deal to *Loaded*. The two met and Bowie produced Reed's second solo album.

Candy man

On *Transformer* (1972), Reed's rhythm guitar was rather slack and his vocals somewhat tranquillised but nonetheless the album worked perfectly. It featured a host of bizarre characters who all seemed to pause in the midst of their abuse and smile for the camera, while the music was an agreeable balance of rock'n'roll, ballads, vaudeville and jazz, carefully arranged for the public ear by Bowie and Mick Ronson.

Sexual ambiguity was everywhere: 'Candy came from out on the island/In the backroom she was everybody's darling' (from 'Walk On The Wild Side') referred to a *man*, while 'Make Up', an exhaustive catalogue of a 'slick little girl' and her cosmetics, suddenly ended with Lou snarling:

'Now we're coming out/Out of our closets' right on time for the growing gay liberation movement. The best tracks were comparatively simple: 'Perfect Day', which told of a beautiful interlude in, a sordid existence, and 'Satellite Of Love', where a lone consumer watches a space launch on television.

Rock'n'roll animal

Transformer sold well in the UK, partly through the prestigious Bowie connection but mainly because of the commercial qualities of the music, and introduced Reed to a wider audience. 'Walk On The Wild Side', meanwhile, was lifted from the album and reached Number 10 in Britain and Number 16 in the US in the spring of 1973. But public reaction wasn't quite the same to Reed's next work, *Berlin*, when it was released that autumn. Produced by Bob Ezrin, the album alternated between lush orchestral passages, simple acoustic strumming and slightly groggy rock. The album told the tale of a doomed liaison in Berlin between two American speed-freaks: Caroline, who liked to climb on top of bars to sing and lived in a hotel, and Jim, a rich young cynic who masked his self-disgust with apathy.

The most disturbing track was probably 'The Kids', in which Jim drunkenly intoned a list of Caroline's affairs – from the Welshman from India to the black Air Force Sergeant – until he snarled, almost in triumph: 'That miserable rotten slut couldn't turn *anyone* away.' Then, behind the acoustic guitar, two children screamed 'Mummy' louder and louder until the track abruptly ended. The second side of *Berlin* contained some of the most harrowing moments in rock's history, and the whole album was one of the few genuine examples of 'rock theatre'.

Perhaps it is no surprise that *Berlin* didn't sell in huge quantities, but Lou Reed was badly affected by the adverse criticism it received. Believing that the public had ignored his masterpiece, he decided to spite himself (and make some money) by touring with a heavy-metal band, massacring his old songs for a new public. Long-standing fans were distressed to see him stumble on without a guitar, kick the microphone like a petulant child, mutter his classic lyrics over a deafening, average backing and stomp off again without a word to the audience. A live album of this debacle, *Rock'n'Roll Animal*, was released in March 1974 and sold very well. Encouraged by such perversity, Lou recorded a consciously trashy album aimed at the gay disco market, entitled *Sally Can't Dance* (1974). Reed played on only one

A rock'n'roll animal with a rock'n'roll heart, Reed's visual image changed throughout the Seventies from decadent ambivalence (right), through self-parody to street-wise leather boy. Reed played up his druggie, camp image mercilessly at this stage in his career to appeal to the gay disco market.

Right: Lou Reed received heavy metal backing at London's Crystal Palace Bowl in the early Seventies. Far right: Reed serenades Paris, 1974. Below: On stage in the early Eighties, Lou plays rhythm guitar to Robert Quine's lead.

track, sang nearly all the vocals in one take and then had them mixed so as to be almost inaudible.

Sally Can't Dance marked a nadir of self-disgust; although he was at the zenith of his mass popularity, Reed seemed to have lost all respect for himself or anyone else. He dyed iron crosses in his hair – two years before punk – and applied a tourniquet and syringe to his arm when he performed 'Heroin' on stage. He played up his bad-guy, 'druggie' image quite shamelessly: 'My week beats your year,' he crowed on the sleeve-notes to *Metal Machine Music*, released in June 1975.

Whether seen as an exercise in the avant-garde, the result of over-indulgence in amphetamines or an attempt to alienate his new audience, *Metal Machine Music* was one of the oddest things ever to emerge under the name of rock music. It comprised four sides of amplifiers and microphones feeding back into each other, with no vocals or instruments. Each side lasted 16 minutes and one second exactly, and was the musical equivalent of a crazed dentist drilling holes in a central heating system. Reed claimed that if you listened carefully, you could hear melodies from Mozart, Beethoven and Vivaldi amid the discordant hammering; a senior executive at RCA, on the other hand, described it as 'torture music'.

Coney Island Baby, released in early 1976, marked the return of Reed's rhythm guitar and natural hair colour, but apart from 'She's My Best Friend', a song about mutilation from the Velvets days, the only arresting track was 'Kicks', on which Reed stuttered a compulsive, sick and fascinating monologue over a two-chord riff about a man who kills people with a flick-knife for amusement.

Hassles of the heart

By now it seemed that Reed was drying up altogether. His last four albums of the Seventies, *Rock'n'Roll Heart* (1976), *Street Hassle, Live – Take No Prisoners* (both 1978) and the embarrassing *The Bells* (1979) all exhibited a distinct loss of power, while Reed's once-incisive voice became increasingly quavering until he seemed to be singing permanently through a tremelo unit. The majority of his songs were garbled, half-finished ideas or old songs dredged up out of his notebooks. With the exception of the title track from *Street Hassle* – a tragic tale of how the body of a young girl, overdosed on drugs, is abandoned in the street to make her look like a hit-and-run victim – these late Seventies albums were depressingly uninspired. Reed seemed doomed to live out his own self-destructive legend, having nothing to say but repeating it endlessly, living proof that drugs only make life boring in the end.

Then, quite unexpectedly, Lou Reed fell in love. His previous marriage, to a waitress named Betty, had petered out in 1973, but his relationship with Sylvia – whom he married in 1980 – had a profound effect on him. *Growing Up In Public* (1980), showed

that the clouds had suddenly lifted. Reed finally stopped relying on drink and drugs and confronted the demons that had been festering in his head for so long. At last he faced up to his boyhood, his unbalanced relationship with his parents, his fear of rejection and the barriers it had caused him to create.

All the music on the album was written and arranged by Reed's long-time keyboard player Michael Fonfara, leaving Lou free to concentrate on his lyric-writing and singing, and providing him with his first decent production since *Berlin*. His voice took on a myriad of expressions, while on 'So Alone' he shouted, yawned, cajoled, admonished, and seduced – all in the space of four minutes.

The last shot

Tearing off the masks of cruelty, sarcasm and apathy, Lou Reed had revealed a surprisingly balanced psyche underneath. But his next album, *The Blue Mask* (1981), was different again. Though peppered with references to Sylvia and slightly ambiguous appraisals of women in general, it marked a return to more sinister preoccupations. Phantoms that crowd into the head of a child lying awake – and alone – at night, muggers, rapists, sado-masochists, the spectre of alcoholism and a fear for the world's future – all came flooding out into the new songs.

The music, minus Fonfara's guiding hand, was rambling, the arrangements, minimal: it was as if it had been neurally recorded straight from Lou Reed's brain. The lyrics, however, were excellent; 'Underneath The Bottle' perfectly captured the tethered vision of an alcoholic, 'The Heroine' was an allegorical tale of a woman in a white robe trying to steer a ship through a howling gale, while 'The Day John Kennedy Died' was a movingly dispassionate account of Reed's feelings on learning of the President's assassination.

By 1982, Reed had given up touring, although he did perform live on occasion – the spring of 1983 saw him playing four nights at the Bottom Line in New York with guitarist Robert Quine. He continued to record, too. 1983's *Legendary Hearts* and 1984's *New Sensations*, which featured the same band as *The Blue Mask*, successfully explored the same musical and lyrical territory; songs like the harrowing 'The Last Shot' showed that the artist's muse had not deserted him. However erratic Lou Reed's career has been, he remains one of the wittiest and most perceptive songwriters in rock; if his influence seems limited, it is because few can follow him.

LUTHER PAISLEY

Lou Reed
Recommended Listening

Transformer (RCA International INTS 5150) (Includes: Vicious, Andy's Chest, Perfect Day, Walk On The Wild Side, Make Up, Satellite Of Love, Goodnight Ladies); *Berlin* (RCA International INTS 5061) (Includes: Men Of Good Fortune, Oh, Jim, The Kids, The Bed, Sad Song).

DESIGNS FOR LIVING

THE ARTISTIC PERSONA of Brian Eno may be summed up by the title of his fourth solo album, *Discreet Music* (1975). Although he had been edged out of Roxy Music in the early Seventies for upstaging Bryan Ferry, self-effacement has subsequently proved to be the key quality of his professional image, both in his solo projects and in his remarkably wide-ranging collaborations with other artists. These have ranged from the comparative obscurity of his dabblings with the Portsmouth Sinfonia (a collective of non-musicians who play amusingly out-of-tune versions of classical favourites) and avant-garde experiments with guitarist Robert Fripp, to his innovative and hugely successful work with David Bowie and Talking Heads.

The body electric
Brian Peter George St John Baptiste de la Salle Eno, born 15 May 1948, was educated by monks and nuns in Suffolk until he was 16, when he left to enrol at Ipswich Art School. It was here that he first began to investigate the music-making potential of

The discreet charm of Brian Eno

tape-recorders. He pursued this interest while studying fine art at Winchester Art School and, by the summer of 1967, was experimenting with electric violins, tape loops, drones and coloured lights, along similar lines to the work of John Cale with the Velvet Underground in New York. At this time he formed his first rock group, the Maxwell Demon. Some of his more idiosyncratic ideas at this time included tying microphones to people to create 'body sounds' and disconnecting the instrument of anyone who played a recognisable riff.

Eno joined Roxy Music in 1971, ostensibly to play synthesiser and keyboards, but more as a sort of roving musical-effects man, randomly manipulating the group's sound from the mixing desk. The combination of Ferry's brilliant amalgamation of Forties and Fifties chic and Eno's untrammelled quirkiness maximised the band's impact on the British music and

fashion scenes. When Roxy first rose to fame, Eno was by far their most exotic-looking member, and he contributed greatly to their outrageous theatrical style. However, it was this very flair for showmanship that was to prove his undoing; in the summer of 1973, Ferry announced that he would 'never get on stage with Eno again'.

Warm Jets and Winkies
If Eno had had a significant share in the creation of Roxy Music's sound and image, Roxy had in turn provided him with a record deal and a public. In two years Eno had developed from obscure theoretician to glam-rock star. In many ways, his subsequent career appears to have been an attempt to reverse this process.

After leaving Roxy Music, Eno rapidly acquired a sober mystique in keeping with his position as rock's foremost éminence grise (above), and a far cry from his earlier, deliberately outrageous high-camp stage persona (right).

His first musical venture after leaving Roxy was an instrumental collaboration with King Crimson guitarist Robert Fripp, *No Pussyfootin'* (1973), in which Eno employed Revox tape machines to create orchestral, multi-textured effects. Two years later the pair once again combined to effect with an album of short, dreamy pieces entitled *Evening Star*.

Here Come The Warm Jets, made with the assistance of Phil Manzanera and Andy Mackay among others, was released in 1973 and marked Eno's debut as a solo artist, but was somewhat disappointing and derivative by his previous high standards. The scratchy guitars were reminiscent of the Velvet Underground and the tunes sounded like early attempts at five-chord songwriting (which they probably were). The record was quite well received, but a promotional tour of England, with Eno being backed by pub-rock hopefuls the Winkies, had to be cancelled when he suffered a collapsed lung. Thereafter Eno gave up all ideas of touring, though he did play a prestigious gig at the Rainbow (captured on the live LP *1 June 1974*) with three other 'left-field' Island acts – Kevin Ayers, Nico and John Cale (with whom he had recently begun a successful collaboration).

There was surprisingly little evidence of Brian Eno's influence on *Fear* (1974), John Cale's first album for Island, which the two co-produced; Cale, however, was perhaps the first person in rock to understand the essence of Eno's contribution to a record, the back cover credits simply reading 'Eno: Eno'. On Cale's next LP, *Slow Dazzle* (1975), Eno's touch was more apparent, particularly his eerie backdrop to John Cale's surrealistic poem 'The Jeweller'.

Eno's second album of songs, *Taking Tiger Mountain (By Strategy)*, released in the winter of 1974, scaled no such hallucinatory heights, featuring instead a rather smug-sounding Eno reeling off a series of short, slick numbers. His voice took on shades of Cale, Robin Williamson and Syd Barrett by turns, yet conveyed little emotion. The most satisfying track was 'Burning Airlines Give You So Much More', featuring a typically quirky Manzanera guitar line.

Relaxez-vous

1975 saw important advances in Eno's music with the release of his third album, *Another Green World*, and the first of his 'ambient music' series on his Obscure label, *Discreet Music*. The former was a soothing mixture of wistful ditties like 'St Elmo's Fire' and 'I'll Come Running To Tie Your Shoe' with drifting instrumentals, such as 'Sombre Reptile' and the title track. Elements of jazz, funk and hard rock were blended into a percussive soundtrack with a pleasing sense of space that his earlier records had lacked. This quality was even more evident on the Obscure albums. Instead of assaulting the eardrums with the traditional rhythmic and musical combinations of rock, Eno preferred to provide a discreet sonic backdrop to people's lives. The resulting shifting waves of sound exercised a gentle, mysterious influence on the listener.

The following year a temporarily jaded David Bowie invited Eno to Berlin to collaborate with him on his forthcoming album. With Eno's help, Bowie, who had nothing much to say lyrically at the time, finally came to terms with *sound* as opposed to *songs* – a direction that Eno, too, was exploring. They evolved an experimental aid to composing whereby various random factors were used to dictate chord changes and song structures. The resulting album, *Low*, shocked fans and critics with its wintry, instrumental second side. Bowie was delighted with the new musical vistas the LP had opened up, remarking that, by not trying to write about anything at all, he and Eno had conveyed more than if they had come up with a concept album.

Their next collection together, *'Heroes'*, was released in the winter of 1977. A creative high-point for both men, the material ranged from the brooding grandeur of the title track and the enchantment of the instrumental 'Moss Garden' to the flippant disco of 'The Secret Life Of Arabia'. Bowie's gift for melodrama blended perfectly with Eno's serene sensuality, prompting the latter's comment: 'I fancy doing things where I keep further back from being the focal point of what's happening; where I take a much more subsidiary role.'

Two in the Bush

Eno's *Before And After Science*, released around the same time as *'Heroes'*, had taken two years to record, yet was the most successful of his cycle of 'song' albums, linking his Sixties origins with his work in the Eighties. Beatles-style pop stood side-by-side with harder rock numbers, while 'Julie With . . .' and 'By This River' were trance-like evocations accompanied by stuttering bass and moody, languid vibraphone. Some of the tracks were created with the aid of Moebius and Rodelius, two German musicians with whom Eno collaborated on the 1978 release *After The Heat*. In many ways a logical development from *Before And After Science*, this LP mainly consisted of short, drifting instrumentals, although it did contain some vocal tracks.

The same year Eno began perhaps his most fruitful partnership, with David Byrne and his band Talking Heads. Though formed in the mid Seventies' Manhattan garage-band boom, Talking Heads had evolved in a completely different direction to the cartoon punk of Blondie and the Ramones. Eno came in as a producer and co-writer on their second album, *More Songs About Buildings And Food* (1978) and accompanied their transition

Right: Eno in the studio in 1979. As well as bass, he is credited as having played a wide variety of synthesisers, guitars and percussive effects on record.

from the disjointed pop of the following year's *Fear Of Music* to the anguish of 1980's *Remain In Light*, at which point they had arguably created more interesting music than any other new wave American band. 'Once In A Lifetime', a single from *Remain In Light*, even bore Eno's voice into the charts, his jaunty chorus counterbalancing Byrne's existential rap.

In 1981 Eno and Byrne released *My Life In The Bush Of Ghosts*, an album that combined percussive, African-style funk with 'found' snatches of dialogue from various radio stations alternating with vocal tracks taken from records made by Middle-Eastern artists. It was – even for Eno – a particularly uncompromising piece; time seemed to have sharpened rather than dulled Eno's commitment to experimentalism.

The following year saw the release of his fourth 'ambient' record, *On Land*. Although the album had broadly similar aims to its predecessors, Eno was still setting himself challenging problems to investigate: 'In multi-track recording . . . perfect erasure is possible . . . I wanted instead to create a situation more analogous to that of painting, where any action I made was not completely retractable, for I

felt that increasing the risk factor in this way would give the action itself a charge and that a concentration of these charges is what makes a work live.

'Consequently I made two working rules: I decided that anything that was recorded on the tape must appear in the final mix in some form (allowing myself the freedom to mutate or reduce it but not to destroy it) and that any piece of music that I worked on, if finally rejected, should be fed into another piece. This technique is like composting: converting what would otherwise have been waste into nourishment.'

Eno continued his idiosyncratic recording career in the Eighties, but achieved most success as a producer with Irish rock supergroup U2.   LUTHER PAISLEY

Eno
Recommended Listening

Before And After Science (Polydor Deluxe 2302 071) (Includes: No One Receiving, Backwater, King's Lead Hat, Julie With . . ., By This River, Here He Comes, Spider And I); *Discreet Music* (Obscure OBS3) (Includes: Discreet Music, Three Variations On The Canon In D Major By Johann Pachelbe(i) Fullness Of Wind (ii) French Catalogues (iii) Brutal Ardour).

Country Life

Bitter-sweet music and dreams for the loser and the little man

The confederate flag flies defiantly outside the Country Music Stars Museum and Mall in Nashville, Tennessee, while the faces of the country and western greats look down.

COUNTRY MUSIC has two seemingly contradictory faces. Its heroes are often rebels – like Waylon Jennings and Willie Nelson – or strongly identify with the underdog, like Johnny Cash. But country itself usually embodies conservative political and social ideas; and the music seems to have no capacity to accommodate radical change, except in so far as commercial pressures have gradually 'sweetened' the sound.

The growing country 'industry' of the Seventies – when films like 1977's *Smokey And The Bandit*, or TV series like 'Dukes Of Hazzard' reflected a growing international awareness of the American South – also demonstrate this duality. Romantic heroes who just want to be left alone but are reluctantly forced into confrontation with the law are frequently the stuff of country legend.

For country music has always directly reflected the economic battles and emotional lives of its audience – the core of which has always been those whose roots are among Southern labouring people. C&W grew out of the folk music of early Scots and Irish settlers, which came in time to absorb elements from other cultures; cajun music, Tex-Mex, the blues and even the Hawaiian influence of the pedal steel guitar.

Drunk again

From anthropologists to pop music writers, middle-class educated city-dwellers have often found country music absurd. David Frizzell's record 'I'm Gonna Hire A Wino (To Decorate Our Home)' was one of the Outstanding Country Songs of 1982 in the annual industry awards. The listener laughs all the way through as the drunk's wife tells him she's going to rip out the carpet, put sawdust on the floor, 'and a neon sign will point the way to our bathroom down the hall'. But beneath the self-deprecating humour is a core of hard social comment and concrete realism.

Marty Robbins' South-western world of inaccessible senoritas and manly courage never existed, and Willie Nelson was never the red-headed stranger wronged by one woman, killing another, with his existence confirmed by the power to possess and defend a horse. But like the South-proud character in blue work shirt that Hank Williams Jr created, spurning the world of the business suit, these myths have an emotional reality. There are many for whom his defiance and humour give strength in the face of everything else being a working-class white Southerner means. There are also those for whom that same strength comes from the gospel quartets who can still be heard coming out of Southern radios singing lines such as: 'This world can't stand long, because it is so filled with hate/This world was destroyed before, it will be destroyed again.' And sometimes they're the same people.

Country music still celebrates ordinariness in a society whose dominant ethic is individual uniqueness and success. The country refrain is scorn of the better side of town – the emptiness of 'satin sheets' and 'crystal chandeliers'. In place of protest, however, country music reaffirms the values of old myths with harsh realism, defiance and humour. ILENE MELISH

THE MAN IN BLACK

How Johnny Cash conquered his darker side

GRUFF, CRAGGY, CLAD always in black and drawling rueful songs about railroad drifters and 'the poor and beaten down' – most characteristically, perhaps, to the ribald cheers of a crowd of convicts – Johnny Cash is a son of the Depression and a sardonic champion of the all-time loser. Born on 26 February 1932 in Kingsland, Arkansas, he emerged from his rural childhood in a government-sponsored settlement – a few hundred families pulling cotton out of virgin land they cleared themselves – with a rebelliousness that took nearly 20 years to subside.

Cash is known universally and utterly mistakenly as a 'founding father of rock 'n'roll' but he is a country singer, a white Southerner whose rage endeared him to a generation of urban youth in the late Sixties – and whose acceptance of authority ultimately provoked their scorn in the Seventies. In the long run, he is likely to be seen in the context of that peculiarly American vision of the folk-poet, a Walt Whitman of military barracks, prison yards, Indian reservations and city jails.

Hometown blues

In 1955, shortly after marrying and leaving the US Air Force, Cash walked into the Sun Record Company studios in Memphis, Tennessee, having quit his job selling used kitchen appliances. Unlike Carl Perkins, who immediately preceded him, and the hundreds who followed, he had chosen Sun as being the local place to record, rather than because of any affiliation with Elvis Presley.

In any case, Cash's music stood clearly apart from Elvis Presley's 'jump-boogie-country'. His conversational songs grew out of the hard and immediately recognisable rhythms played by his original backing musicians – string-bass player Marshall Grant and electric guitarist Luther Perkins, both mechanics from the garage where his older brother worked. Cash himself played acoustic guitar with paper occasionally shoved under the strings to add to the sandpaper-grit sound. To this line-up, Sun added a drummer – but only after songs like 'Folsom Prison Blues', 'I Walk The Line', 'Big River' and 'Ballad Of A Teen-Age Queen' had made Cash's name and given him an image.

What was that image? Sun boss Sam Phillips says today he saw Cash right from the start as 'kind of a religious storyteller . . . his songs stood out so well he could have stood up and spoke them. Johnny did not necessarily want to "go rock"; even if he had I'd have said, "Well Johnny, you'll have to find another recording studio".'

From simple beginnings in the Fifties (top right), Cash became a spokesman for the oppressed (above left). In 1971 he starred in the movie The Gunfight *(right).*

As for Cash being a rock artist, mostly he just happened to be in the same room while his contemporaries were creating their fusion of urban black pop, blues and hard country. From the 1956 Sun track 'Luther Played The Boogie', named after his original guitarist, to 1978's 'I Will Rock And Roll With You (If I Have To)', Cash remained deeply affectionate towards what happened at Sun, but professed himself a contemporary rather than a catalyst.

There was a desperate urgency to his own music on Sun that has the appeal of early rock, and it was certainly a long way from the crooning country and western of the Forties. But that urgency was as likely to be found in the gospel doom of 'Belshazzar', the song he auditioned with, as on anything that could be described as 'rock 'n'roll'. Where Cash really captured a rock audience, beyond the bold guitar-based simplicity of those early tracks, was in albums of the gritty defiance of the series of albums he recorded in the early Sixties after leaving Sun. These fused his rural conscience with the social consciousness of the urban folk revival, and the culmination of this stage in Cash's career came at the end of the decade with his live recordings at Folsom and San Quentin prisons in California.

Walking the line

Signing for Columbia in 1958, Cash headed for new pastures. He moved his family to California, tried films, logged hundreds of dates a year with his band and adopted a lifestyle that led to the frenzy of amphetamine addiction, as chronicled thoroughly in his 1975 autobiography *Man In Black*. At the same time, however, he was exploring Greenwich Village and the folk scene when it was at its most vital in the late Fifties and early Sixties, and forging ties with Bob Dylan, Ramblin' Jack Elliott and others that were to endure over the years.

On the LPs *Ride This Train* (1960) and *Blood, Sweat And Tears* (1963), Cash included a number of songs that lasted for up to eight minutes and were like small plays. In them he adopted the persona of the underdog: he was the lumberjack risking death at the top of tall trees; the cowboy convicted of a crime he doesn't remember; the chain-gang prisoner overworked and sadistically abused; the man beaten, hungry, worked to death but never defeated. The tales of desperation with which Cash introduces each song on *Ride This Train* almost cross the line from the poor man's traditional resentment of authority to a personal obsession.

Cash's private rebellion was also taking form at this point. It necessitated roaming at night alone with light and gun in woods and deserts; a large intake of alcohol as well as pills; one-night stands in local jails; seeing how fast he could drive or how close to the edge of a cliff he could bring a tractor

Below: Cash surveys the set of the 1974 ABC-TV special 'Riding the Rails'. Opposite: Duetting in concert with his wife, country singer June Carter.

(it went over); and the physical collapse that followed this train of events.

The other side of that rural, lonesome rebellion was his sense of absolute right and wrong, where authority is ultimately upheld and only its abuses condemned, and victory lies not in political change but individual defiance and finding the moral strength to survive. Even when Cash plays the man on top for the only time on *Ride This Train*, the moral code is invoked; in the dialogue between master and slave introducing 'Boss Jack', he is the slave-owner choosing decency over cruelty.

Within months of that recording, black students were sitting in at segregated lunch counters in the South and the Civil Rights movement of the Sixties had begun. Southerners were obliged to declare loyalties, black or white: Johnny Cash, via a grandmother's ancestry, declared himself on the side of the American Indian. Indian themes had been dealt with earlier by Cash, but in 1964, on the *Bitter Tears* album, he recorded angrier pieces by Peter La Farge, the folksinger-son of an Indian historian.

One such composition was 'The Ballad of Ira Hayes', a song about the Marine who raised the flag at Iwo Jima in the Second World War and died a 'whisky-drinking Indian' years later. Both this and Cash's version of La Farge's 'Drums' – a number scorning racial distinctions and asserting Indian resistance, by rebellion if necessary – raised a storm of objection, and Cash was threatened by the Ku Klux Klan.

He refused to bow down, however, to any

side. *Orange Blossom Special* (1965) included 'All God's Children Ain't Free', whose gospel phrases linked the black, the poor and the imprisoned. But, calling himself 'a Southerner', Cash also disparaged the 'young folk-music authorities' and 'the customers in the coffee houses of New York' – obvious targets in Cash's war against complacency – yet the album also included three Dylan songs.

Jailhouse rock
This period of protest produced commercially lean years for Cash (interrupted only by the blazing horns and love balladry of 1963's *Ring Of Fire* album), but it otherwise consolidated his public character. He was proving capable of an honesty and an ease that made the live albums *At Folsom Prison* (1968) and *At San Quentin* (1969) artistic and commercial triumphs.

Cash gave the first of his prison concerts in 1957, and they became a regular feature of his live work. By the late Sixties he had developed a unique rapport with this audience: the intensity of the men's response to Cash and his gentleness towards them made him a major folk hero. This particular social quest continued through 1972's *Man In Black* – 'I'll try to carry off a little darkness on my back/'Till things are brighter I'm the man in black' – and the same year's *In Sweden*, recorded in a Swedish prison and including 'City Jail', an angry condemnation of a small-town arrest delivered with wry humour.

By the early Seventies Cash was remarried – to country singer June Carter, with whom he had a son and who joined his roadshow – and had finally overcome his addiction to pills. He now remoulded his personality, and the tension between defiance and decency that he had turned into an art-form (and which had brought him near to emotional and physical collapse) made way for a sense of affirmation. Having avoided the reality of wealth for a decade through the embattled obduracy of his music and the rootlessness and despair of his lifestyle, he began to embrace a domesticity marked by very great wealth indeed. Domestic decency, religion (Cash toured with evangelist Billy Graham) and identification with the traditions of country music and US history became mainstays of his work from the Seventies onward.

But Cash had not deserted his songwriting roots. Homely sketches of the Seventies like 'While I've Got It On My Mind' and 'Saturday Night In Hickman County' had the same conversational quality as much of his earlier work, and he continued to produce stark songs like 'Lonesome To The Bone' and rapid-fire romantic pieces such as 'Kate' and 'Cold Lonesome Morning', which could just as easily have graced his Sun repertoire. He continued to go beyond the country audience with the occasional pop or novelty song in the charts – 1969's 'A Boy Named Sue' reached Number 2 in the US and Number 4 in the UK, for example.

Cash on delivery
Cash did not join in with other musicians' protests against the Vietnam War, but wrote of the soldiers' plight 'whether we belong there or not'. Along with his prison concerts, he made regular fund-raising appearances on behalf of Indian education and bankrupt rural state fairs.

His concerts have become shows where once they were 'statements'. And since his backing group the Tennessee Three became (with the tragic death in a house-fire in 1969 of Luther Perkins and departure in 1979 of Marshall Grant) the Great Eighties Eight, the stage can be filled with slick brass and tinkling piano. But, in time-honoured tradition, Cash still persuades June Carter to pick up a banjo, reminisce about Uncle Dave Macon ('King of the Hillbillies') and Carter family travels in the Forties, and toss off her shoes and dance while her husband excitedly declares: 'That's June Carter from Poor Valley, Virginia, and the Tennessee Flatfoot!'

Johnny Cash's journey from rural poet-protester to showbiz entertainer earned him many critics in the Seventies, even though he was no less conscientious or committed to the people he was singing about and for. Reaching the age of 50 in 1982, he continued to go his own way, while that dark, rock-hard voice remained one of the most powerful to be heard in any sphere of American music. ILENE MELISH

Johhny Cash
Recommended Listening

Biggest Hits (CBS 32304) (Includes: Ring Of Fire, Folsom Prison Blues, A Boy Named Sue, Kate, Riders In The Sky, The Baron, Daddy Sang Bass).

OUTLAW MAN

Willie Nelson
Recommended Listening

20 Of The Best (RCA International INTS 5208)
(Includes: Funny How Time Slips Away, Hello
Walls, Family Bible, Good Times, Yesterday's
Wine, Good Hearted Woman, Phases And Stages,
Circles, Cycles And Scenes).

Willie Nelson: true grit from Texas

WITHIN WEEKS OF ARRIVING in Nashville at the start of the Sixties, Willie Nelson found success as a writer and was soon making a small fortune from compositions like 'Crazy', 'Funny (How Time Slips Away)' and 'Hello Walls', all of which have since become country classics. His main ambition was to perform, but he had an extremely frustrating time getting anyone to take him seriously or to buy his records. Fifteen years later he finally had a Country Number 1, 'Blue Eyes Crying In The Rain', a breakthrough that came only after he had rejected the Nashville studio system and begun making records in his own way with his road band.

Willie Nelson was born on 30 April 1933 in Abbott, a small farming community near Fort Worth, Texas. His parents divorced when he was six months old and he was brought up, along with his sister Bobby (who later played piano in his band), by his music-loving grandparents.

His grandmother wrote gospel songs, while his grandfather gave Willie his first guitar when he was just five; a year later the boy was writing and singing his own songs. His first professional gig was at the age of nine, playing guitar for a Bohemian polka band, but his first regular group was formed when he was 15. They played at local social functions and had a weekly radio show.

Songs for sale
The 'other jobs' included selling encyclopedias, giving away a free Bible with every purchase (which inspired the Nelson song 'Family Bible'), disc jockey, janitor and a two-year spell in the Air Force. By night he'd play in Texas honky tonks, including Gray's Bar in Fort Worth, which was so tough that chicken wire was strung between the audience and the stage to protect musicians from flying bottles.

While working as a DJ in Oregon in the late Fifties, Willie made his first record, a single called 'No Place To Go', which was released on his own label and sold 2000 copies. His ambitions grew, but he knew little about the music business and parted with two of his best songs for a pittance; the publishing rights to 'Family Bible' was sold for 50 dollars 'to pay the rent', while 'Night Life', an autobiographical tale of a honky tonk musician, went for 150 dollars.

Nelson moved to Nashville and soon discovered the true value of his songs after established writer Hank Cochran 'spotted' him singing at Tootsie's Orchid Lounge, a famous Nashville musical starting-point. Nelson signed to Pamper Music and had success writing hits for Faron Young, Ray Price (who employed Nelson briefly as bass-player) and Patsy Cline.

Money brought Willie and his family material comforts, but the young songwriter was frequently unhappy; his private life was in almost constant turmoil

and his recording ambitions were frustrated. No Nashville company would take him on, although he finally got a deal with the California-based Liberty Records in 1961, making a string of singles that resulted in one small hit before the label collapsed. In 1964, after a brief and un-

Opposite: From the Seventies onwards, Nelson replaced his former conventionality (inset) with a frontiersman's braids, bandana and battered guitar. Above: With Dyan Cannon in Honeysuckle Rose.

successful sojourn with Monument, Nelson became disgusted at his failures and retired to become a farmer, setting up home on a 100-acre farm near Nashville.

The retirement was brief, and Willie returned to recording in 1965, this time for the Nashville-based RCA label with which he cut several albums and singles, most of which featured his pure country vocals submerged in an over-produced welter of strings and sweetened back-up vocals.

A lot of people in the record industry liked Nelson's singing, but no-one saw him as a potential star; he dressed scruffily at a time when the country music norm was smart suits and short hair, and he sang in an old-fashioned style that was at odds with the slick, urbane 'Nashville Sound' of the Sixties. He was, however, recognised as a songwriter of note, having composed several hundred songs that had been recorded by a wide range of popular singers, including Elvis Presley, Frank Sinatra, Bing Crosby, Al Green, Aretha Franklin and Ray Charles.

Redneck rock
In 1969, Nelson reached the lowest emotional point of his life and made the decision to quit Nashville. 'Hank Cochran and I had been sitting in the basement writing songs,' he recalls. 'That year I went through a divorce and had four cars wrecked. We were kicking all this around and we wrote the song, "What Can You Do

To Me Now". The next day my house burned down.' Willie managed to rescue his beloved Martin guitar and a pound of Columbian marijuana from the flames, then moved to Texas where he made a final, determined effort to become a star.

He was surprised to discover a growing number of young people in his audiences, particularly at the Armadillo World Headquarters in Austin. The Texan capital became his base and he soon became the focal point of the early Seventies' progressive country movement, which featured musicians who mixed rock music with country.

In 1971 Nelson was signed to the New York-based Atlantic Records, where Jerry Wexler gave him the freedom to record with his own choice of musicians – his band, and friend Leon Russell. The result, *Shotgun Willie* (1973), came close to capturing his live sound and, although not a major success, outsold all his previous records combined. The follow-up, *Phases And Stages* (1974), also sold moderately well, but suffered through being released at a time when Atlantic were closing down their country division.

Nelson then moved to CBS and recorded the concept album, *The Red Headed Stranger* (1975), which included the single release, 'Blue Eyes Crying In The Rain'. Picked up by radio stations across the country, it was soon a huge country and pop hit, reaching Number 21 in the Hot Hundred. Songwriter Willie Nelson had finally broken through as a singer, ironically with a composition that was not his own but a Fred Rose song from 1945. His career was boosted still further when he appeared with his close friend Waylon Jennings on the 1976 RCA compilation, *Wanted: The Outlaws*; this became one of the best-selling country albums, and earned them three Country Music Association awards.

Nelson had supplied songs for films before his real screen debut in *The Electric Horseman* (1979); his success in portraying the manager of an ex-rodeo star (played by Robert Redford) led to the leading role in *Honeysuckle Rose* (1980), the semi-autobiographical story of a tough, warm-hearted honky-tonk singer from Texas. 1983 saw him starring opposite Gary Busey in *Barbarosa*, once more in an outlaw role, to good reviews.

Success finally brought Willie Nelson the personal happiness and contentment he had long sought, but had the significant effect of slowing down his songwriting – which always seems to have been inspired by hard times and depression – to a trickle. Subsequent recordings heavily featured new versions of his old songs, or reworkings of classics – notably the *Stardust* album (1978), a collection of pop standards from the Thirties and Forties, performed with basic country instrumentation, that stayed on the country charts for five years. By the beginning of the Eighties, Willie Nelson was established as one of the most popular country singers of all time.

RICHARD WOOTTON

The troubled life of a country great

THERE ARE VERY FEW, if any, country artists who have distinguished themselves in so many different areas of their craft as has Merle Haggard. Initially recognised as a brilliant singer-songwriter, he has also proven himself as an exceptional musician (on guitar and fiddle), the leader of one of the most accomplished bands in the business (the Strangers, whose freewheeling style of music Haggard describes as 'country jazz'), and as a musical historian.

It is Haggard's work as a recording artist and songwriter that has been most significant since 1963, when he scored his first chart success. With over 25 Number 1 hits in the country charts and many hundreds of original songs in his catalogue, Haggard has proved to be one of the most prolific and successful performers in his field. One of his songs, the classic 'Today I Started Loving You Again', has been recorded by over 400 different artists.

Life in prison

Merle Haggard was born on 6 March 1937, in Oildale, California, the son of migrant parents who, three years earlier, had arrived from East Oklahoma, the victims of the Dust Bowl droughts. In his early years Haggard was confronted with the harsh realities of labour camps, poverty and unemployment – the world so vividly depicted by John Steinbeck in *The Grapes Of Wrath* – and, by his own admission, he grew up too fast.

When his father died in 1946, Merle began to display an open hostility towards the restrictions of authority and, five years later, he ran away from home. By the time he had reached his 23rd birthday he had spent seven years in reform schools and jail, including a three-year stretch at San Quentin for burglary. It was, as he explained in his autobiography *Sing Me Back Home*, through having conversations (via a ventilation system) with infamous condemned rapist Caryl Chessman that he quit his life of crime. 'Just ask me about hell,' Haggard wrote, 'I've been there.'

Finally paroled in 1960, he moved to Bakersfield, California, where he began working for his elder brother, an electrical contractor, as an 80-dollar-a-week ditch-digger while moonlighting as a guitar-player in the town's rough-and-tumble bar and nightclub area, known locally as 'beer can hill'. Until that time, Haggard's only connections with music came from his father and grandfather, both fiddle players, and through the music of Jimmie Rodgers, Bob Wills and Lefty Frizzell played on the radio.

Eventually he landed a gig as guitarist in the band of new chart artist Wynn Stewart and, shortly afterwards, was discovered by Lewis Talley and Charles 'Fuzzy' Owens who owned a small label, Talley Records. Haggard's initial recordings were made in a small garage behind

MERLE HAGGARD

Talley's house, and he debuted in the country charts in 1963 with 'Sing A Sad Song'. A couple of years later, his third chart single '(My Friends Are Gonna Be) Strangers', penned by Liz Anderson, brought a deal with Capitol Records and opened up a highly successful 12 year association with the label.

From the first, there were shades of biography in many of Haggard's raw, rhythmic compositions; 'Life In Prison' and 'Sing Me Back Home' – the tale of a condemned prisoner's final walk – told of life behind bars, while 'Misery And Gin' and 'I Can't Hold Myself In Line' concerned themselves with relationships destroyed by drink. But the song that was to change his life, penned in the back of a bus with Strangers member Eddie Burris, was released in 1969.

It was called 'Okie From Muskogee' and has been described as everything from 'an unabashed call for old fashioned

Above: Merle Haggard in the cap of a railroad engineer. Opposite: On stage with the Strangers.

patriotism' to 'a reactionary hellraiser's' anthem'. In fact, the words—'We don't smoke marijuana in Muskogee/We don't make our trips on LSD/We don't burn our draft cards down on Main Street/We like living right and being free'—contained more than a hint of irony, but the song was accepted at face value by Southern country fans and became an enormous hit, even making the national Top Fifty.

Released during the height of domestic unrest brought on by the Vietnam conflict, 'Okie From Muskogee' earned Merle an invitation to perform at the White House from President Nixon, while George Wallace, the Governor of Alabama, asked the singer to support him in his re-election campaign (Haggard declined and later admitted that the song had been intended as a joke). But by now, Haggard had established himself as one of country music's top attractions; his *Okie From Muskogee* (1970) album became a best-seller and the follow-up, *The Fightin' Side Of Me*, released the same year, sold a million.

Land of many barrooms
Although he had now made a name for himself as a singer-songwriter in his own right, Merle Haggard had become more interested in exploring his musical heritage and, in 1969, came up with the first of his 'tribute' releases, a double album of Jimmie Rodgers material titled *Same Train, Different Time*. A year later, after considerable preparation, he presented his *A Tribute To The Best Damn Fiddle Player In The World*, a salute to Western swing innovator Bob Wills, which reunited many of Wills's former Texas Playboys on the sessions as well as Haggard's own Strangers.

The ambitious album *A Land Of Many Churches* (1973) provided an almost documentary glimpse of gospel worship in contemporary America and used the Carter Family on a series of location recordings – *I Love Dixie Blues* (1974) was a live tribute to Dixieland music, while the 1976 tribute to the railroads, *My Love Affair With Trains*, reflected a lifelong interest.

By comparison with his Capitol years, Haggard's association with MCA Records from 1977 to 1981 represented a lean period. 1977 saw the release of the somewhat hastily-compiled *My Farewell To Elvis*, which contained the hit single 'From Graceland To The Promised Land', although 1980 saw the singer back on top form with a superlative collection of drinking songs – *Back To The Barrooms*. The MCA period was marked by times of turmoil and transition in Haggard's life – his marriage to Bonnie Owens broke up – but by 1981 he had re-married, to country singer Leona Williams, settled near Redding on the shores of Lake Shasta and signed a new contract with Epic.

Big City, his first release for the new label, was a collection of songs produced by Haggard and longtime associate Lewis Talley and showed that the singer's natural, unmannered vocals were as good as ever. The following year, Haggard duetted with country legend George Jones on *A Taste Of Yesterday's Wine* and with modern-day country phenomenon Willie Nelson on *Poncho And Lefty*. The latter turned out to be a classic album, presenting a brilliant combination of talents that share a common interest and background of Western swing heritage.

Merle Haggard has always shied away from 'Hollywood' country and the star process and remained true to his roots – whether, like Jimmie Rodgers and Hank Williams before him, writing and singing from bitter experience or documenting the country traditions and heritage of the American South. For these reasons alone, Haggard will always be remembered in country's hall of fame. TONY BYWORTH

Merle Haggard Recommended Listening

Capitol Country Classics—Merle Haggard (Capitol CAPS 1034) (Includes: The Fightin' Side Of Me, It's Not Love But It's Not Bad, Movin' On, The Roots Of My Raising, Things Aren't Funny Anymore, Everybody Had The Blues).

TO BEAT THE DEVIL

Kris Kristofferson took on Nashville and won

ONE OF THE FEW artists successfully to make the transition from pop music to film is singer-songwriter-actor Kris Kristofferson. On record, he is remembered for such classics as 'Me And Bobby McGee', 'Help Me Make It Through The Night' and 'For The Good Times', while on film he has been acclaimed for his performances in *Pat Garrett And Billy The Kid* (1973), *A Star Is Born* (1976) and *Heaven's Gate* (1980). Since the mid Seventies, Kristofferson became better-known for his screen roles, although his headlining appearance at the 1981 Silk Cut Country Festival in London showed he had lost none of his musical abilities.

Oxford scholar

Born in Brownsville, Texas, on 22 June 1936, Kristofferson was the son of an Air Force officer. At high school, he combined scholastic and sporting talents, winning a coveted Rhodes scholarship to Oxford in 1958, where he spent two years specialising in the works of William Blake. At Oxford he began seriously to explore his literary gifts, completing two (unpublished) novels and writing songs. The latter brought him to the attention of Tommy Steele's agent, John Kennedy, who paraded him, with little success, as 'Kris Carson'.

Unable to make headway as a novelist or singer, he enlisted in the US Air Force, serving in Europe as a helicopter pilot.

While stationed in Germany, he began performing his material at service clubs and submitting tapes to publishers back in the United States.

Following his discharge from the service in 1965, Kristofferson returned to the US. A meeting with Johnny Cash encouraged him to persevere with his songwriting and to turn down an opportunity to teach literature at West Point Military Academy. Determined to push his own songs, he headed for Nashville, taking a job as a janitor at CBS. For a few years, it looked as though that was the nearest Kristofferson would get to a recording studio.

While striving for acceptance in the cutthroat Nashville scene – a period of his life he later recounted in 'To Beat The Devil' – Kristofferson took a number of jobs, including that of helicopter pilot, flying workers to the oil rigs in the Gulf of Mexico. He was on the verge of quitting music altogether and becoming a construction worker when, in 1969, Roger Miller decided to cover the number 'Me And Bobby McGee'.

The song was immediately hailed as a classic and was snapped up by many mainstream performers. Probably the best-remembered version, however, was that recorded by Janis Joplin, which went to Number 1 in the US in early 1971. By then, Kristofferson's potential had been realised and stars like Johnny Cash, Willie Nelson and Gordon Lightfoot were eager to record his work. Kristofferson's own distinctive versions of his best-known songs may be heard on his two finest albums, both recorded for Monument: *Me And Bobby McGee* (1970) and *The Silver Tongued Devil And I* (1971), and on the compilation *The Songs Of Kristofferson* (1977).

Kristofferson's rise coincided with that of the singer-songwriter cult, epitomised by James Taylor and Carole King. Kristofferson's songs were less inward-looking

than those of his contemporaries, however, his age and experience bringing a harder edge to his work.

Outlaw blues

Kristofferson's early Seventies albums exemplified a brand of country music that avoided romantic clichés and was gaining a wider, younger audience, thanks largely to the Byrds' *Sweetheart Of The Rodeo* (1968) and Bob Dylan's *Nashville Skyline* (1969). His songs told of losers and dreamers, of idealists who, as he sang in 'Billy Dee', roved 'lookin' for a home they'll never find'.

Kristofferson could come up with a memorable melody, such as 'Help Me Make It Through The Night', but made his main contribution to country music as a lyricist. In 'Me And Bobby McGee', for

Left: Kris Kristofferson at home on the range in the Eighties (left), in concert with former wife Rita Coolidge (right) and acting with Bob Dylan in Sam Peckinpah's Pat Garrett And Billy The Kid *(below right).*

example, his writing was typically earthy and accessible, with a nicely-judged line in cornball wit ('Busted flat in Baton Rouge and headed for the trains/Feelin' nearly faded as my jeans. . .') and homespun philosophising ('Freedom's just another word for nothing left to lose/Nothing ain't worth nothing but it's free. . .'). Perhaps more significantly, however, he brought a distinctly modern sensuality to his love songs as the first verse of 'Help Me Make It Through The Night' shows: 'Take the ribbon from your hair/Shake it loose and let it fall/Layin' soft against my skin/Like the shadows on the wall. Come and lay down by my side/Til the early mornin' light/All I'm taking is your time/Help me make it through the night.'

Although his work has been covered by so many other artists, familiarity has not robbed it of its poignant authenticity. 'Me And Bobby McGee' remains one of the classic 'road' songs; 'Sunday Mornin' Comin' Down' acutely captures the loneliness and desperation of big city life; 'Billy Dee' is a touching portrait of a young friend driven to death by disillusion and drug addiction; 'Casey's Last Ride' depicts the failed aspirations of an ordinary man; while 'The Pilgrim – Chapter 33' is an affectionate portrait based on several of Kristofferson's hard-living buddies, such as Johnny Cash, Dennis Hopper and Ramblin' Jack Eliott: 'He's a poet, he's a picker/He's a prophet, he's a pusher/He's a pilgrim and a preacher/And a problem when he's stoned/He's a walking contradiction/Partly truth and partly fiction/Taking every wrong direction/On his lonely way back home.' It featured on the soundtrack of Cisco Pike (1971), in which Kristofferson had his first major screen role. (He had made his debut in Dennis Hopper's The Last Movie, completed in 1971, that did not see official release until 1982.)

In 1973 Kristofferson became a genuine movie celebrity, co-starring with James Coburn and Bob Dylan in Sam Peckinpah's Pat Garrett And Billy The Kid. The film was severely cut by the studio without the director's approval, although Kristofferson's fine performance as the legendary outlaw Billy remains intact. From then on, Kristofferson's music was to take second place to his acting.

Hangover street
Kristofferson's performances in such films as Martin Scorsese's Alice Doesn't Live Here Any More (1974) and Lewis John Carlino's The Sailor Who Fell From Grace With The Sea (1976) were widely acclaimed. But while Kristofferson's professional star was rising, his private life was entering a troubled phase.

Although to outward appearances happily married to singer Rita Coolidge (they had wed in 1973), he had begun drinking heavily. His albums, whether solo efforts or recorded with his wife, were disappointing and he was becoming less selective about his film roles. From singing about losers, Kristofferson suddenly seemed in

A bove: Kris kisses and makes up with Barbra Streisand in Frank Pierson's A Star Is Born, the film that consolidated Kristofferson's position as a major box-office draw in 1976.

danger of becoming a loser himself.

His personal problems were to some extent reflected by A Star Is Born, in which he played Barbra Streisand's husband; his career wanes as hers waxes, driving him to drink. Kristofferson turned in a disturbingly convincing performance despite the fact that he was only third choice for the role, both Elvis Presley and Mick Jagger having turned it down.

Although his 1978 album, Easter Island, showed him back on form as a songwriter, numbers like 'Living Legend' and 'The Sabre And The Rose' being worthy additions to his early work, his acting career suddenly seemed in jeopardy. He abruptly withdrew from filming Hanover Street (1979) and, following a starring role in the disastrous television series Freedom Road – in which he was cast opposite Muhammad Ali – he announced his retirement from the screen. However he was unable to resist the temptation to star in Michael Cimino's Heaven's Gate in 1980. Enshrined in Hollywood as the most expensive movie ever made, it was a disastrous commercial failure.

To his credit, Kristofferson believed in the film and – possibly with bitter memories of the fate Pat Garrett And Billy The Kid had suffered in the studio cutting-rooms – appeared with Cimino to promote Heaven's Gate at the Cannes Film Festival,

where it was favourably received by critics. Kristofferson seemed back on course, starring with Jane Fonda in Roll Over in 1982. He also began gigging again, delighting audiences with his impressive repertoire.

Straight from the heart
Kristofferson's contribution to the country-rock style defined by artists such as Gram Parsons and Nashville 'outlaws' Waylon Jennings and Willie Nelson, should not be overlooked. His songs, born out of genuine and often bitter experience, admittedly displayed a sentimentality for their subjects, but were never facile or cloying. While his singer-songwriter contemporaries generally opted for meditations on love and reflections on the pressures of fame, Kristofferson's best work spoke from the heart, reflecting a generation's aimless and frustrated idealism.

When success assuaged the hunger and anger which had prompted those early songs, the standard of Kristofferson's writing deteriorated. But with a successful film career and an impressive roster of hits behind him, he has fully vindicated his stubborn belief in his own talents.

PATRICK HUMPHRIES

Kris Kristofferson
Recommended Listening

Me And Bobby McGee (Monument MNT 64631) (Includes: Help Me Make It Through The Night, For The Good Times, Me And Bobby McGee, To Beat The Devil, Darby's Castle, The Law Is For The Protection Of The People).

HONKY-TONK HERO

Waylon Jennings put the soul back into country

WITH HIS TANGLED MANE of dark hair framing a fierce, aquiline, grizzled face, Waylon Jennings at once appears the antithesis of the bland, bejewelled and smiling Grand Ole Opry star. He has had to struggle long and hard to achieve recognition as one of the most influential and forceful figures in contemporary country music, his dynamic personality and gritty baritone voice cutting through the run-of-the-mill Nashville sweetness, sentimentality and rhinestone glitter to create music that is passionate, uncluttered and timeless.

The party's over

Born on 15 June 1937 in Littlefield, Texas, Jennings came from a musical family; both parents played guitar, his father performing in a local country dance band. Waylon consequently became committed to music at an early age – at 12 he had established himself as 'the youngest DJ in America' with his own radio show, and he formed his first group, the Texas Longhorns, when barely in his teens.

In 1954 Jennings met Buddy Holly – who, at the time, was a member of the group Buddy, Bob (Montgomery) and Larry (Wilburn) – on the popular KLLL radio show, 'Country Party'; the two quickly became friends. When Holly had achieved international success four years later, he took Jennings under his wing and produced his first recordings, 'Jole Blon' and 'When Sin Stops', at Norman Petty's Clovis studio. However, when released back-to-back on the Brunswick label, the single quickly disappeared from sight. Holly's faith in Jennings' talent remained undiminished despite this setback; when he decided to form a new band after splitting with the Crickets, he hired Jennings as the bass-player. Sadly their association was to be short-lived, being terminated by the plane crash that took the lives of Buddy Holly, the Big Bopper and Ritchie Valens on 3 February 1959.

Nashville cat

Jennings' next period of activity came in 1964 when, after returning to disc jockeying in Lubbock and cutting some tracks for the Trend label, he moved to Phoenix, Arizona. He formed his own band, the Waylors, and began a residency at a newly-opened supper club, JD's. He quickly became a local celebrity, leading to an album being made that year at the city's Audio Recorders studio. *Waylon Jennings At JD's* was reissued, with the inclusion of the Brunswick tracks, by MCA Records in 1979 as *The Early Years*. The record helped bring him to the attention of Herb Alpert, who had just launched A&M records with Jerry Moss.

Jennings subsequently recorded an album, *Don't Think Twice*, for A&M. Like the preceding LP, it was mainly comprised of then-popular titles such as 'Kisses Sweeter Than Wine' and 'Twelfth Of Never'. Although not officially released until 1970, it was heard by others in the music business. Among those who heard it was Bobby Bare, an artist riding high in both country and pop charts with 'Shame On Me'.

Bare heard Jennings' original song, 'Just To Satisfy You', and immediately decided to cover it. When Bare saw Jennings on stage in Phoenix shortly afterwards, he phoned his producer, Chet Atkins, in Nashville, recommending he sign the singer. Atkins heeded Bare's advice and, on 16 March 1965, Jennings cut his first session for RCA. Five months later a single, 'That's The Chance I'll Have To Take', appeared briefly in the country charts. Jennings' second single for RCA, 'Stop The World (And Let Me Off)', fared better and, by the time of his fifth release, 'That's What You Get For Loving Me', in late 1966, he was regularly to be seen in the country Top Ten. Atkins slotted his new signing into the lucrative 'folk-country' category that had already brought success to Bobby Bare and George Hamilton IV.

This approach fitted RCA's very conservative treatment of its country roster, and the label's executives undoubtedly failed to understand Jennings' dissatisfaction at the end of the decade when his track record displayed nearly 20 country chart hits and several successful album releases. Jennings insisted on a broader musical approach, but all he was permitted was the album *Country Folk* (1969), on which he shared artist credits with the Kimberlys, a vocal quartet from Oklahoma. The record's

material included 'Games People Play', 'MacArthur Park' and a cover of the Seekers' 'A World Of Our Own'. Despite this mish-mash of popular music, the LP retained its own peculiar charm.

Jennings reacted angrily to accusations that he might be 'selling out' by covering contemporary hits, commenting: 'I couldn't go pop with a mouthful of firecrackers. Instruments don't make country. We're entitled to a heavy rock beat if it complements our songs. Or if we want to use a kazoo played through a sewer pipe, that's all right too. Why should we lock ourselves in?'

This revolutionary attitude to country – which, in addition to exploring contemporary musical directions, involved getting back to the emotional wellsprings of the music – was crucial to Jennings' development as an artist and informed all his subsequent recordings.

The following year's *Singer Of Sad Songs* presented material that ranged from mainstream country, such as the Louvin Brothers' 'Must You Throw Dirt In My Face?', to contemporary rock numbers like the Rolling Stones' 'Honky Tonk Women', and plainly showed the contrasting styles that Jennings could handle. Yet, in spite of the album's success and a country chart hit with a cover of Chuck Berry's 'Brown Eyed Handsome Man', his wrangles with RCA continued. In an effort to ease the situation, Atkins matched the artist with an array of producers – including Lee Hazlewood, Ronnie Light and Nashville brass innovator Danny Lewis – on a succession of albums. Some, like the excellent *Lonesome, Orn'ry And Mean* (1972) and *Honky Tonk Heroes* (1973) had lengthy producer credits, including participation by Jennings himself.

The outlaw trail
In 1973 Jennings renegotiated his RCA contract, achieving complete control over his recorded work. Within 12 months he had teamed with Willie Nelson to produce an album named *This Time* (1974), the title track bringing him his first ever Number 1 country single. Further successes with 'I'm A Ramblin' Man' and a double A-side 'Are You Sure Hank Done It This Way'/'Bob Wills Is Still The King' – two songs that paid tribute to Jennings' innovations and musical roots – further consolidated his reputation.

The mid Seventies saw the release of the album that would change the face of country music and turn Jennings from a respected artist dabbling in new ideas to a genuine force to be reckoned with. The record was the brainchild of RCA executive Jerry Bradley (one of Waylon's closest allies at the label). He decided to band all of Nashville's non-conformists together on one album.

Entitled *Wanted: The Outlaws* and presenting the talents of Jennings, Willie Nelson, Tompall Glaser and Jessi Colter (also known as Miriam Eddy, the former wife of guitarist Duane Eddy but, by this

Opposite: Jennings in 1973. Above: With the Waylors, featuring Ralph Mooney on pedal steel. Below: The star shows off his customised 'Waylon Jennings Special'.

time, married to Jennings), the album became the most talked-about release of 1976. It subsequently found its way into the record books as the first country LP to go platinum, indicating that a number of rock fans were being drawn to country music for the first time.

After *Wanted: The Outlaws*, Jennings could do no wrong with the public, with ever-increasing receipts at the box-office and a string of single hits, including 'Luckenbach, Texas' (a Hot Hundred Number 25 in 1977), 'Wurlitzer Prize', 'I've Always Been Crazy' and 'I Ain't Living Long Like This'. Albums were just as successful; his LP with Willie Nelson, *Waylon And Willie* (1978) created almost as much excitement as *Wanted: The Outlaws*, while *I've Always Been Crazy* (1978) and *What Goes Around Comes Around* (1979) represented country-rock music at its best.

With his musical beliefs vindicated, it was perhaps not surprising that Jennings seemed a mellower, less strident figure in the Eighties – an attitude that could be glimpsed in his delicate 1979 version of C. B. Robertson's 'Ivory Tower': 'Here we are in our ivory tower/All our fears left behind/Looking down from our ivory tower/Like everyone else has lost their minds.' His albums, which included a duet presentation with Jessi Colter, *Leather And Lace* (1981), and *Black On Black* (1982), cut across a wide musical spectrum but were noticeably gentler than in the days when he was consciously trying to rock Nashville's very foundations.   TONY BYWORTH

Waylon Jennings
Recommended Listening

Greatest Hits (RCA 3031) (Includes: Good Hearted Woman, Luckenbach, Texas, Mammas Don't Let Your Babies Grow Up To Be Cowboys, Are You Sure Hank Done It This Way, Ladies Love Outlaws, I'm A Ramblin' Man).

STEELIN' AWAY

PROBABLY NO OTHER instrument in the world is as closely associated with country music as the pedal steel guitar. Yet its roots are found not in some rural hamlet in the Southern reaches of America, but in an exotic, hybrid Polynesian culture located in the middle of the Pacific Ocean.

The steel guitar's most venerable ancestor was born in the Hawaii of a century past, after the guitar had been introduced to the islands by Mexican and Portuguese cowboys who came following a cattle boom. According to legend, a man named Joseph Kekuku one day happened to drop his comb across his guitar's strings, becoming enchanted with the slithering, slinky sound it made. By 1894, he was giving impromptu concerts accompanied by his cousin Sam on violin and, by the turn of the century, had begun to move past mere novelty into serious study of the instrument. He designed a steel bar, held in the left hand and moved across the strings, to make the sound brighter and cleaner.

The instrument was imported to the United States on the wave of a Hawaiian craze that washed over American shores

Pedal steel power from country pickers

after the First World War. Coinciding with the growing popularity of phonograph records, such 'hula blues' masters as Sol Hoopii, Frank Ferara and Roy Smeck were soon making the 'lap' guitar a fashionable instrument.

Mongrel music
Related somewhat to the bottleneck style, the Hawaiian legacy was picked up by the mongrel music known as Western swing in the Thirties. Bob Dunn, of Fort Worth, Texas, became the first to apply electricity to the acoustic lap steel, and from there, such guitarists as Leon McAuliffe, Noel Boggs and the legendary Joaquin Murphy (who would often walk off-stage in mid-song if he was somehow dissatisfied) set the perimeters of the new style.

The problem with the steel was the bar, which often forced players into strange tunings and awkward 'slants' to obtain some degree of musical sophistication.

This would eventually result in the addition of pedals to the instrument, whose function would be the same as placing fingers on a guitar neck. The Forties saw many players attempting to bridge this technical gap, from Herb Remington – whose 'Remington Ride' is an acknowledged steel classic – through the pure-toned Jerry Byrd, to Speedy West, the Jimi Hendrix of steel, whose bar crashes and wild swoops created sounds that remain unique decades later.

All of the above used some form of pedal guitar, but it wasn't until 1954 that the steel guitar entered widespread use. With Bud Isaacs providing support for singer Webb Pierce, a song called 'Slowly' captured the imagination of country hit parades everywhere, and the 'crying' sound of a steel soon became *de rigeur* on every Nashville session.

The instrument was growing in sophistication as well. Buddy Emmons recorded *Steel Guitar Jazz* in 1963, backed by a jazz quartet. For those who had thought the steel confined to mere weeping, Emmons showed harmonic possibilities on a par with the broadest of keyboards. Top session man and producer Pete Drake took the instrument another step further when he employed a voice-box to make his steel 'talk' – a move that resulted in the 1964 million-seller, 'Forever'.

Increasingly, steel musicians began to look past their own little world, intent on promoting the concept of pedal steel to outside listeners and players. Dobroist Shot Jackson and Buddy Emmons teamed up early on to design the Sho-Bud guitar, thereafter a perennial favourite. Others, like the tireless Jeff Newman, began to teach the steel by means of mail-order courses, with play-along cassettes.

Steel sweethearts

The annual high point of this activity comes during Labor Day weekend every year, when pedal steel guitarists and fans meet in St Louis to pay homage to their instrument.

With all this seeming versatility, it seems strange that the instrument has continued to be so resolutely identified with country music. Early country-oriented rock and roll – Bill Haley and the Comets, Sid King and the Five Strings – did feature large helpings of steel, but the attraction of the easily-mastered orthodox guitar probably discouraged many would-be steelers. The instrument, with its pedal choices, knee levers, different tunings and usual ten strings per neck requires a degree of expertise and concentration that conflicts with rock's teenage impatience.

The country-rock boom of the late Sixties and early Seventies did produce some interesting hybrids, however. Rusty Young of Poco would slap effects devices galore on his stand-up steel, delighting audiences at both Fillmores, East and West. The Flying Burrito Brothers featured Sneaky Pete Kleinow, while the Byrds repaid the crossover by bringing Nashville regulars Lloyd Green and Jaydee Maness into the world of rock on their 1968 album *Sweetheart Of The Rodeo*. Clarence White, who played on the set, later devised a B-string bender for his Telecaster to simulate the steel's sound.

In the Eighties, the steel guitar found itself at a crossroads. Long identified with country music, it was in real danger of becoming an easy stereotype: nevertheless, the ornate richness of the steel texture is still capable of sweetening any form of sound. That it might become an instrument used worldwide was shown when it appeared within the Afrikan Beat Band of Nigeria's King Sunny Ade in a neat trick of cultural transformation. It had been a long journey for the steel guitar from 'Aloha Oe' to the backbone of country and beyond.

LENNY KAYE

Above left: Lloyd Green and Sho-Bud pedal steel. The Sho-Bud was co-designed by Buddy Emmons (right). Top right: Leon McAuliffe plays an archaic steel with the Texas Playboys. Above right: Poco's Rusty Young.

Music City USA

The Seventies were boom years for the Nashville music industry. Country music – which hardly anyone called 'country and western' any more – became big business, taking off in different directions to win huge new audiences across America in the rock and easy-listening markets. Moreover, the Nashville studios became increasingly popular with non-country musicians, who saw the Tennessee city and its top-notch session men as a stimulating alternative to the recording centres in New York, Los Angeles and London.

Rich pickings

Country music's growth was nurtured by successful producers like Billy Sherrill, Allen Reynolds and Tom Collins, who made subtle but significant changes to the 'Nashville sound' – the string-soaked concoction created by Owen Bradley, Chet Atkins and others in the late Fifties and Sixties – to arrive at 'crossover pop', so-called because of the behaviour of records that appeared in the country charts before crossing over into the pop listings. Their sophisticated, urbane recordings, usually shorn of fiddles, steel guitars and other traditional instrumentation, took country music uptown and away from its rural roots.

There had been country million-sellers before, but the new 'crossover' stars were

Change and challenge in Seventies Nashville

different; they were consistently successful and became established with a middle-class, middle-of-the-road audience that had previously shunned country music. The major breakthrough was made by Charlie Rich in 1973 with two Billy Sherrill-produced singles, 'Behind Closed Doors' and 'The Most Beautiful Girl', which each sold over two million copies. Rich, who had recorded for several labels in a variety of styles since the mid Fifties

with only limited success, suddenly found that he could command the same huge fees as rock and pop stars. He paved the way for others – most notably Kenny Rogers, who emulated Rich's success with a very similar country crooning style, scoring international best-sellers with 'Lucille', 'The Gambler' and others.

This new-found mass popularity for country music was not welcomed by everyone; hard-core country fans feared that the frequently bland, easy-listening style of many potential 'crossover' artists was eroding the distinctive qualities of their music. This fear was shared by some long-established performers, especially when non-country singers like Anne Murray, John Denver and Olivia Newton-John began flavouring their lightweight pop material with country, sold well in both markets and then began scooping prestigious music industry awards that had previously been the exclusive property of Nashville-based performers.

When Olivia Newton-John was voted Best Female Vocalist Of 1974 by the Country Music Association (CMA), after scoring country hits, including 'Let Me Be There' and 'If You Love Me (Let Me Know)', several outraged Nashville singers formed the Association of Country Entertainers (ACE), which argued that only 'authentic' singers should thenceforth

Opposite: The skyline of Nashville, country capital of the world. Two of the city's favourite sons were Charlie Rich (left) and Kenny Rogers (right), both specialists in the soft-voiced, urbane country style.

be eligible for country awards. The trend of non-country acts winning did not continue, but ACE's cause was blunted by the continuing growth of 'crossover' as more and more supposedly 'authentic' singers, including ACE founder-member Dolly Parton, joined the pop bandwagon and made records that were a long way from their roots.

Stand by your fans

Country music had now become such big business that the established stars were subject to heavy commercial pressures and did not have a lot of choice about the direction their music should take. Prior to the Seventies, the country market was in the South of the USA, where the predominantly blue-collar audience was small but reliable and was guaranteed to buy similar-sounding albums by the same stars year after year. Albums that sold only in tens of thousands were considered successful because they were made cheaply on a conveyor-belt system that utilised a small group of very accomplished session men and a seasoned producer who could help a singer make a 10-song album in a matter of hours, far quicker than the rock and pop

process. But when country music began competing for a larger share of the American record market, more time, money and effort was lavished on country product and modest sales were thus no longer acceptable.

Many country stars struggled to change in order to survive, although a few of the best – including George Jones, Johnny Cash and Tammy Wynette – had built up such a strong and loyal audience that they were able to continue recording without making any concessions to pop. But they tended to be the exceptions; by the end of the decade many of the major names of the

> 'I left because there are elements in Nashville I couldn't combat, set ways that I wanted to change. I wanted to do things another way but was told: "This is the way things will be done, this is the way they've always been done".'
> **Willie Nelson**

Fifties and Sixties had been dropped by the big labels. The important new stars were youngsters with a less obvious country twang in their voices and a broader appeal for the market, which now stretched from Maine to California. These performers included Eddie Rabbitt, who had been born and bred in New Jersey; Crystal Gayle – little sister of Sixties country queen Loretta Lynn – whose sophisticated city-girl image was miles from Loretta's down-home appeal; and Barbara Mandrell, who won a huge following with a slick TV show that used the old-fashioned hillbilly image of country music only to raise a laugh.

Yet some brave performers broke new ground in the Seventies by deliberately going against the prevailing trends and earning a reputation as country-music 'outlaws'. Most notable of these were Waylon Jennings and Willie Nelson, who, from around 1972, changed their only moderately successful mainstream country sound by kicking back at what they considered the limitations and restrictions of the Nashville studio system.

The 'outlaw' revolt came, somewhat ironically, at a time when a growing number of rock musicians were coming to Nashville to record, including Bob Dylan (who started the trend back in 1966), Ringo Starr, Neil Young and Joan Baez. All focused attention on and brought respect to the city's studios and session men. Yet while those artists embraced the Nashville

system, Jennings and Nelson rejected it, preferring to make music with their own bands that was rough-edged and unadorned – a sharp and popular antidote to 'crossover'.

The surprising success of Jennings and Nelson meant that their rebellious behaviour and unkind words were soon forgotten. They were lauded by the Nashville establishment and showered with awards, particularly in 1976 when they topped the country charts with the album *Wanted: The Outlaws* and the single, 'Good Hearted Woman'. They had proved that country music could succeed in a wide marketplace without having to make compromises, and they had also changed the popular image of the country performer. In the Sixties, short hair, clean-shaven faces and smart clothes were mandatory, but Waylon and Willie's success ensured that beards, long hair and scruffy denims were to become equally acceptable.

Another man who helped change the look of country artists was Kris Kristofferson, although his most significant achievement was in opening the door for a new breed of mainly college-educated songwriters to break through in Nashville. His

Nashville has justifiably prided itself on its women stars; Crystal Gayle (left) younger sister of Loretta Lynn, and Dolly Parton (right) were two country stars to emerge in the Seventies.

1971 CMA award as Songwriter of the Year for 'Sunday Morning Coming Down' led to the acceptance of writers like Lee Clayton, Guy Clark, Shel Silverstein, Rodney Crowell, Billy Joe Shaver and Dean Dillon.

Hollywood cashes in

By the late Seventies, the country boom had expanded into TV, radio and movies. Although there were few regular country series on the major TV networks, country stars were turning up on a daily basis on specials and the prestige talk-shows. The expansion of country music on radio was very dramatic; 81 radio stations in the US had been programming country music in 1961, but the total had risen to 525 by 1971 and tripled during the Seventies, with over 1500 having emerged by 1980. Hollywood discovered the new selling power of country music and there was a surfeit of films that used country themes and/or soundtracks, including box-office hits like *Smokey And The Bandit* (1977) and *Every Which Way But Loose* (1978).

Although Robert Altman's *Nashville* (1975) brilliantly satirised many aspects of Nashville life, neither that film nor the romantic views of the old-style Nashville music industry expressed in movies like the Oscar-winning *Coal Miner's Daughter* (1980), which celebrated the achievements of Loretta Lynn, accurately reflected the way the industry operated in the Seventies. Instead of the pioneering musical adventurers who first made Nashville into 'Music City USA' from small offices in the Lower Broadway area after the war, lawyers and accountants ran the business from smart offices in Music Row (16th and 17th Avenues and their connecting streets). The downtown of Nashville had been abandoned to seedy bars, strip joints, down-and-outs and country fans who come

to gaze at the dilapidated Ryman Auditorium, home of the Grand Ole Opry for many years.

Country music was still growing in popularity at the end of 1980, a time when the rest of the music industry was in the doldrums. It defied the critics and continued this growth largely due to the New Country movement which in the mid-Eighties replaced MOR-bound stars like Dolly Parton with younger, fresher faces. Singers such as Nanci Griffith, Steve Earle, Hank Williams Jr, Ricky Scaggs,

Above: Tompall Glaser, Waylon Jennings, Jessi Colter and Willie Nelson proudly display platinum albums for Wanted: The Outlaws. *Below: Opryland.*

Rosanne Cash and Randy Travis were bringing a young audience back to the music, eschewing the synthesiser for more traditional instrumentation like mandolins, fiddles and steel guitar. And despite the rise of Austin as Texas' second musical centre, Nashville still reigned supreme.

RICHARD WOOTTON

One-Man Bands

The return of the solo performer in the Seventies

IF THE SUCCESS of the Beatles inspired the formation of a multitude of bands that changed the face of rock in the Sixties, then perhaps it was predictable that the following decade was to see the pendulum swing back towards the solo performer that such groups had displaced. As the Beatles themselves split into four variously talented individuals, so the solo star returned to the popular music scene in numbers unknown since the early Sixties.

A certain breed of solo performer emerged as the superstar of the Seventies – one determined to break free from a cult audience, and, significantly, one who could project his (or her) image and personality on stage as well as on record.

The show goes on

The career of Elton John fulfilled both these conditions. He was a shy, bespectacled pianist whose sensitive, emotional songs had gleaned him a respectable following – yet it was not until he hit his songwriting stride, simultaneously affecting a sweeping change of image to that of a space-age Jerry Lee Lewis, that he hit the headlines.

Stevie Wonder, meanwhile, distinguished himself not only by proving bigger than

Above left: Stevie Wonder. The child-star of the Sixties transformed himself, in the early Seventies, into a multi-talented superstar and became Motown's biggest money-spinner. Right: Elton John hid his shy persona behind eccentric spectacles and glittering stage suits, but it was his sensitive, emotional songs more than anything else that projected him into the spotlight.

Motown's all-consuming production-line star system, but also by overcoming the handicap of blindness. Yet in graduating from formula music-making to the more personal statements of 1971-72 onwards, he embraced not only the concerns of the black man, but also wider issues including ecology, human rights and the like.

It might be said that that colour was literally unimportant to a blind performer, but this would be to ignore the deeply-felt racial injustice mirrored in such songs as 'Living For The City'. Wonder was also keenly aware of the need to broaden his audience, touring the US as opening act for the Rolling Stones in 1972 to reach a generation of (white) rock fans to whom he had previously been 'Little' Stevie, child-star and harmonica-player. The fact that they received his new music as enthusiastically as his old black audience had done swiftly elevated him to superstar status.

Of the four ex-Beatles, it was Paul McCartney who found greatest success as a solo star. Although he had chosen the relative anonymity of Wings as an antidote to the media overkill of Beatles days, he was to find that an individual is considerably more likely to sustain a long and profitable career in rock' than a band. In 1974, he split Wings, adopted star billing and found 1974's *Band On The Run* his biggest-selling album to date. Moreover, McCartney's shrewd purchase of Buddy Holly's publishing rights and associated ventures have marked him as one of the more successful of the growing breed of rock-stars-turned-entrepreneurs. The attempts of other performers to start record labels have generally met with little success.

Change of clothes
Rock, of course, is subject to constant change, and an individual can often adapt more easily to prevailing trends. Thus it was that Gilbert O'Sullivan could trade his flat cap and short trousers image for that of roll-neck sophisticate while peddling essentially the same music – he had merely discarded an image that had served the purpose of attracting public (and media) attention. Similarly, Leo Sayer threw away his clown-suit after his dramatic appearance in 1973 with 'The Show Must Go On', eventually

Below: Paul McCartney. The ex-Beatle became one of the richest men in rock through a combination of commercial musical offerings and shrewd business ventures. Inset below left: Gilbert O'Sullivan arrived on the scene in a flat cap and pudding-basin haircut. He soon adopted a more sophisticated image, but his music – middle-of-the-road ballads – remained the same. Inset below right: Leo Sayer dressed as a clown to promote his first single, 'The Show Must Go On'.

achieving an audience that spanned several generations. Like Elton John, he moved from a left-field rock audience into mainstream pop while retaining the loyalty of a hard-core of fans. Performers like Barry Manilow, who aim solely at the MOR market, are unable to sustain such a wide following.

Togetherness
Ironically for two solo performers, Elton John and Stevie Wonder shared the distinction of achieving their highest UK chart placings with duets – Elton in 1976 with Kiki Dee ('Don't Go Breaking My Heart') and Stevie in 1982 with Paul McCartney ('Ebony And Ivory'). Yet perhaps this is indicative of the adaptability that is a hallmark of rock's new solo superstars, who learned from the eclipse of the Philly teen idols and so many others in succeeding decades that the fickleness of the teenage record-buying public is no guarantee of longevity in the ever-changing world of rock music. MICHAEL HEATLEY

ROCKET MAN

From Reg to riches . . . Elton John embroiders the stylish trappings of success with touches of witty eccentricity.

Elton John: shooting to the top of rock

THE NAME Elton John conjures up various images, ranging from 'gigantic specs' and 'oversize platform boots', to the Pinball Wizard or the quiet ballad 'Your Song'. He has achieved the status of 'pop personality', providing regular material for the news hounds with his outrageous antics and self-revelations, a popular family entertainer and the ideal chat-show guest. His gimmicky image even won him a place of honour in wax in London's Madame Tussaud's.

The singer's immense success must owe much to his wide appeal to a number of different tastes and audiences, his commercial opportunism – cashing in on the glam-rock wave of the early Seventies, for instance – and his prolific output during his heyday. By the Eighties, when Elton was reputedly grossing £7 million a year, his output was largely slanted towards the middle of the road, but it was certainly among the best of its kind.

Multi-millionaire superstar Elton John started life as Reginald Kenneth Dwight, born in Pinner, Middlesex, on 25 March 1947. At the age of four he began taking piano lessons, and at 11 won a scholarship to London's Royal Academy of Music, where he studied every Saturday morning for five years. As a schoolboy Reg cut a chubby, ungainly figure, and when it was discovered that he needed glasses, he chose a pair with thick horn-rimmed frames in emulation of his early hero Buddy Holly. He left school at 16 and worked by day as a messenger for West End music publishers Mills Music, spending the evenings entertaining the locals on the bar piano at the Northwood Hills Hotel in Pinner. After joining a group called the Corvettes, who re-christened themselves Bluesology after the title of a Django Reinhardt number, Reg bought a Hohner electric piano and devoted his evenings to more demanding stuff than 'Roll Out The Barrel' and 'Goodnight Irene'.

Goodbye Reg

Dwight stayed with Bluesology for five years and, although they never made it in their own right, they made a couple of singles – 'Come Back Baby' and 'Mr Fran-

tic' for Fontana – and supported visiting American soul artists such as Doris Troy, Major Lance and Patti LaBelle and the Bluebelles. Reg's role was limited to keyboards; his image was not considered appropriate as a frontman. It was during one of their regular spots at London's Cromwellian Club that they were spotted by 6ft 7in blues singer Long John Baldry, who asked the band to become his full-time backing group. In 1966 Bluesology toured the UK, playing R&B in the smooth, soft-edged Baldry style. At this time, the band included future Roxy Music guitarist Neil Hubbard, along with saxophonist Elton Dean, who later joined Soft Machine.

In late 1967 Baldry had a Number 1 hit with the maudlin ballad 'Let The Heartaches Begin' and entered the cabaret circuit. Bluesology abandoned him and then split up. Realising that his name was acutely mundane by pop standards, Reg Dwight decided on a change. Amalgamating the names of Elton Dean and John Baldry, he adopted the stage name Elton John; with the addition of the nickname 'Hercules', this was later legalised.

In June of that year, a subsidiary of Liberty Records placed an advertisement for 'new talent' in *New Musical Express*. Elton failed the audition by performing five Jim Reeves numbers in a row, but was offered a pile of lyrics and invited to compose some music for them. The lyrics had been submitted by a would-be poet from Lincolnshire called Bernie Taupin (born 22 May 1950). The two did not meet until six months later, but Elton prepared 20 songs from the material handed to him. Liberty showed no interest in the results, so Elton and Bernie took their wares to Dick James, a tubby, balding, cigar-smoking music publisher in the Tin Pan Alley tradition.

James' subsidiary company, Northern Songs, had struck gold in 1963 when the Beatles came its way. James offered Elton and Bernie a three-year songwriting contract at £10 a week and encouraged them to write Top Twenty material for MOR artists like Tom Jones and Engelbert Humperdinck. For two years they produced such songs as 'Mirrors Of My Mind' and 'Lemonade Lake', Elton keeping his day job (he now worked at a music store) and Bernie commuting from Lincolnshire with his manuscripts. Frustrated with

From small scales at the age of eight (top), Reg teamed up with Bernie Taupin (above), and went on to find success on a grand scale, playing to a packed Dodgers Stadium in LA in 1975 (left). Inset far left: Elton as the Pinball Wizard in Tommy.

their lack of success, the two set to work on their own material and Bernie moved into a flat with Elton in London. In 1969, they released the single 'Lady Samantha' on Phillips and the album *Empty Sky* on DJM's new label.

The guitar-based single and the folk-styled album, laced with harpsichord and flute, aroused enough interest for the second LP, *Elton John* (1970), to enter the UK album charts at Number 45. Elton John was now being produced by Gus Dudgeon, who brought in arranger Paul Buckmaster to embellish the songs with strings. The album remains one of Elton's classiest. Its mood was serious and poetic, the highly personal lyrics set to lilting melodies; the highlight was 'Your Song', which was released as a single in 1971 and reached Number 7 in the UK charts. Other tracks such as 'Border Song' and 'Take Me To The Pilot' had strong hooks and intriguing, elusive lyrics. As American critic Robert Christgau has pointed out, Taupin's lyrics, though catchy, often made little sense. Apart from composing the melodies, Elton's talent lay in his vocal ability to inject Taupin's lines with significance and emotion.

Frantic antics
Elton recruited drummer Nigel Olsson (formerly of Plastic Penny) and one-time Mirage bassist Dee Murray – both previously in the Spencer Davis Group – and went on the road. He developed a frenzied stage routine during which he would kick over the piano stool, jump over the keys and dance on the lid, and wore outlandish clothes in cheerful self-mockery. Grace was never one of his attributes. His appearance at the Troubador Club in LA, attended by Bob Dylan, heralded his success in the States, and was followed up with a prolific output of albums and singles.

The LP *Tumbleweed Connection* (1970) revealed Taupin's obsession with Americana and the mythology of the old West, a nostalgia later reflected in the song 'Indian Sunset' on the album *Madman Across The Water* (1971). *Tumbleweed* featured backing vocals by Dusty Springfield, Madeline Bell and Lesley Duncan and had a country-blues feel to it, with a gospel-tinged treatment given to numbers like 'Burn Down The Mission'. *Honky Chateau*, recorded at Strawberry Studios in France and released in 1972, signified a move away from ballads towards more commercial material; it reached Number 1 in America, Number 2 in the UK and contained a hit single in 'Rocket Man'. Both the 1973 albums, *Don't Shoot Me I'm Only The Piano Player* and

Elton John may have had some quiet songs in his repertoire, but he always made a loud spectacle of himself on stage – from playing the pantomime turkey (inset far left) to breaking out in a rash of pinballs (inset above left). Elton entertained his audience with a frenzied knees-up of a stage routine, doing handstands on his grand piano (left).

Goodbye Yellow Brick Road, topped US and UK charts.

Elton John's albums were notable, thenceforth, for their varied content and tone; the double album *Goodbye Yellow Brick Road* featured commercial uptempo numbers like 'Bennie And The Jets' and 'Saturday Night's Alright For Fighting' alongside the uneven, embarrassingly melodramatic 'Funeral For A Friend' and the wistful 'Candle In The Wind', a 'tribute' to Marilyn Monroe. Of the albums that followed, *Captain Fantastic And The Brown Dirt Cowboy* (1975) stood out for its overladen autobiographical concept – a parable about stardom versus the ordinary life – recalling the duo's struggles in their early days, their time spent sharing a basement flat in North London, the 'Tin Pan Alley twins' at Denmark Street, and the bitter self-pity of 'Someone Saved My Life Tonight', documenting Elton's break-up with a fiancée. The album went straight to the top of the US album charts.

Buried within Elton John's albums – and often surrounded by easily forgettable tracks – are a number of minor masterpieces. For every popular toe-tapper like 'Philadelphia Freedom' and 'Island Girl',

> 'I've never been a sex symbol and the clothes I wear have always been to conceal the fact that I'm horribly shy. Look at me; I'm plump, I'm hairy, I've never been part of what they call The Bare Chest Brigade. I'm more "Oh, ain't he lovely? Take 'im home and make 'im a cup of tea!"'
> **Elton John,** 1978

there are songs such as 'Mona Lisas And Mad Hatters' (a picturesque description of life in New York), 'Texas Love Song' (which exudes redneck venom with understated malignancy), and 'Your Sister Can't Twist (But She Can Rock'n'Roll)' (a doowop number with surfing undertones).

Garden gnome
Elton John toured relentlessly during his heyday, having recruited ex-Magna Carta guitarist Davey Johnstone to the line-up in 1972. Elton carried with him several wardrobes full of exotic outfits – jump-suits trimmed with feathers and a reputed £20,000 worth of customised specs, some illuminated, others so large they nearly obscured his whole face. His performances contained all the razzamatazz of Barnum and Bailey: a sequinned dwarf, he was a giant in the glitter era. He attracted huge audiences, breaking attendance records at venues such as the 20,000-seater Madison Square Garden in New York.

Changes came gradually, however. When his hair began to fall out, Elton had a much-publicised transplant and the tinted specs were eventually replaced by contact lenses. Murray and Olsson were replaced and Elton's backing band grew to include six musicians and a trio of back-up

singers. When his contract with Dick James Music expired, he formed his own record label, Rocket Records, in a blaze of publicity. Rocket's first signing, Kiki Dee, had a UK Top Twenty hit in 1973 with 'Amoureuse'. Davey Johnstone's solo album appeared on the label, whose artists included Neil Sedaka, Longdancer and Judie Tzuke, while Elton signed Cliff Richard to Rocket in the US in 1976.

In five years, Elton John made nine albums (one of them a double) and a string of singles ranging from pop rockers like 'Crocodile Rock' and 'Saturday Night's Alright For Fighting' to reflective, sentimental ballads like 'Rocket Man', 'Daniel', 'Goodbye Yellow Brick Road', 'Candle In The Wind' and 'Don't Let The Sun Go Down On Me'. He also produced some excellent hook-lines on such numbers as 'Honky Cat' and 'Bennie And The Jets'. Most of these made the Top Ten on both sides of the Atlantic, 'Crocodile Rock' giving him his first US Number 1 in 1973. In the UK, he had to wait until 1976 before he topped the charts with 'Don't Go Breaking My Heart', a duet with Kiki Dee.

Flights of fancy
Besides pursuing his music and football interests, Elton also ventured into films, making a memorable appearance as the Pinball Wizard in the Who film *Tommy* (1975) to follow his cameo role in Marc Bolan's *Born To Boogie* (1972). His private life mirrored the extravagances of his public image, while the business style of his new manager, Scottish whizz-kid John Reid, ensured that both their bank balances reached well into seven figures. Elton was unashamed of this vast wealth and was determined to enjoy it in a flamboyant way that somehow endeared him to fans and critics alike. His generosity was well-publicised – in 1975 he flew his British office staff and their families to see him on tour in America; the following year he gave two concerts at Earl's Court on behalf of the Sports Aid Foundation.

Elton's home in Bel Air, California, once belonged to Greta Garbo, while his Windsor home, set in 37 acres of woodland, lakes and vineyards, boasted a 100-seat cinema. His fleet of Rolls Royces each has a colour TV and phone, while his private jet has its own bar and piano for in-flight entertainment. Cartier, the New York jewellers, opened on a Sunday on one occasion to let Elton do a little shopping; he spent over £30,000 on gifts for friends. Elton has also demonstrated extravagance in his stage shows. In 1976, he appeared at Madison Square Garden dressed as the Statue of Liberty, while for his 1982 concerts at London's Hammersmith Odeon, he had the venue decorated like a huge gift-wrapped Christmas present, complete with bow, at a cost of £8000. Among Elton's most loyal fans are the Royal Family; in 1981, the performer played at Prince Andrew's 21st birthday party at Windsor Castle.

In 1977, with 14 albums and two hits compilations to his credit, Elton decided

enough was enough. The previous year's album release, the double *Blue Moves*, had been badly received by critics. Wavering between self-doubt, self-pity and self-hatred, it contained a dull mixture of dirge-paced melodies with pretentiously obscure lyrics. Elton decided to split with lyricist Taupin and his other musical allies, cut back on live performances and restrict his output to an album every 18 months – a productivity rate that bordered on stagnation by his previous standards. Elton's other interests began to occupy more of his time, energy and money; he acquired a controlling share in Watford Football Club and, having been elected chairman of the board, devoted his attention to advancing their fortunes.

Rocking Russia

His enthusiasm for life landed him on the front pages of the national newspapers in late 1978; after playing in a football tournament, followed by a gruelling afternoon's tennis with Billie-Jean King, Elton collapsed and was rushed to hospital amid rumours of a heart attack. It turned out he was suffering from severe exhaustion, although this did not dampen his spirits for long. By 1979 he was back on the road again, backed by percussionist Ray Cooper, and played over 100 concerts, including a trip to Moscow and Leningrad.

The album *A Single Man* (1978) had been his first without Taupin and, perhaps significantly, provided Elton with his first instrumental hit single with 'Song For Guy'. It also featured his collaborations with songwriter Gary Osborne for the first time. *Victim Of Love* (1979) was written almost entirely by producer Pete Bellotte; it abandoned ballads and melodies for disco and included a 15-minute version of 'Johnny B. Goode', while the same year Elton released a number of tracks recorded some time earlier with Philadelphia producer Thom Bell. In 1980, he recruited a new line-up that included James Newton-Howard, Richie Zito and Tim Renwick

Top left: Lord Choc Ice checks out his band (from left Davey Johnstone, Nigel Olsson and Dee Murray). Top right: Three of a kind – Elton with his glam-rock buddies Rod Stewart and Gary Glitter. Above: Elton whispers a joke to his chart-topping partner Kiki Dee. Opposite: The singer dons a chic bonnet to woo fashion-conscious fans in Paris in 1979.

alongside Murray and Olsson to play over 40 dates in the US, including an open-air concert in New York's Central Park before an audience of more than 400,000. The same year, at the age of 33, Elton released his 21st album, *21 At 33*.

By the Eighties, Elton John's record sales were beginning to level out and hit singles were becoming thin on the ground. The albums *Jump Up* (1982) and *Too Low*

For Zero (1983) were recorded on the Caribbean island of Montserrat, and the single 'I Guess That's Why They Call It The Blues', released in April 1983, with lyrics by Taupin, featured Stevie Wonder on harmonica. Elton continued to draw the crowds to his live shows, however. Touring Britain for the first time in three years in 1982, he played 42 dates, earning the nickname 'Lord Choc Ice' because of his bizarre Ruritanian general's outfit – and providing the title 'Lord Choc Ice Goes Mental' for the B-side of his 1983 single.

The end of the tour was marred rather by reports of Elton John's temperamental behaviour. On one of the nights at the Hammersmith Odeon, Olsson (apparently suffering from influenza) failed to turn up and Elton complained of poor sound quality. When his piano stool broke, he hurled it aside; it bounced off the stage and hit a girl in the audience. The fan was later taken backstage and given a leather tour jacket, a bottle of champagne and two tickets for the Christmas Eve show as compensation.

In 1983, Elton was still making the headlines – having been presented with a gem-encrusted pair of spectacles at a star-studded Cartier event in Tunisia, Elton dropped his trousers to provide entertainment for the guests. The following year he married recording engineer Renate Blauel in Sydney, Australia.

Elton John became one of the world's most successful recording artists, with in Sydney Australia, but the couple split in late 1988.

Elton had continued in the media spotlight, recording an album a year, 1984's *Breaking Hearts* made Number 2 and the following year's *Ice On Fire* made Number 3 in the UK, but *Leather Jackets* (1986), *Live In Australia* (1987) and *Reg Strikes Back* (1988) did not fare so well. Part of the problem was a vindictive tabloid press campaign which sought to exploit his self-confessed bisexuality; some of the mud was bound to stick.   CHRIS CHARLESWORTH

ELTON JOHN
Discography to 1984

Singles

With Bluesology
Come Back Baby/Times Getting Tougher Than
Tough (Fontana TF 594, 1965); Mr Frantic/Every
Day (I Have The Blues) (Fontana TF 668, 1966);
Since I Found You Baby/Just A Little Bit (Polydor
56195, 1967).

As Elton John
I've Been Loving You/Here's To The Next Time
(Philips BF 1643, 1968); Lady Samantha/All
Across The Heavens (Philips BF 1739, 1969); It's
Me That You Need/Just Like Strange Rain (DJM
DJS 205, 1969); Border Song/Bad Side Of The Moon
(DJM DJS 217, 1970); Rock And Roll Madonna/
Grey Seal (DJM DJS 222, 1970); Your Song/Into
The Old Man's Shoes (DJM DJS 233, 1971);
Friends/Honey Roll (DJM DJS 244, 1971); Rocket
Man/Holiday Inn/Goodbye (DJM DJX 501, 1972);
Honky Cat/Lady Samantha/It's Me That You Need
(DJM DJS 269, 1972); Crocodile Rock/Elderberry
Wine (DJM DJS 271, 1972); Daniel/Skyline Pigeon
(DJM DJS 275, 1973); Saturday Night's Alright
For Fighting/Jack Rabbit/Whenever You're Ready
(We'll Go Steady Again) (DJM DJX 502, 1973);
Goodbye Yellow Brick Road/Screw You (DJM DJS
285, 1973); Step Into Christmas/Ho! Ho! Ho! Who'd
Be A Turkey At Christmas (DJM DJS 290, 1973);
Candle In The Wind/Bennie And The Jets (DJM
DJS 297, 1974); Don't Let The Sun Go Down On
Me/Sick City (DJM DJS 302, 1974); The Bitch Is
Back/Cold Highway (DJM DJS 322, 1974); Lucy In
The Sky With Diamonds/One Day At A Time (DJM
DJS 340, 1974); Philadelphia Freedom/I Saw Her
Standing There (DJM DJS 354, 1975); Someone
Saved My Life Tonight/House Of Cards (DJM DJS
385, 1975); Island Girl/Sugar On The Floor (DJM
DJS 610, 1975); Grow Some Funk Of Your Own/I
Feel Like A Bullet (In The Gun Of Robert Ford)
(DJM DJS 629, 1976); Pinball Wizard/Harmony
(DJM DJS 652, 1976); Don't Go Breaking My
Heart/Snow Queen (With Kiki Dee) (Rocket ROKN
512, 1976); Bennie And The Jets/Rock And Roll
Madonna (DJM DJS 10705, 1976); Sorry Seems To
Be The Hardest Word/Shoulder Holster (Rocket
ROKN 517, 1976); Crazy Winter/Chameleon
(Rocket ROKN 521, 1977); Bite Your Lip (Get Up
And Dance)/Chicago (B-side – Kiki Dee only)
(Rocket ROKN 526, 1977); Ego/Flintstone Boy
(Rocket ROKN 538, 1978); Part Time Love/I Cry At
Night (Rocket XPRES 1, 1978); Song For Guy/
Lovesick (Rocket XPRES 5, 1978); Are You Ready
For Love Part 1/Are You Ready For Love Part 2
(Rocket XPRES 13, 1979); Mama Can't Buy You
Love/Strangers (Rocket XPRES 20, 1979); Victim
Of Love/Strangers (Rocket XPRES 21, 1979);
Johnny B. Goode/Thunder In The Night (Rocket
XPRES 24, 1979); Little Jeannie/Conquer The Sun
(Rocket XPRES 32, 1980); Sartorial Eloquence/
White Man Danger: Cartier (Rocket XPRES 41,
1980); Harmony/Mona Lisas And Mad Hatters
(DJM DJS 10961, 1980); Dear God/Tactics (Rocket
XPRES 45, 1980); I Saw Her Standing There/
Whatever Gets You Through The Night/Lucy In
The Sky With Diamonds (DJM DJS 10965, 1981);
Nobody Wins/Fools In Fashions (Rocket XPRES
54, 1981); Just Like Belgium/Can't Get Over
Losing You (Rocket XPRES 59, 1981); Loving You
Is Sweeter Than Ever/24 Hours (with Kiki Dee)
(Ariola ARO 269, 1981); Blue Eyes/Hey Papa
Legba (Rocket XPRES 71, 1982); Empty Garden/
Take Me Down To The Ocean (Rocket XPRES 77,
1982); Princess/The Retreat (Rocket XPRES 85,
1982); All Quiet On The Western Front/Where
Have All The Good Times Gone? (Rocket XPRES
88, 1982); I Guess That's Why They Call It The
Blues/Choc Ice Goes Mental (Rocket XPRES 91,
1983); I'm Still Standing (EJS1, 1983); Kiss The
Bride (EJS2, 1983); Cold As Christmas/Crystal
(EJS3, 1983); Sad Song (Say So Much) (PH7, 1984);
Passengers (EJS5, 1984); Who Wears These Shoes
(EJS6, 1984); Breaking Hearts (Ain't What It Used
To Be) (EJS7, 1985); Act Of War (With Millie
Jackson) (EJS8, 1985).

Albums

Empty Sky (DJM DJLPS 403, 1969); *Elton John*
(DJM DJLPS 406, 1970); *Tumbleweed Connection*
(DJM DJLPS 410, 1970); *17.11.70* (DJM DJLPS
414, 1971); *Friends* (Paramount SPFL 269, 1971);
Madman Across The Water (DJM DJLPH 420,
1971); *Honky Chateau* (DJM DJLPH 423, 1972);
Don't Shoot Me I'm Only The Piano Player (DJM
DJLPH 427, 1973); *Goodbye Yellow Brick Road*
(DJM DJLPD 1001/2, 1973); *Caribou* (DJM DJLPH
439, 1974); *Greatest Hits* (DJM DJLPH 442, 1974);
Captain Fantastic And The Brown Dirt Cowboy
(DJM DJLPX 1, 1975); *Rock Of The Westies* (DJM
DJLPH 464, 1975); *Here And There* (DJM DJLPH
473, 1976); *Blue Moves* (Rocket ROSP 1, 1976);
Greatest Hits Volume II (DJM DJLPH 20520,
1977); *Candle In The Wind* (St Michael 2094 0102,
1978); *Elton John Live* (Hallmark SHM 942, 1978);
London And New York Live (Hallmark SHM 966,
1978); *A Single Man* (Rocket TRAIN 1, 1978); *The
Elton John Live Collection* (Pickwick PDA 047,
1979); *Victim Of Love* (Rocket HISPD 125, 1979);
21 At 33 (Rocket HISPD 126, 1980); *Lady
Samantha* (DJM 22085, 1980); *The Fox* (Rocket
TRAIN 16, 1981); *The Album* (Hallmark SHM
3088, 1981); *Jump Up* (Rocket HISPD 127, 1982);
Love Songs (TV Records TVA 3, 1982); *Too Low For
Zero* (Rocket HISPD 128, 1983); *Breaking Hearts*
(Rocket HISPD 25, 1984).

INNERVISIONS

*Two faces of a soul superstar: the
Harmonica Man of 1963 (opposite) and the
cornrowed Eighties look (above).*

Sweet sounds and insight from Stevie Wonder

IT IS LIKELY that with modern medical technology Steveland Morris would never have been blind. As it was, on 13 May 1950, too much oxygen found its way into two incubators in a hospital in Saginaw, Michigan; in one a girl died, while in the other the month-premature Stevie survived, but lost his sight.

The mother, Lula Hardaway, had already had two healthy children, Milton and Calvin, and while her youngest son's handicap was unexpected, she did her best to bring him up the same way as his elder brothers. Stevie's father, however, could not accept the burden, and eventually left the family.

As with most blind people, Stevie's other senses compensated for his lack of sight – in particular his hearing. Friendly neighbours would toss coins onto the kitchen table, and those that Stevie correctly guessed he kept. 'I could almost always get it right, except a penny and a nickel confused me.'

By the time he was four, Stevie's family had moved to Detroit in search of a better life. They settled, though, in Breckenridge, on the East side of the city – one of the worse slums – with most of its inhabitants working for the Ford Motor Company and the kids always in trouble. Stevie's interest in music was aroused by listening to radio station WCHB, on which he heard various R&B singers, including Johnny Ace. Other early influences included Little Walter, Jimmy Reed, the Coasters and Nat 'King' Cole.

After enduring all manner of pots and pans being banged all year round, his family found Christmas presents easy to buy for Stevie: toy drums, which, by Boxing Day, were invariably smashed to bits. Eventually a friendly barber gave him a four-holed harmonica on a chain, and an uncle later gave him a Hohner. His musical development was further assisted at the age of seven by two further gifts: a neighbour leaving the West side housing project where the family now lived left him her piano, while the local Lions club gave him a decent set of drums one Christmas.

Kerbside audition
Word of Stevie's talent soon spread further afield. Ron White, a member of Motown's successful group the Miracles, had heard his brother Gerald talk glowingly of the little blind boy, and went to hear him play. Suitably impressed by the multi-talented 11-year-old, White arranged to take him to Motown's studios the next day and introduce him to Brian Holland. As Brian was busy doing a session at the time, Stevie's

Little Stevie Wonder in the shade. Unlike many a child prodigy in rock, Wonder transcended record company hyperbole and public adulation to prove an enduring performer.

'audition' took place on the kerb of Woodward Boulevard.

After founder Berry Gordy had heard Stevie play, the company offered him a contract. As a minor, Stevie was not old enough to negotiate or sign for himself, so an official from the State of Michigan was appointed to make sure his contract guaranteed time for tutoring, that he wouldn't work long hours and that he was protected from the vices associated with the music world.

Little success
Stevie's friendliness, unspoilt nature and energetic love for his craft did not readily convert into healthy record sales: 'I Call It Pretty Music' (with Marvin Gaye on drums), 'Waterboy' (a duet with Clarence Paul) and 'Contract On Love' all failed to sell in quantity, giving Berry Gordy a problem. Motown was still in its infancy and could not subsidise singles failures indefinitely; it was obvious that Gordy needed a new image for his young charge.

Somewhere along the way, Steveland Morris had become Little Stevie Wonder: he wasn't yet in his teens, which accounted for the 'Little', and the staff and producers at Motown had taken to calling him 'the Boy Wonder'. Although there is some dispute as to who finally put the name together, by early June 1963 everyone in the United States knew who Little Stevie Wonder was. Berry Gordy had made his decision – since Stevie's charm transmitted perfectly during live performance, then why not put out a live record? It didn't matter that the song Gordy had chosen, 'Fingertips', was too long; he would simply chop it in half and promote the second side as 'Fingertips Part II'.

This decision proved to be a masterstroke; in barely six weeks, the single was Number 1 in the Hot Hundred (one week after it had topped the R&B charts). The song itself was slight, basically a harmonica-led 12-bar, with a chant-like vocal. But its vitality and infectious enthusiasm was typical of Stevie Wonder's music of the time. Gordy's packaging ideas extended to albums too. Wonder's first album, *Tribute To Uncle Ray* (1963), had been intended to capitalise on the fame of Ray Charles. In the wake of 'Fingertips', the youth aspect was played on in the title of the accompanying album, *Recorded Live – 12 Year Old Genius* (also 1963).

The success of the single made Stevie hot property, and in the next months he toured America to consolidate his position, also making his first visit to Europe. While Berry Gordy would have been happy to have Stevie continue to win over new fans on the road, the Board of Education was not. Although it had ratified his tours to date, it wanted them to be the exception rather than the rule, and requested Stevie to return to school until he graduated in 1968. Despite Gordy's fear that Stevie's career would subsequently lose its momentum (the follow-up single, 'Workout Stevie Workout', reached only Number 33), the

singer was enrolled in the Michigan School for the Blind in Lansing.

The authorities did, however, make one or two concessions; Ted Hull, a Michigan State University graduate was appointed to accompany Stevie when he was on the road in order to ensure that the young singer had four or five lessons a day. Together with producer Clarence Paul and Ardena Johnston, employed by Motown to be a mother figure for Stevie during the six months he was on the road, Ted Hull had to endure Stevie's developing sense of humour. He would deliberately walk into cars, miss a step and fall down the stairs or frighten fellow air passengers, claiming that 'This is judgement day' whenever the plane hit turbulence.

Just after Stevie commenced work on *With A Song In My Heart* (1963), his fourth album in barely five months, his voice began to break. Clarence Paul felt that the best way of helping Stevie through his voice change was to get him singing as much as possible. Ballads proved a problem, but Clarence smoothed over the cracks in Stevie's voice by singing along himself, thereby turning them into duets.

Stevie grows up
Although not a major hit, 'Castles In The Sand' continued to keep Stevie in the spotlight early in 1964; more importantly, it brought him to the attention of the Hollywood film producers. His appearances in *Muscle Beach Party* and *Bikini Beach* (both 1964) were hardly straight acting parts, but stuck in his mind as they brought him to California for the first time, 'Because . . . it is warm enough to grow oranges there and I knew those didn't grow in Detroit.'

'Hey Harmonica Man' was Wonder's only other hit single in 1964 – and the first to be issued without his diminutive prefix – but by the end of the year something far more important for his long-term career was taking place: he was beginning to write songs. Although it would be a couple of years yet before Berry Gordy would allow him to record his own numbers exclusively, there is no doubt that the early collaborations Stevie was working on with Clarence Paul, Hank Cosby and Sylvia Moy were the first fruits of a major talent. Stevie invariably came up with the tune, Sylvia did the lyrics and Hank arranged the song.

From one such afternoon's fun came 'Uptight (Everything's Alright)', the chorus of which derived from one of Wonder's favourite phrases. It reached Number 3 in the Hot Hundred and Number 14 in Britain. This UK chart debut was followed up by a short tour and a number of TV appearances. The hit single had also proved important in his homeland in winning new fans. Fan letters sent to Stevie after 'Uptight' would often be addressed simply to 'Stevie Wonder, Detroit'.

Stevie's next hit was 'Blowin' In The Wind', a Bob Dylan song that had already been a US Number 1 for Peter, Paul and

Mary in 1963, but which had been part of Stevie's live show for over a year. The version released was, in fact, a duet with Clarence Paul; it came about not only because Stevie had enjoyed singing with Clarence when his voice was breaking, but also because Stevie was in the habit of forgetting the words, and needed Clarence to prompt him. That Stevie had even got his way in having 'Blowin' In The Wind' released was remarkable enough, for Motown had hitherto steered clear of protest songs. Stevie's faith in the song was proven by its US Top Ten success.

When it became time for a new contract, Berry Gordy wasted no time in offering Wonder a further five-year pact – and, to his relief, Stevie was just as eager to continue their relationship. The year ended with *Billboard* naming him one of the top singles artists. Wonder was rapidly registering a succession of hit singles in the US charts: 'I Was Made To Love Her' (Number 2, 1967) 'Shoo-Be-Doo-Be-Doo-Da-Day' (Number 9, 1968), 'For Once In My Life' (Number 2, 1968), 'My Cherie Amour' (Number 4, 1969) and 'Yester-Me, Yester-You, Yesterday' (Number 7, 1969) all hit the Top Ten in a little over two years, while a further five singles hit the Hot Hundred.

Team work
The start of the Seventies saw Wonder in harness with some new writing partners – 'Signed, Sealed, Delivered (I'm Yours)', for example, was co-written with his mother Lula, Lee Garrett and Syreeta Wright. Lee had been a friend of Stevie's for a long time, and he, too, was black and blind. Lula was suspicious of Lee at first, as Stevie had suddenly acquired many new 'friends' and Lee's own career as a singer hadn't taken off, but he was eventually accepted.

Syreeta had recorded one unsuccessful single for Motown, and was working as a secretary at the company when Wonder got to know her and invited her along to a writing session. 'Signed, Sealed, Delivered' became one of Stevie's biggest hits, reaching Number 3 in the US and Number 15 in the UK. The same team also wrote 'It's A Shame' for the Motown (later Detroit) Spinners, notching another transatlantic hit as a result. That this was the result of more than a working relationship was confirmed when Stevie and Syreeta married in Detroit on 14 September 1970.

The time was fast approaching when Stevie would have to sign a new, self-negotiated contract, and Berry Gordy therefore chose to grant the singer control over his forthcoming album release. Since Stevie's previous albums hadn't sold in great quantity, there was no album-buying public to disappoint, and even if the project failed it would surely realise at least one hit single. While Stevie and Syreeta began work on *Where I'm Coming From*, Motown released Stevie's cover of the Beatles' 'We Can Work It Out' to keep his name in the public eye.

Where I'm Coming From was released on 12 April 1971, nearly one year after Stevie and Syreeta had begun writing the songs for it. Gordy got his hit single with 'If You Really Love Me', but was not over-impressed with the rest of the album, which dealt variously with ghetto life, on 'Do Yourself A Favor', and the discovery of love in the lyrical 'Something Out Of The Blue'. Not surprisingly, Stevie's view was somewhat different from that of his label: 'People are not interested in "Baby, baby" songs any more. There is more to life than that. I also think that singles are very important but I don't want to do singles only. There are some rock artists who don't want to do singles at all. I don't mind – as long as they come off an album but for me they are generally only one page in the book.'

On Stevie's reaching the age of 21, Berry Gordy and his executives praised him for all he had achieved during his ten years with the company – of the 27 singles Motown had released, eight had gone gold with US sales of one million copies and one was a platinum two-million-seller. One single had reached Number 1 in the Hot Hundred, ten had hit the Top Ten, while no fewer than 25 had figured on the *Billboard* charts. Total record sales exceeded 30 million, and Berry Gordy said he would be more than happy if Stevie would like to continue their relationship further.

All Wonder would sign, however, was a receipt for the one million dollars that the record company held in trust. Telling Motown that he wanted some time to think, he and Syreeta set up home in a New York hotel to work on the music that Stevie had wanted to do for a long time.

Freedom fighter
To handle any future business deals he appointed Johannan Vigoda, a top show-business lawyer who had previously worked with Jimi Hendrix and Richie Havens. To help him make his music, he brought in Robert Margouleff and Malcolm Cecil, electronic keyboards pioneers who had recorded as Tonto's Expanding Headband. They were to spend many hours at Electric Lady studios acquainting Wonder with the Arp and Moog synthesisers that he wanted to use on his next album. Once Stevie felt happy with what he had learned, he and Syreeta began writing the songs.

After nearly 100 songs had been recorded, Wonder was ready to talk to Motown again. The contract worked out between Stevie, Motown and Vigoda ran to a rumoured 120 pages. However, it was the content that was infinitely more important than the quantity – Stevie got the long sought-after artistic freedom to decide what tracks would go on an album, which would be released as singles, when he would go on tour, and who his support bands would be. He also formed his own publishing company, Black Bull, and production company, Taurus Productions (named after his birth sign), and his own backing group, Wonderlove.

Mind-blowing music
On 3 March 1972 Motown released *Music Of My Mind*, the album that first fulfilled Stevie's ambition to be taken seriously as an artist. In the years to come, Motown was to reap colossal reward from allowing both Stevie and Marvin Gaye the freedom to exploit the album market. (Indeed, Gaye's *What's Going On*, had just been released with scant promotion, yet was to become one of black music's biggest-selling albums.)

Music Of My Mind represented a tremendous advance on its predecessor, with breathtaking electronic keyboard textures on tracks like 'Love Having You Around' announcing that Wonder had mastered the Seventies technology he had taken such trouble to master. Sadly, its release coincided with Stevie and Syreeta's breakup, his need for a traditional marriage being at odds with her personal and musical ambitions.

By the time 1972 came, Stevie was ready to release a new album. He chose to promote the record by supporting the Rolling Stones on their mammoth US tour, and the Stones fans loved the 'new' Stevie they were hearing: *Talking Book* was to prove his finest release up to that time. It showed that Stevie's new music depended as much on white audience support as it did on his traditional black support. Wonder's image, too, was changing: gone were the jackets and crew-cut, discarded in favour of colourful African robes and beaded hairstyle.

Talking Book gave Wonder his first platinum album – and deservedly so. Jeff Beck's guitar-playing added rock credibility, while the album also included the political comment of 'Big Brother', with its lyrics clearly aimed at Richard Nixon. The album's breadth of material pleased rock and soul fans alike. The hard rhythms and funky Clavinet of 'Superstition' contrasted with the easy-listening charm of 'You Are The Sunshine Of My Life', and both songs made Number 1 in the Hot Hundred when released as singles.

Stevie's next project, for which he had set a release date of March 1973, was originally titled *Last Days Of Easter*. In his own words, it was 'about the last day of beauty. All the horror and hypocrisy in the world today. People neglecting other people's problems. And what needs doing socially, spiritually and domestically. I can only do it through my songs and I try to be positive about it.'

When the album finally appeared in August 1973, it had been re-titled *Innervisions*. Motown had previewed the album with the single 'Higher Ground', one of several tracks with a spiritual aspect. Some of Wonder's best lyrics appeared on the album, 'Visions' in particular containing visual imagery astonishing for a blind man. The album's *tour de force* was 'Living For The City', a cautionary tale of a boy from 'hard-time Mississippi' who comes to New York and is unwittingly caught up in crime and violence.

On 6 August, just three days after the

'I want to reach the people. I feel there is so much through music that can be said, and there's so many people you can reach by listening to another kind of music. That's why I hate labels where they say "This Is Stevie Wonder And For The Rest Of His Life He Will Sing 'Fingertips' . . ."'
Stevie Wonder

album had been released, Stevie was a passenger in a car bound for Durham, South Carolina, when it was involved in a smash. He was rushed to hospital in a coma, remaining unconscious for some five days; many papers had already pronounced him dead, while rumour had it that, even if he survived, he had suffered lasting damage. Eventually the hospital was able to ascertain that Stevie would not suffer any permanent brain damage, and the long haul back to recovery could begin.

After two weeks in North Carolina, Motown had him moved to Los Angeles, which was considered 'closer to home', but Stevie felt alienated in LA. Still, Motown had shown good intentions, and Stevie was far more concerned with whether his musical ability had been impaired. Eventually, personal aide Ira Tucker had a Clavinet brought into Stevie's room, and it soon became apparent that all was well with the singer.

Finales and encores

Stevie made a speedy recovery from his accident, and in late September made his first public appearance on stage with Elton John during the latter's concert date in Boston. His doctors had advised against any major concerts at least until the end of the year, so Stevie was free to write songs for his next album, *Fullfillingness' First Finale*. Motown in the meantime released 'Living For The City' as a single, and it sailed into the US Top Ten.

By January 1974 Stevie had recovered enough to go back on the road. On 20 January he opened the first gala at the Midem Convention in Cannes, and then went to London to play the Rainbow Theatre. He then returned to the US to collect five Grammy awards.

At the end of March, Stevie Wonder announced that he was retiring. He intended to tour North America extensively for two years, raising money for charity, embark on a Farewell World Tour at the end of 1975, and then move to Africa to work with handicapped, blind and underprivileged children. Motown were able to convince him that he would better be able to help Africa by staying in America gaining publicity for those causes. So Stevie stayed, and in July 1974 gave Motown *Fullfillingness' First Finale* which, by the end of the year, had become his third platinum album. 'Boogie On Reggae Woman' reached Number 3 when released as a single, while the anti-Nixon sentiments of 'You Haven't Done Nothin'' took it to the top of the US charts.

While plans for an album and (abortive) world tour were mooted, Wonder cashed in

Stevie Wonder shares the spotlight with Motown chief Berry Gordy (top right), his mother and sometime co-writer Lula Hardaway (above right) and labelmate Lionel Richie (right). Left: Although better-known as a keyboardist, Stevie proved an influential drummer on his Seventies albums and, on occasion, in concert.

on past achievements by picking up another five Grammies in March 1975. A month later his girlfriend Yolanda Simmons gave birth to a baby daughter, Aisha. Stevie had met Yolanda when she had called Black Bull enquiring about a secretarial job; as Stevie was in the office he had answered the call and, liking the sound of her voice had invited her in. The birth of a son, Keita Sawandi, on 16 April 1977, confirmed Stevie and Yolanda's commitment to each other despite the shelving of marriage plans.

In spite of the signing of a seven-year contract worth 13 million dollars in August – reputedly the biggest of any recording artist – the chance of Stevie's new album, now entitled *Let's See Life The Way It Is* and scheduled as a double album, appearing that year were rapidly fading. Release dates of September 1975 and January 1976 passed and speculation mounted. All anyone now knew for certain was that the title had again changed; it would now be called *Songs In The Key Of Life*.

The collection of songs finally selected for release in early October fully merited a double album; four more were squeezed onto an accompanying EP. The highlights were many – 'Sir Duke' paid joyous homage to jazzman Duke Ellington and 'Isn't She Lovely' was dedicated to Stevie's daughter, while the haunting melody of 'Pastime Paradise' highlighted the sensitive side of Stevie's writing. *Songs In The Key Of Life*'s appearance just qualified it for inclusion in the Grammy Award nominations for that year. Some six months previously, Paul Simon had collected the Grammy Award for album of the year and had publicly thanked Stevie for not releasing an album in 1975. In 1976, Wonder was back with a vengeance; he picked up eight nominations and subsequently collected four awards which included Album of the Year.

Celluloid collaborations

The wait for Stevie's next project was to prove even longer, taking three years. Some time before the release of *Songs*, he was approached by two authors, Peter Tompkins and Christopher Bird, whose book, *The Secret Life Of Plants*, had just been published. They were working on a film version of the book, to be produced by Michael Braun, and wondered whether Wonder would be interested in scoring the music. After much thought, Stevie announced that he would begin work on it as soon as *Songs* was released.

Wonder's sightlessness meant that the very process of scoring a film was to take longer than any other project with which he had been involved. Each scene and each frame had to be carefully explained to him, while the special effects were even more complex – he taped the sounds at an airport, the sounds at a wildlife park, and the sound of waves breaking on a shore. The problematical film was never generally released, but since the project had eaten up

three years of Stevie's life, it was too late to abandon the album.

Reaction to the double LP released in October 1979 was poor. Pre-sale demand ensured that the album made Top Ten around the world, but it quickly slipped down the charts again, while three singles failed to halt the slide. Few reviewers had seen the film, and most therefore had nothing to relate the album to; nevertheless, *Journey Through The Secret Life Of Plants* undoubtedly contained some of Stevie's finest melodies.

Whatever Wonder's thoughts about his artistic credibility after *Secret Life Of Plants*, he realised that his commercial standing had taken a severe jolt, and wasted no time in launching a new album to remedy matters. It was soon evident that *Secret Life Of Plants* had had no adverse effect on his drawing power as a live performer – six nights at London's Wembley Arena in September 1980 sold out within days. Wonder chose the UK appearances to preview his new album,

Above: A friendly word of advice from Wonder to Beatle Paul McCartney in the late Sixties. The duo recorded a worldwide hit in 1982 with 'Ebony And Ivory'. Below: On stage in Paris, 1981. Opposite: Songs in the key of Stevie.

Hotter Than July, and the public acclaim that followed proved that *Secret Life Of Plants* had been no more than a slight hiccup in his career.

No fewer than four singles, each in widely differing styles, hit the UK Top Ten – a tribute to Bob Marley in 'Masterblaster (Jammin')', the country-flavoured 'I Ain't Gonna Stand For It', the classic ballad 'Lately' and 'Happy Birthday'. The last track paid tribute to the assassinated Civil Rights leader Martin Luther King, whose 15 January birthday Wonder campaigned to make a national holiday.

For his next project, Stevie felt it was time for a retrospective of his career. He had forbidden Motown to release their 1974 *Anthology*, but had relented three years later. *Original Musiquarium I* covered 1972 to 1982, together with a side of new material. In 1984, Stevie did the soundtrack for the film *The Woman In Red* and had a UK Number 1 hit single with 'I Just Called To Say I Love You'.

The track, from the film *The Woman In Red,* hit the top in the US, too—as did his next effort, 'Part Time Lover', from 1985's *In Square Circle.* The pace then slowed somewhat until the late 1987 release of *Characters,* although he had made cameo appearances on record with the likes of Cliff Richard, Michael Jackson, Julio Iglesias and the Eurythmics.

GRAHAM BETTS

STEVIE WONDER
Discography to 1984

Singles

I Call It Pretty Music (But The Old People Call It The Blues) Part 1/Part 2 (Tamla 54061, 1962); Little Water Boy/La La La La La (Tamla 54070, 1962); Contract On Love/Sunset (Tamla 54074, 1962); Fingertips Pt 2/Pt 1 (Tamla 54080, 1963); Workout, Stevie, Workout/Monkey Talk (Tamla 54086, 1963); Castles In The Sand/Thank You For Loving Me (All The Way) (Tamla 54090, 1964); Hey Harmonica Man/This Little Girl (Tamla 54096, 1964); Happy Street/Sad Boy (Tamla 54103, 1964); Kiss Me Baby/Tears In Vain (Tamla 54114, 1965); High Heel Sneakers/Music Talk (Tamla 54119, 1965); Uptight (Everything's Alright)/Purple Raindrops (Tamla 54124, 1965); Nothing's Too Good For My Baby/With A Child's Heart (Tamla 54130, 1966); Blowin' In The Wind/Ain't That Asking For Trouble (Tamla 54136, 1966); A Place In The Sun/Sylvia (Tamla 54139, 1966); Someday At Christmas/The Miracles Of Christmas (Tamla 54142, 1966); Travelin' Man/Hey Love (Tamla 54147, 1967); I Was Made To Love Her/Hold Me (Tamla 54151, 1967); I'm Wondering/Every Time I See You I Go Wild (Tamla 54157, 1967); Shoo-Be-Doo-Be-Doo-Da-Day/Why Don't You Lead Me To Love (Tamla 54165, 1968); You Met Your Match/My Girl (Tamla 54168, 1967); Alfie/More Than A Dream (Gordy 7076, 1968); For Once In My Life/Angie Girl (Tamla 54174, 1968); I Don't Know Why I Love You/My Cherie Amour (Tamla 54180, 1969); Yester-Me, Yester-You, Yesterday/I'd Be A Fool Right Now (Tamla 54188, 1969); Never Had A Dream Come True/Somebody Knows (Somebody Cares) (Tamla 54191, 1970); Signed, Sealed, Delivered/I'm More Than Happy (I'm Satisfied) (Tamla 54196, 1970); Heaven Help Us All/I Gotta Have A Song (Tamla 54200, 1970); We Can Work It Out/Never Dreamed You'd Leave In Summer (Tamla 54202, 1971); If You Really Love Me/Think Of Me As Your Soldier (Tamla 54208, 1971); What Christmas Means To Me/Bedtime For Toys (Tamla 54214, 1971); Superwoman/I Love Everything About You (Tamla 54216, 1972); Keep On Running/Evil (Tamla 54223, 1972); Superstition/You've Got It Bad Girl (Tamla 54226, 1972); You Are The Sunshine Of My Life/Tuesday Heartbreak (Tamla 54232, 1973); Higher Ground/ Too High (Tamla 54235, 1973); Living For The City/Visions (Tamla 54242, 1973); Don't You Worry 'Bout A Thing/Blame It On The Sun (Tamla 54245, 1974); You Haven't Done Nothing/Big Brother (Tamla 54252, 1974); Boogie On Reggae Woman/Seems So Long (Tamla 54254, 1974); I Wish/You And I (Tamla 54274, 1976); Sir Duke/ He's Misstra Know It All (Tamla 54280, 1977); Another Star/Creepin' (Tamla 54286, 1977); As/ Contusion (Tamla 54291, 1977); Send One Your Love/Instrumental (Tamla 54303, 1979); Outside My Window/Same Old Story (Tamla 54308, 1980); Master Blaster (Jammin')/Dub (Tamla 54317, 1980); I Ain't Gonna Stand For It/Knocks Me Off My Feet (Tamla 54320, 1980); Lately/If It's Magic (Tamla 54323, 1981); Did I Hear You Say You Love Me/As If You Read My Mind (Tamla 54328, 1981); That Girl/All I Do (Tamla 1602, 1981); Do I Do/ Rocket Love (Tamla 1612, 1982); Ribbon In The Sky/Black Orchid (Tamla 1639, 1982); Used To Be (with Charlene)/(B-side – Charlene solo) (Motown 1650, 1982); I Just Called To Say I Love You (TMG 1349, 1984); Love Light In Flight (TMG 1364, 1984); Don't Drive Drunk (TMG 1372, 1984).

Albums

The Jazz Soul Of Little Stevie (Tamla 233, 1963); *Tribute To Uncle Ray* (Tamla 323, 1963); *Recorded Live – 12 Year Old Genius* (Tamla 240, 1963); *With A Song In My Heart* (Tamla 250, 1963); *Stevie At The Beach* (Tamla 255, 1964); *Uptight* (Tamla 268, 1966); *Down To Earth* (Tamla 272, 1966); *I Was Made To Love Her* (Tamla 279, 1967); *Someday At Christmas* (Tamla 281, 1967); *Greatest Hits* (Tamla 282, 1968); *For Once In My Life* (Tamla 291, 1968); *Eivets Rednow* (Gordy 932, 1968); *My Cherie Amour* (Tamla 296, 1969); *Live!* (Tamla 298, 1970); *Signed, Sealed, Delivered* (Tamla 304, 1970); *Where I'm Coming From* (Tamla 308, 1971); *Greatest Hits Vol 2* (Tamla 313, 1971); *Music Of My Mind* (Tamla 314, 1972); *Talking Book* (Tamla 319, 1972); *Innervisions* (Tamla 326, 1972); *Fulfillingness' First Finale* (Tamla 332, 1974); *Songs In The Key Of Life* (Tamla 340, 1976); *Anthology* (Motown M9-804A3, 1977); *Journey Through The Secret Life Of Plants* (Tamla 371, 1979); *Hotter Than July* (Tamla 373, 1980); *Stevie Wonder's Original Musiquarium I* (Tamla 6002, 1982); *The Woman In Red* (Motown ZL72285, 1984).

Fame & Fortune

How rock stars save and squander their royalties

SINCE THE EARLY Sixties the earning power of top rock musicians has been considerable, with many amassing large fortunes. Those at the top of the popular entertainment pyramid have always been richly rewarded; the rock millionaires of the Sixties and Seventies can be seen as the modern-day equivalents of the film stars of the Twenties.

There is a clear distinction between the way money has been handled by artists in the US and by their British counterparts; this in turn reflects crucial differences in attitude towards the acquisition of wealth in their respective countries. In the US, rock stars tend to surround themselves not only with a manager and a legal adviser, but also a financial adviser who assiduously looks after their financial interests.

Their money is frequently invested on their behalf, the interest alone enabling them, if they so wish, to retire to a lifestyle of considerable luxury.

In the US, financial investments are rarely scrutinised by the media; people thus feel more comfortable using large sums of money and living off the proceeds than in Britain. Michael Jackson was reputed in the early Eighties to be personally worth 35 million dollars, yet what he was doing with a sum of such vast proportions was not made public knowledge. In like manner, American-based groups like Fleetwood Mac, the Eagles and Boston have all reaped rich rewards, yet virtually nothing is known about what they do with their money.

Guilt-edged wealth

Things are very different in the UK, largely because of the country's existing social structure. In the first place, working-class people (and many rock stars have come from such a background) have difficulty escaping feelings of guilt at having rapidly acquired considerable sums of money. Consequently, there is a tendency for them to be extravagant in its use. In addition, they are naturally unsure of how to dispose of their new-found wealth. The country's best financial brains are unlikely to come to their assistance in this; city financiers have always found the music scene to be irredeemably vulgar and have remained aloof from most aspects of it. Prominent UK rock stars thus frequently have to rely for advice on second-rate accountants. Those who do demonstrate an ability to handle their money without fuss, feelings of guilt or unwelcome publicity tend to be those who have had middle-class upbringings – the Rolling Stones' Mick Jagger being an obvious example.

In the matter of wealthy rock stars trying to become entrepreneurs, the Beatles were innovators. In 1967 they began by opening their own Apple boutique in Baker Street, London. This venture proved unsuccessful, however: the shop closed within eight months and the stock was given away to passers-by.

The group subsequently set up their own multi-media arts company, also called Apple. This was started more or less as a tax loss, although tax was not all that was lost. The biggest fortune that any rock group had at that time amassed was virtually squandered through chronically bad management – in one sense the whole enterprise was simply an illustration of how the Beatles set about expunging their guilt feelings at having acquired so much money. Electronics, films and publishing divisions had been visualised for Apple, but none was ever seriously inaugurated.

The Apple recording company was a slightly different matter, because that benefited from the Beatles' own recordings. One of the group's primary aims had been to discover and foster new talent, but this was only fitfully achieved. Paul McCartney acquired his own protégés in

Opposite above: Abba in the boardroom. Opposite: Lol Creme and Kevin Godley in the video directors' chairs. Above: Paul and Linda at a Buddy Holly party.

Mary Hopkin and Badfinger, and George Harrison had his in Billy Preston and the Radha Krishna Temple; however, the massive potential of the company was far from realised. With considerable perception, the Beatles had installed Peter Asher as head of A&R, but he was frustrated by the organisational chaos surrounding him. Had he been able to finish the job, there is little doubt that Apple would have become a major company. Even in the short time he was there, he discovered James Taylor, who later joined Warner Brothers and became one of the top-selling acts of the early Seventies.

Any other UK rock stars would have been bankrupted by such inefficiency; the Beatles, however, had reached a position of such pre-eminence that they were able to earn fresh millions to replace those lost. It is noticeable that they did not make the same mistakes twice; three of the four group members have used their money to achieve major investment coups.

Paul's Buddy

McCartney invested in song-publishing so successfully that he became one of the world's most prominent song-publishers. He purchased the entire Buddy Holly catalogue, as well as the rights to musicals such as *Grease, Annie* and *A Chorus Line*. It is a masterstroke of irony that the world's most successful song composer

could, if he so wished, live comfortably off other people's royalties.

Harrison began HandMade films in 1978 when EMI withdrew its money from *Monty Python's Life Of Brian* (1979). He agreed to finance the movie, and thus one of the UK's most successful film production companies was born. Subsequent successes have included the distribution of *The Long Good Friday* (1980), and the production of films by individual members of the Python team – Terry Gilliam's *Time Bandits* (1981) and Michael Palin's *The Missionary* (1982).

John Lennon's fortune was adroitly managed for him in the last years of his life by Yoko Ono who invested in real estate and, strangely, in dairy cattle – with spectacular results. Ringo Starr was the only one of the four not to have used his fortune as the rock on which to build another one, although he was involved in a cable consortium bidding for a franchise in Liverpool in the early Eighties.

Rock stars who sought to become entrepreneurs in their own right have frequently stuck to their own field of activity and several have tried to establish their own record label. Such labels were customarily launched with the best of philanthropic intentions, but either rapidly failed or, if moderately successful, became indistinguishable from the very companies to which they had originally sought to provide a viable alternative. The Moody Blues began Threshold, Melanie had Neighborhood, Elton John got Rocket under way and the Rolling Stones acquired their own custom label. None developed properly as an active company, although Elton John should at least be given credit for perseverance.

A number of acts have invested in recording studios – with considerably more success. The Rolling Stones mobile, for example, became very popular with other artists at one time. Pete Townshend's Eel Pie studios have remained in use, as have 10cc's Strawberry Studios in Stockport. Elsewhere in the field of the arts, Townshend started his own bookshop, Magic Bus, in Richmond, and publishing company, also called Eel Pie, although neither venture survived for long. Jimmy Page also opened his own bookshop – specialising in the occult – in West London and the Moody Blues went into the retail business, opening two Threshold record shops in Birmingham and Cobham.

More ambitious artists have decided to risk money in film and video; Kevin Godley and Lol Creme, once of 10cc, enjoyed particular success through being in at the start of the video revolution. McCartney has provided money for his wife, Linda, to make short films, and has financed two full-length ones of his own – *Rockshow* (1980) and *Give My Regards To Broad Street*, in production in 1983 – while Pink Floyd put up much of the capital for their film, *The Wall* (1982). The Who's own company produced *The Kids Are Alright* (1979) and *McVicar* (1980). On the whole, UK artists have enjoyed reasonable returns from film investment. Certainly, none has suffered the chastening experience of Robbie Robertson of The Band, who underwrote *Carny* (1980) with much of his own money. The film fared disastrously at the box-office.

Footing the bill

The subject that apparently interests most UK rock stars, after music itself, is soccer. Elton John led the way by becoming chairman of Watford, and the club has been transformed under his enthusiastic patronage. His involvement could hardly be termed a business investment, however: accounts have revealed that Watford's achievements have been largely due to the superstar's loan of over £1.2 million.

Other rock stars who have dabbled in the sport include Rick Wakeman, who joined the board of Brentford FC. Both he and Mick Jagger were also part of a group which owned the Philadelphia club in the North American soccer league.

The most notorious instances of commercial ill-fortune have concerned Abba and Pink Floyd. The Swedes' reputation for shrewd business management was blemished when a cargo of crude oil which they owned lost most of its value (about £2 million) after a sudden fall in the spot market price, while Pink Floyd lost substantial sums when Norton Warburg, the investment trust which had handled their income throughout the Seventies, went into liquidation.

Many rock stars have spent lavishly – and some have almost relished contriving their own financial ruin, largely because that was the only way they could come to terms with their wealth. Extrovert personalities like P. J. Proby and Gary Glitter, for example, have found it necessary to file for bankruptcy. In the US, Willie Nelson has been forthright about his own attitude to money: 'I hope that when I die I owe a million. That's my goal. That may be what an outlaw is – to go out owing a million. That's the only way to beat the system.'

His views, however fiercely held, are eccentric in an American context, where rock stars who acquire wealth do not feel at all abashed by it. The words are, however, more typical of attitudes in the UK, where few make money without simultaneously acquiring complex personality traits which leave them ill-equipped to deal with it.   BOB WOFFINDEN

Elton John, the wealthy chairman of Watford FC, with his squad.

INDEX

U.S. HIT SINGLES

1976

JANUARY

3 SATURDAY NIGHT *Bay City Rollers*
10 CONVOY *CW McCall*
17 I WRITE THE SONGS *Barry Manilow*
24 THEME FROM MAHOGANY *Diana Ross*
31 LOVE ROLLERCOASTER *Ohio Players*

FEBRUARY

7 50 WAYS TO LEAVE YOUR LOVER *Paul Simon*
14 50 WAYS TO LEAVE YOUR LOVER *Paul Simon*
21 50 WAYS TO LEAVE YOUR LOVER *Paul Simon*
28 THEME FROM S.W.A.T. *Rhythm Heritage*

MARCH

6 LOVE MACHINE PT. 1 *Miracles*
13 DECEMBER, '63 (OH, WHAT A NIGHT) *Four Seasons*
20 DECEMBER, '63 (OH, WHAT A NIGHT) *Four Seasons*
27 DECEMBER, '63 (OH, WHAT A NIGHT) *Four Seasons*

APRIL

3 DISCO LADY *Johnny Taylor*
10 DISCO LADY *Johnny Taylor*
17 DISCO LADY *Johnny Taylor*
24 DISCO LADY *Johnny Taylor*

MAY

1 LET YOUR LOVE FLOW *Bellamy Brothers*
8 WELCOME BACK *John Sebastian*
15 BOOGIE FEVER *Sylvers*
22 SILLY LOVE SONGS *Wings*
29 LOVE HANGOVER *Diana Ross*

JUNE

5 LOVE HANGOVER *Diana Ross*
12 SILLY LOVE SONGS *Wings*
19 SILLY LOVE SONGS *Wings*
26 SILLY LOVE SONGS *Wings*

JULY

3 SILLY LOVE SONGS *Wings*
10 AFTERNOON DELIGHT *Starland Vocal Band*
17 AFTERNOON DELIGHT *Starland Vocal Band*
24 KISS AND SAY GOODBYE *Manhattans*
31 KISS AND SAY GOODBYE *Manhattans*

AUGUST

7 DON'T GO BREAKING MY HEART
  Elton John and Kiki Dee
14 DON'T GO BREAKING MY HEART
  Elton John and Kiki Dee
21 DON'T GO BREAKING MY HEART
  Elton John and Kiki Dee
28 DON'T GO BREAKING MY HEART
  Elton John and Kiki Dee

SEPTEMBER

4 YOU SHOULD BE DANCING *Bee Gees*
11 (SHAKE, SHAKE, SHAKE) SHAKE YOUR BOOTY
  KC and the Sunshine Band
18 PLAY THAT FUNKY MUSIC *Wild Cherry*
25 PLAY THAT FUNKY MUSIC *Wild Cherry*

OCTOBER

2 PLAY THAT FUNKY MUSIC *Wild Cherry*
9 A FIFTH OF BEETHOVEN
  Walter Murphy/The Big Apple Band
16 DISCO DUCK (PART 1) *Rick Dees and His Cast of Idiot*
23 IF YOU LEAVE ME NOW *Chicago*
30 IF YOU LEAVE ME NOW *Chicago*

NOVEMBER

6 ROCK N' ME *Steve Miller*
13 TONIGHT'S THE NIGHT (GONNA BE ALRIGHT)
  Rod Stewart
20 TONIGHT'S THE NIGHT (GONNA BE ALRIGHT)
  Rod Stewart
27 TONIGHT'S THE NIGHT (GONNA BE ALRIGHT)
  Rod Stewart

DECEMBER

4 TONIGHT'S THE NIGHT (GONNA BE ALRIGHT)
  Rod Stewart
11 TONIGHT'S THE NIGHT (GONNA BE ALRIGHT)
  Rod Stewart
18 TONIGHT'S THE NIGHT (GONNA BE ALRIGHT)
  Rod Stewart
25 TONIGHT'S THE NIGHT (GONNA BE ALRIGHT)
  Rod Stewart

1977

JANUARY

1 TONIGHT'S THE NIGHT (GONNA BE ALRIGHT)
   Rod Stewart
8 YOU DON'T HAVE TO BE A STAR
   Marilyn McCoo/Billy Davis Jr
15 YOU MAKE ME FEEL LIKE DANCING   *Leo Sayer*
22 I WISH   *Stevie Wonder*
29 CAR WASH   *Rose Royce*

FEBRUARY

5 TORN BETWEEN TWO LOVERS   *Mary MacGregor*
12 TORN BETWEEN TWO LOVERS   *Mary MacGregor*
19 BLINDED BY THE NIGHT   *Manfred Mann's Earth Band*
26 NEW KID IN TOWN   *Eagles*

MARCH

5 LOVE THEME FROM *A STAR IS BORN*   Barbra Streisand
12 LOVE THEME FROM *A STAR IS BORN*   Barbra Streisand
19 LOVE THEME FROM *A STAR IS BORN*   Barbra Streisand
26 RICH GIRL   *Darryl Hall and John Oates*

APRIL

2 RICH GIRL   *Darryl Hall and John Oates*
9 DANCING QUEEN   *Abba*
16 DON'T GIVE UP ON US   *David Soul*
23 DON'T LEAVE ME THIS WAY   *Thelma Houston*
30 SOUTHERN NIGHTS   *Glen Campbell*

MAY

7 HOTEL CALIFORNIA   *Eagles*
14 WHEN I NEED YOU   *Leo Sayer*
21 SIR DUKE   *Stevie Wonder*
28 SIR DUKE   *Stevie Wonder*

JUNE

4 SIR DUKE   *Stevie Wonder*
11 I'M YOUR BOOGIE MAN   *KC and the Sunshine Band*
18 DREAMS   *Fleetwood Mac*
25 GOT TO GIVE IT UP, PART 1   *Marvin Gaye*

JULY

2 GONNA FLY NOW (THEME FROM *ROCKY*)   *Bill Conti*
9 UNDERCOVER ANGEL   *Alan O'Day*
16 DA DOO RON RON   *Shaun Cassidy*
23 LOOKS LIKE WE MADE IT   *Barry Manilow*
30 I JUST WANT TO BE YOUR EVERYTHING   *Andy Gibb*

AUGUST

6 I JUST WANT TO BE YOUR EVERYTHING   *Andy Gibb*
13 I JUST WANT TO BE YOUR EVERYTHING   *Andy Gibb*
20 BEST OF MY LOVE   *Emotions*
27 BEST OF MY LOVE   *Emotions*

SEPTEMBER

3 BEST OF MY LOVE   *Emotions*
10 BEST OF MY LOVE   *Emotions*
17 I JUST WANT TO BE YOUR EVERYTHING   *Andy Gibb*
24 BEST OF MY LOVE   *Emotions*

OCTOBER

1 STAR WARS THEME/CANTINA BAND   *Meco*
8 STAR WARS THEME/CANTINA BAND   *Meco*
15 YOU LIGHT UP MY LIFE   *Debby Boone*
22 YOU LIGHT UP MY LIFE   *Debby Boone*
29 YOU LIGHT UP MY LIFE   *Debby Boone*

NOVEMBER

5 YOU LIGHT UP MY LIFE   *Debby Boone*
12 YOU LIGHT UP MY LIFE   *Debby Boone*
19 YOU LIGHT UP MY LIFE   *Debby Boone*
26 YOU LIGHT UP MY LIFE   *Debby Boone*

DECEMBER

3 YOU LIGHT UP MY LIFE   *Debby Boone*
10 YOU LIGHT UP MY LIFE   *Debby Boone*
17 YOU LIGHT UP MY LIFE   *Debby Boone*
24 HOW DEEP IS YOUR LOVE   *Bee Gees*
31 HOW DEEP IS YOUR LOVE   *Bee Gees*

U.K. HIT SINGLES

1976

JANUARY

3 BOHEMIAN RHAPSODY *Queen*
10 BOHEMIAN RHAPSODY *Queen*
17 BOHEMIAN RHAPSODY *Queen*
24 BOHEMIAN RHAPSODY *Queen*
31 MAMMA MIA *Abba*

FEBRUARY

7 MAMMA MIA *Abba*
14 FOREVER AND EVER *Silk*
21 DECEMBER, '63 (OH, WHAT A NIGHT)
   Four Seasons
28 DECEMBER, '63 (OH, WHAT A NIGHT)
   Four Seasons

MARCH

6 I LOVE TO LOVE *Tina Charles*
13 I LOVE TO LOVE *Tina Charles*
20 I LOVE TO LOVE *Tina Charles*
27 SAVE YOUR KISSES FOR ME
   Brotherhood of Man

APRIL

3 SAVE YOUR KISSES FOR ME
   Brotherhood of Man
10 SAVE YOUR KISSES FOR ME
   Brotherhood of Man
17 SAVE YOUR KISSES FOR ME
   Brotherhood of Man
24 SAVE YOUR KISSES FOR ME
   Brotherhood of Man

MAY

1 SAVE YOUR KISSES FOR ME
   Brotherhood of Man
8 FERNANDO *Abba*
15 FERNANDO *Abba*
22 FERNANDO *Abba*
29 FERNANDO *Abba*

JUNE

5 NO CHARGE *JJ Barrie*
12 COMBINE HARVESTER *Wurzels*
19 COMBINE HARVESTER *Wurzels*
26 YOU TO ME ARE EVERYTHING *Real Thing*

JULY

3 YOU TO ME ARE EVERYTHING *Real Thing*
10 YOU TO ME ARE EVERYTHING *Real Thing*
17 THE ROUSSOS PHENOMENON (EP)
   Demis Roussos

24 DON'T GO BREAKING MY HEART
   Elton John and Kiki Dee
31 DON'T GO BREAKING MY HEART
   Elton John and Kiki Dee

AUGUST

7 DON'T GO BREAKING MY HEART
   Elton John and Kiki Dee
14 DON'T GO BREAKING MY HEART
   Elton John and Kiki Dee
21 DON'T GO BREAKING MY HEART
   Elton John and Kiki Dee
28 DON'T GO BREAKING MY HEART
   Elton John and Kiki Dee

SEPTEMBER

4 DANCING QUEEN *Abba*
11 DANCING QUEEN *Abba*
18 DANCING QUEEN *Abba*
25 DANCING QUEEN *Abba*

VOLUME 14/15

OCTOBER

2 DANCING QUEEN *Abba*
9 DANCING QUEEN *Abba*
16 MISSISSIPPI *Pussycat*
23 MISSISSIPPI *Pussycat*
30 MISSISSIPPI *Pussycat*

NOVEMBER

6 MISSISSIPPI *Pussycat*
13 IF YOU LEAVE ME NOW *Chicago*
20 IF YOU LEAVE ME NOW *Chicago*
27 IF YOU LEAVE ME NOW *Chicago*

DECEMBER

4 UNDER THE MOON OF LOVE
   Showaddywaddy
11 UNDER THE MOON OF LOVE
   Showaddywaddy
18 UNDER THE MOON OF LOVE
   Showaddywaddy
25 WHEN A CHILD IS BORN *Johnny Mathis*

1977

JANUARY

1	WHEN A CHILD IS BORN	*Johnny Mathis*
8	WHEN A CHILD IS BORN	*Johnny Mathis*
15	DON'T GIVE UP ON US	*David Soul*
22	DON'T GIVE UP ON US	*David Soul*
29	DON'T GIVE UP ON US	*David Soul*

FEBRUARY

5	DON'T GIVE UP ON US	*David Soul*
12	DON'T CRY FOR ME ARGENTINA	
	Julie Covington	
19	WHEN I NEED YOU	*Leo Sayer*
26	WHEN I NEED YOU	*Leo Sayer*

MARCH

5	WHEN I NEED YOU	*Leo Sayer*
12	CHANSON D'AMOUR	*Manhattan Transfer*
19	CHANSON D'AMOUR	*Manhattan Transfer*
26	CHANSON D'AMOUR	*Manhattan Transfer*

APRIL

2	KNOWING ME KNOWING YOU	*Abba*
9	KNOWING ME KNOWING YOU	*Abba*
16	KNOWING ME KNOWING YOU	*Abba*
23	KNOWING ME KNOWING YOU	*Abba*
30	KNOWING ME KNOWING YOU	*Abba*

MAY

7	FREE	*Deniece Williams*
14	FREE	*Deniece Williams*
21	I DON'T WANT TO TALK ABOUT IT/	
	FIRST CUT IS THE DEEPEST	*Rod Stewart*
28	I DON'T WANT TO TALK ABOUT IT/	
	FIRST CUT IS THE DEEPEST	*Rod Stewart*

JUNE

4	I DON'T WANT TO TALK ABOUT IT/	
	FIRST CUT IS THE DEEPEST	*Rod Stewart*
11	I DON'T WANT TO TALK ABOUT IT/	
	FIRST CUT IS THE DEEPEST	*Rod Stewart*
18	LUCILLE	*Kenny Rogers*
25	SHOW YOU THE WAY TO GO	*Jacksons*

JULY

2	SO YOU WIN AGAIN	*Hot Chocolate*
9	SO YOU WIN AGAIN	*Hot Chocolate*
16	SO YOU WIN AGAIN	*Hot Chocolate*
23	I FEEL LOVE	*Donna Summer*
30	I FEEL LOVE	*Donna Summer*

AUGUST

6	I FEEL LOVE	*Donna Summer*
13	I FEEL LOVE	*Donna Summer*
20	ANGELO	*Brotherhood of Man*
27	FLOAT ON	*Floaters*

SEPTEMBER

3	WAY DOWN	*Elvis Presley*
10	WAY DOWN	*Elvis Presley*
17	WAY DOWN	*Elvis Presley*
24	WAY DOWN	*Elvis Presley*

OCTOBER

1	WAY DOWN	*Elvis Presley*
8	SILVER LADY	*David Soul*
15	SILVER LADY	*David Soul*
22	SILVER LADY	*David Soul*
29	YES SIR I CAN BOOGIE	*Baccara*

NOVEMBER

5	NAME OF THE GAME	*Abba*
12	NAME OF THE GAME	*Abba*
19	NAME OF THE GAME	*Abba*
26	NAME OF THE GAME	*Abba*

DECEMBER

3	MULL OF KINTYRE	*Wings*
10	MULL OF KINTYRE	*Wings*
17	MULL OF KINTYRE	*Wings*
24	MULL OF KINTYRE	*Wings*
31	MULL OF KINTYRE	*Wings*